CURRENCY

DOUBLEDAY

DATE DUE

"This book is a not-to-be-missed opportunity to visit the 'front lines' of service with some memorable people. The service providers you will meet are creating the future of our businesses as they work to delight their customers—every call, every day!"

—W. R. GRIFFIN
President & CEO,
Roto-Rooter, Inc.

THE REAL

HEROES OF

BUSINESS

. . . AND NOT A CEO AMONG THEM

CURRENCY

DOUBLEDAY

NEW YORK   TORONTO   LONDON
SYDNEY   AUCKLAND

THE REAL HEROES OF BUSINESS

. . . AND NOT A CEO AMONG THEM

WORLD-CLASS FRONTLINE

SERVICE WORKERS:

HOW DO YOU FIND THEM?

TRAIN THEM?

MANAGE THEM?

RETAIN THEM?

BILL FROMM

AND LEN SCHLESINGER

A CURRENCY BOOK

PUBLISHED BY DOUBLEDAY
a division of Bantam Doubleday Dell Publishing Group, Inc.
1540 Broadway, New York, New York 10036

CURRENCY and DOUBLEDAY are trademarks of Doubleday, a division
of Bantam Doubleday Dell Publishing Group, Inc.

Library of Congress Cataloging-in-Publication Data
Fromm, Bill.
The real heroes of business— and not a CEO among them / Bill
Fromm & Leonard A. Schlesinger. — 1st ed.
p.   cm.
"A Currency book."
Includes index.
1. Customer service—Management.   2. Employees—Recruiting.
I. Schlesinger, Leonard A.   II. Title.
HF5415.5.F76   1994
658.8'12—dc20   93-39817
CIP

ISBN 0-385-42555-4

5   7   9   10   8   6

Not all heroes are engaged in events that make headlines, not all are enshrined in halls of fame. Many heroes in our business are the people who do their best every day, and succeed more often than not.

—HAROLD A. POLING

chairman and CEO of Ford Motor Co., quoted in a

hand-lettered sign hanging in one of Ford's factories

DEDICATION

Too many business books rely on the "wisdom" of people who have long-since ceased to do the "real work" at their companies. Most of those companies would not exist without the people who answer phones and wait tables, who open doors and give directions, who load planes and serve drinks, who fix cars and stack apples, who sell recliners and cash register tapes, who clean drains and fix telephones, who make bank loans and manage frontline workers.

And, surely, this book would not exist without those people and their colleagues across the country. What insight it contains owes to Paula Doricchi and Marie Williams, Phil Adelman and Joe Sabelli, Jorge Alvarez and Joni Strong, Keith Spring and Wally Bojorquez, David Greene and Rich Ciotti, Alan Wilk and Danny Williams, Jacob Smith and Marian Goodman.

ACKNOWLEDGMENTS

How do a busy advertising executive and an over-committed Harvard Business School professor find the time to travel around the country, meeting world-class service performers who might be candidates for this book? They don't.

Instead, we found the time to find Charles Fishman, and he did our chasing for us. Charles started out as our legs, eyes, and ears. He crisscrossed the country—from South Florida to Boston, from Washington to Dallas, from Charlotte to San Diego—spending days shadowing potential candidates for this book. He watched them work, interviewed their coworkers and supervisors and friends, spent hours on the phone talking to their colleagues and relatives. Then he drafted rich character profiles that became the foundation for the lessons you'll find in this book.

In addition to all that, Fishman, a former *Washington Post* reporter, continually challenged us to make this book the best, and the best-written, it could possibly be. Just as the people in this book are the unsung heroes who create the results managers get credit for, so Charles Fishman has been the unsung hero of this book. We couldn't have done it without him.

This is the second book Andy Fromm has worked on, and he clearly figured that he had picked an easier role on this book than he had on the last. Thankfully for all the rest of us, he guessed wrong. From coordinating the selection of candidates for the book, to making travel arrangements, seeing that everybody in the book was properly photographed, getting copyright permissions, keeping track of the tens of thousands of dollars of expenses a national project like this entails, and handling a hundred administrative details, Andy has been the person who literally made the book happen. He has also been a cool-headed voice of experience and wisdom—on everything from the conceptual underpinnings of the book to its title—when the more emotional members of the team were busy being loud and hotheaded.

Our colleague and friend Mark Pelofsky was instrumental in coming up with the concept for the book, and had the courage to suggest we bring Charles Fishman into the project. He has heard every sentence of the book, most more than once, and he has, in his gentle but uncanny manner, pointed out flaws, sloppy thinking, and gawky wording on every page. The book makes a good deal more sense, and is easier to read, because of him.

During its creation, this book has had many additional anonymous defenders and protectors, people whose contribution has been critical, who have lent their thoughts, their wit, their judgment, and hours of their time to make the book better, through no stronger connection to the project than friendship.

Kevin Spear and Jaine LaFay provided the kind of support that helped make it possible to research and write in nine months a book that required eighteen months of work.

Along with Mark Pelofsky, others listened to nearly every word of the book read aloud to them, and listened with equal patience to the revisions resulting from their suggestions: Jeff Brazil, Geoff Calkins, and Peter Mitchell. Amy Leviton read every word of every chapter with a well-aimed red pen. All five had to endure storms of protest and bad temper over brilliant editing suggestions (criticisms that were in fact *invited*), and did so with humor, encouragement, and enthusiasm. Their excitement for the book and its characters never wavered, and every page is better because of a suggestion from one of them.

Len Schlesinger's faculty colleagues in the Service Management Interest Group at Harvard have been a never-ending source of ideas, inspiration, and friendship. Jim Heskett, Earl Sasser, Tom Jones, and Gary Loveman each, in his own way, put a stamp on this book. Roger Hallowell, in his role as a research associate, and Kathy Ivanciw, as Len's assistant, have provided the best support network a human being could have (one probably better than Len is entitled to).

Bill Fromm's associates at Barkley & Evergreen continually gave input to Bill, Andy Fromm, Mark Pelofsky, Charles Fishman, and anybody else who would listen. Bill's assistant, Shelly DeMotte, was collator, mail service expert, and scheduler.

Arthur Pine had the inspiration for the final title. Harriet Rubin and Janet Coleman, our editors at Doubleday, provided a valuable perspective.

We cannot close without thanking Shop 'N Chek for mystery shopping the candidates, Manatech for providing us the opportunity to review their Personalysis profiles, and Fred Mancheski for providing the quote from Harold "Red" Poling.

CONTENTS

"EXCUSE ME, CAN I GET SOME HELP HERE?"

FIGURING OUT SERVICE ONCE AND FOR ALL

"Do you work here . . . ? Hi, can I just ask . . . Do you know where I can find . . . ?

"Excuse me, but can I get some help here?"

Such has become the cry of the customer in the nineties. The customer just wants a little help, a little attention, a little service.

And the companies have caught on.

Oh, how they've caught on.

Customer service has become the most discussed—perhaps overdiscussed—topic in American business today.

There isn't a single major company that hasn't devoted at least one long management meeting to the topic. Many have hired legions of consultants to assist in developing service improvement programs.

The shelves of bookstores groan with books complaining about service, extolling service, explaining service.

So why do we propose to add one more book to the pile?

Because, for the moment, almost no one gets it.

We're both in the service business, we've read the books, we've attended the seminars—heck, we've *taught* the seminars—and, until very recently, even we didn't fully get it.

All these years, all these words, all these ideas—but in all of it, one very important element has been overlooked: the people who actually deliver great service.

Where was the book that, instead of theorizing and postulating and pontificating, went straight to the frontline workers who deliver great service every day and asked them how they do it, why they do it, what kind of management silliness they had to overcome to do it?

Where was *that* book?

To get it, we had to write it. You now hold it in your hands.

This is a book with a very simple set of premises:

If you want to know how to give great customer service, find people who do it and watch them work.

If you want to know how important great customer service is, find people who deliver it and see what impact they have on their companies and their customers.

If you want to know how to find and hire great customer service providers, find people who are great service performers, see what they look like and sound like and think like, so when a great service performer walks into your business, you'll recognize him or her instantly.

If you want to keep great customer service performers in your company, find people who are great service performers and ask them what's important to them, how they like to be managed, what makes them happy in their work.

Before we plunged in, we had only the vaguest of ideas what a project like this would produce.

We were surprised in a dozen different ways—first, and most happily, at the quality of people we found who are out there every day, doing what all the professors, bosses, and consultants only talk about.

But one thing we were not surprised about: the people who deliver great service know just what they're doing; they are the people to learn from; and what wisdom and insight this book contains comes from them.

■

To start this project, we undertook a yearlong search to identify some of our nation's finest service workers. We solicited nominations from each of *Fortune* magazine's top 500 service companies and from three hundred additional companies we identified. We also targeted a number of companies where, from our personal experiences or from the writings of other service experts, we knew there were likely to be some outstanding folks.

We ended up with several hundred nominations, which we narrowed down to approximately forty possible subjects. Our criteria for this narrowing were admittedly unscientific: Did the nomination packets include stories about the candidate that left us saying "Wow"? Did we have a comprehensive set of service-work categories? Did we have a reasonable geographic spread?

With our list narrowed, we turned to Shop 'N Chek of Atlanta, Georgia, and had them "mystery shop" each of our semifinalists. A researcher then shadowed and interviewed thirty candidates, each over a two-day period.

In this book are the stories of fourteen of these people, folks we believe are the *real* heroes of business.

We do not claim that we have unearthed the *best* service workers in America. In fact, one very heartening thing we've discovered is that although on the whole customer service is not very good across a broad range of industries (a fact borne out by years of consumer research), great individual service workers are all around us.

What we do claim is that we have discovered fourteen people who, as a group, are as remarkable a collection of American service workers as anyone could assemble. They are not the only people who perform the way they do, but they unquestionably represent the best frontline service workers in the nation.

Our fourteen heroes know far more about delivering good service than most market researchers and expensive consultants.

Why? Because they do it every day. And most of them have figured out how to do it on their own.

They see what they do not as jobs, but as roles. They feel a sense of obligation—to their own standards, and to their customers. In the richest sense, they see themselves not as service workers, but as service *performers*. And it makes all the difference in how they do their jobs. They have refined their experiences in dealing with customers to a fine art—one that carefully balances the needs of the customers and those of the business.

■

Our presentation of these heroes starts in Cambridge, Massachusetts, where we meet a doorman who has turned what many could perceive as a relatively minor job at the front door of a Marriott hotel into a franchise from which he virtually creates the entire personality of the hotel.

We visit Greenville, South Carolina, and meet a waitress so good that customers wait in line up to an hour to eat at one of her tables—passing up empty tables elsewhere in the restaurant so they can be served by her.

In Reno, Nevada, you'll meet an eighty-five-year-old hotel security guard who is so important to the property that a part of its casino has been named after him.

The eleven other people in the book are equally amazing—their performances and personalities so rich and compelling, we are concerned only that we have had to flatten them unfairly to fit them into a book.

Before you plunge into the body of this book, there is something you need to understand: this is really two books braided together.

It is a book of the stories of the people profiled in each of its chapters. And it is a book of practical advice on how to find, hire, manage, and nurture people like these—world-class frontline service workers.

The stories of each of our heroes are supplemented with our commentary. As each chapter unfolds, we stop the action to point out lessons for managers—to help them find an employee like the one being profiled, or to help their current employees grow and develop.

The more impatient among our readers may have wondered why we bothered with the storytelling part. In fact, the book is set up physically so those who are only interested in the bottom line—in the lessons—can get them with a quick skim.

But it's not just that the people are entertaining, or that their work habits so vividly illustrate the lessons, showing how those lessons apply in real situations. You really need to meet these people to understand how they work, to understand how to bring people like this into your business.

If you skip their stories, you'll be missing the point.

·

As you read, there is one critical question you should keep asking yourself:

What if this person worked for me, for my company?

While most companies espouse a desire to focus on customer satisfaction, very few deliver, often because of a set of false assumptions with which they approach the people who occupy frontline service jobs:

There is an abundant (and cheap) labor market to draw from;

Employee turnover is inevitable, so one should minimize both selection and training costs;

Technology will ultimately eliminate most of this kind of work.

All of these assumptions are, at best, naive and, at worst, simply wrong. And if these assumptions pervade your company, there is little chance of you identifying or retaining performers such as our fourteen heroes. Because one thing that came through loud and clear is that people of this caliber, this energy level, this imagination and devotion, don't stay long in organizations that don't appreciate them, that don't allow them to perform.

When you have people like these, you need to help them do their best work. As you will see in the profiles, these folks are not always the easiest employees to have, but that is only because they never settle into complacency. Great service performers require understanding and supportive management—and management that is not threatened by being challenged.

The lessons in the book can help make anyone a better manager, and help give almost anyone a better and more profitable company. We think you can use them to learn:

How to change your hiring procedures to increase your chances of finding and hiring world-class service workers;

How to make your company a more attractive place for the best service workers to work—which will reduce turnover, reduce your costs, and increase customer satisfaction;

How to manage your employees so more of them will be able to do work of the quality and consistency of the people you'll meet in this book;

How to manage world-class service workers, so when you hire them you are able not only to retain them, but to use their skills and attitude to raise the general level of performance at your company.

Perhaps most important, we hope to show you exactly what the standards of world-class service are, what it means to your customers, and how vitally important it is to your bottom line and your competitiveness. We want to make it clear that people like the heroes in this book are anything but replaceable—that they perform a role technology never can.

And we hope to persuade even the most hard-line manager of the economic logic that requires an appreciation of these people. In each of our fourteen chapters, we calculate the monetary value of the work the service performers do. These calculations surprised even us. And, in an appendix, we show you how to do similar calculations for your own workers.

We end each chapter with some hints on how to find someone like the person you'll have just read about. Our sense of the more general lessons we've learned is collected in a conclusion and in an appendix with twenty interview questions that will help you find people like these during the hiring process.

.

Finally, it's worth asking the question, Who are we, and why did we write this book? Both of us have devoted a substantial portion of our professional careers to issues of frontline service.

Barkley & Evergreen, the Kansas City marketing and advertising agency Bill Fromm has led since 1964, is a stunning example of the importance of high-quality customer contact. Fromm's insights on service firms and service strategies have created a company that has sustained double-digit growth rates in good economic times and bad. In 1991, Fromm and Schlesinger formed an internal marketing division of Barkley & Evergreen. This division develops and implements programs to improve customer service, employee morale, and employee productivity.

Fromm's management and employment strategies were highlighted in his recent book, *The Ten Commandments of Business and How to Break Them*. Many of his fundamental ideas about how to run a business represent the institutional embodiment of the way our fourteen heroes perform as individuals.

Len Schlesinger has addressed these issues as both a management practitioner and an academic. In the middle of a fifteen-year career on the faculty of Harvard Business School, he took out three and a half years to serve as executive vice president and then chief operating officer at Au Bon Pain, a chain of quick-service French bakery-cafés.

During his time at Au Bon Pain, Len went to bed each night praying for the appearance of great service performers in each of his restaurants. He quickly learned that, although divine intervention and fate were a portion of every firm's hiring strategy, there was a lot more you could do to provide great service. Over the last five years, Len has devoted all of his research time and attention to the issues raised by this book.

Rather than create another how-to manual, we've chosen to compile a textbook through the stories of some extraordinary people. Whatever you think are the problems of American business today, we know that those problems evaporate in the face of performances like those from the people in this book. It is not just their insistence on quality, and their sensitivity to customers, it is their ability to adjust and adapt as the world changes.

In learning what motivates these fourteen people and in discovering the lengths to which they go to deliver outstanding service, we got positively giddy. You will too.

THE REAL

HEROES OF

BUSINESS

. . . AND NOT A CEO AMONG THEM

FIRST

IMPRESSION

SERVICE

photo by FAYFOTO

PHIL ADELMAN

ROLLING OUT THE RED CARPET

A THOUSAND TIMES A DAY

Everyone has had the kinds of experiences that instantly sour them on a business or service establishment, even before they actually do any business with it. The electronics store you call to find out if an advertised item is in stock, only to be put on hold for so long you begin to think the place has filed for Chapter 11 since answering the phone; the doctor's office where the receptionist behind the sliding glass window acts as if she's doing you a favor to glare at you; the rental-car agent who seems to be just learning how to use a computer keyboard when there's a seven-person line of impatient drivers; the restaurant with a sign that says PLEASE WAIT TO BE SEATED, where you stand expectantly as uniformed employees whisk by, looking at you with a mixture of pity and incomprehension, as if there could be no possible explanation of why you are standing at the entrance to the dining room.

Yet one of the oldest rules of human interaction—business or personal—is that the impression you first make on someone will be what sets the tone and expectations for the rest of the relationship. In everything from dating and job hunting to making multi-million-dollar takeover deals, the first impression may determine whether there is any relationship at all.

Given that the value of first impressions is underscored from Sunday schools to the nation's most elite MBA programs, what is remarkable is how many businesses overlook the power of first impressions—the good they can do, and the damage.

Studies have shown that 35 percent of business-to-business callers are put on hold when they first place a call. Every one of those encounters is off to a bad start—even if the person answering the phone is gracious and ultimately helpful. Of course, in most cases the person answering the phone is overworked, underpaid, under pressure, and quite likely to be curt, rushed, and unhelpful. So much for giving customers a sense that you value their business.

But first impressions work both ways. Hotels have discovered that guests form their overall impressions during the first ten minutes of a stay—the time when a guest pulls up, unloads, checks in, and locates and explores the room. If the check-in process is smooth, understandable, and relaxed, if the staff is helpful, the halls well lit, the room clean, and the luggage cheerfully delivered, then guests are left not just with a feeling of competence and comfort. They are inclined to dismiss subsequent problems—room service that's a little slow, a burned-out light bulb in a room lamp—as aberrations.

By the same token, a guest who arrives at the room already

irritated by a confusing welter of carparkers, doormen, and bell-men, by a slow and supercilious desk clerk, by a room with two twin beds when one queen was requested—such a guest is likely to view the entire stay as unpleasant, regardless of how the hotel and its staff subsequently perform.

Jan Carlzon, the former CEO of SAS Airlines, who has thought about service encounters extensively, has broken them down into "moments of truth"—key points when a customer's expectations are met or disappointed. The first encounter between a customer and a business is always a moment of truth—it is the point at which a customer first forms an impression of a business, and an expectation of the level of quality and helpfulness to be provided.

Indeed, the first impression may be the most important moment of truth. How many times have you yourself, as a customer, simply turned on your heel in the first five minutes of dealing with a business if you couldn't get some attention? If you've done it at a restaurant, the place might have missed out on a thirty-dollar meal—or on five years of weekly thirty-dollar meals. If you've done it at a doctor's office or a furniture store or a car dealership, the financial stakes for that business were considerably higher. The place that bungles that first moment of truth doesn't ever get the chance to show what kind of work it can do.

If you are a manager reading this book, do you have any idea what kind of first impression your business conveys? There are all kinds of ways to seek feedback. To find out what customers think, you can use surveys, focus groups, performance review cards. You can also assess how you're doing by shopping your competition, and by hiring mystery shoppers to shop your own business and report their experiences—and not just their first impressions.

If you are a service worker reading this book, do you know what kind of first impression you make? We're not talking about artificial, Hi-my-name-is-Mandy chirpiness. We're talking about looking crisp and professional, being engaged in what you're doing, paying attention to the customers as if they were people you might actually be interested in (they might be), and moving the work along without being brusque.

It's not merely a matter of symbolism. Wal-Mart pioneered the concept of greeters at its stores—friendly, alert, uniformed employees stationed near the entrances to welcome each customer. Wal-Mart often seems to use senior citizens for this post. The benefits have been widely acknowledged—from setting the mood to establishing a subtle security presence. But Wal-Mart undertook this task more carefully than some people realized, as became apparent when a competitor tried the same thing. Kmart followed Wal-Mart's lead, but often staffed the position with disinterested, awkward teenagers who didn't have any idea what they were supposed to do. The result actually backfired—the sullen, bored greeters at Kmart did more harm than having no one at the door.

Phil Adelman works the door at the Marriott Hotel in Cambridge, Massachusetts, and he could not be a more persuasive embodiment of the power of first impressions in the service industry.

We found Phil through a friend and colleague who is related to him, and who gave us five handwritten pages Phil had composed about how to be a doorman: an essay and list of suggestions he titled "An Observation of Our Guests."

The advice combines simplicity of expression with sophisticated understanding. "We are basically a businessmen's hotel," Phil writes. "From Monday through Friday, our guest arrives either by taxi or a rental car. He is carrying a briefcase in one hand and a carry-on over his shoulder. He is usually in a rush. He wants his car parked and immediately runs over to the front desk to check in. He does not need a bellman to assist him. When he comes down the following morning, he wants his breakfast or coffee at once. He is usually in a big hurry. He wants his car immediately and does not like waiting. One minute waiting is ten minutes waiting for the guest."

Among Phil's suggestions:

"If a guest is alone, eating in our restaurant, say hello. Be friendly. He misses his home."

"Take care of the guest's needs and wants. If possible, give that little extra something."

"Smile. However you come into work in the A.M. will rub off on your associates. Leave your personal problems at home."

4

In person, Phil Adelman turns out to be his own advice come to life in big-screen Technicolor.

Many customers treat jobs like Phil's—doorman, greeter, security guard—as if those roles and those people didn't exist. But the real problem is that many companies treat them that way as well. Jobs that involve constant customer contact are by their very definition highly visible. Companies that make the most of the service opportunities these jobs present gain great competitive advantage.

Phil has taken just such a job and turned it into a position from which he sets the tone and personality of his hotel. He leaves a first impression of extraordinary helpfulness, knowledge, hospitality, and security. He knows how to make customers welcome. And, as a bonus, he is also often the last person guests encounter at the hotel, sending them off with a lasting *last* impression.

PHIL'S KINGDOM

The immediate patch of territory over which Phil Adelman presides is a red carpet twenty-four steps long and seven steps wide. This is Phil's office and his stage and his kingdom, and he is determined to see that no one passes through it without receiving some sort of favor—luggage lifted cheerfully into a cab, permission granted to park briefly in the driveway, the front door pulled open eagerly and with a certain flourish.

Under Phil's reign, the curb at the Cambridge Marriott Hotel, which often teeters on the edge of chaos and confusion, is a place of order and humor, precision and hospitality. It is also a place to discover how much intricacy, importance, and warmth can be infused into a job that these days is most commonly done by an electric eye.

Phil Adelman is fully outfitted for his role—creased black pants, shiny black shoes, and a white blazer with black epaulets, red shoulder braid, and gold buttons. On his head is a white pith helmet topped by a spray of bright red feathers.

THERE ARE NO INVISIBLE JOBS

Companies that employ doormen and security guards have an advantage over most firms. Marriott, for instance, uses Phil to help set the tone for the hotel, to acknowledge customers when they arrive, to help them get checked in and get settled. The uniform is an important tool for preventing Phil—or the valets, or the security guards—from becoming invisible. The uniform sends the clear message to the customers that this person is here to help.

More important, Phil is a good example of the opportunity to win and secure customers presented any time a company has an employee in contact with the public. Many such jobs—not just doormen or security guards, but restaurant hostesses, airline reservation agents, retail clerks—are staffed as an afterthought. These jobs often don't demand much in the way of technical skills, but they should still be filled with care. The people you select to present your company to the public say as much about you as your advertising or your logo—perhaps more. Pick people who enjoy working with the public, who do it with enthusiasm and patience and good humor.

The uniform aside, Adelman doesn't seem like a classic doorman type. He's sixty-five years old. He's not tall or stern or broad-shouldered. He's a man of moderate build, and his mind is a constant whirl of cheerful observations and suggestions. He is constitutionally incapable of remaining still. His manic energy level is exceeded only by his capacity to talk. If you were going to build a television situation comedy around a doorman, Phil would be your model. He has a story about everything.

The only thing Phil likes better than working or talking is talking about his work. And the apparent simplicity of a doorman's job has not fooled Phil. His style is a mix of worrying about tiny details and thinking in the broadest terms about how the hotel should approach its guests. He is, in that sense, entrepreneurial. He has a vision of both the ideal doorman and the ideal hotel, but he realizes that the vision is irrelevant if the details aren't taken care of.

Each morning he's on duty, Phil arrives at his station at seven o'clock with a combination barometer/thermometer tucked under his arm, and his first act is to mount it on a brick pillar just outside the hotel's front door. "It's my idea," he says. "The guests want to know how cold it is. And it's a great conversation piece. While they're waiting for their cars, they have something to keep them occupied."

WHY ELEVATOR LANDINGS HAVE MIRRORS

Elevator landings in hotels and office buildings often have mirrors so people have something to do—check their appearances—while they wait for the elevator to arrive. Studies have shown people perceive the wait for an elevator to be much less onerous when there is a mirror for them to use while they wait.

Disney World does the same thing. Long lines at the theme park are ingeniously wrapped around themselves, and around landscaping, so guests don't stand still for long, and so they never have to stare at forty minutes of people queued up in front of them. Lately, the park has installed video monitors along some of the lines to entertain guests while they wait.

Phil Adelman instinctively understands this principle—his barometer/thermometer is just something to keep guests from getting fidgety and impatient while they wait for cabs or for their cars to be brought around. There are many circumstances when a customer will be waiting, even when the customer doesn't seem to be in line. Look for those "hidden lines" and find ways to distract your customers while they're in them.

The expansive glass and steel canopy that shelters the hotel's driveway is also Phil's idea. When the Marriott first opened, there was no canopy, just a small brick overhang that barely covered the sidewalk.

"People would pull up in their cars in the rain," says Bill

Munck, the general manager who opened the Cambridge Marriott, "and the person on the passenger side was nice and dry and the driver would get soaked. Phil came into my office and he said, 'You gotta do something. Come on out and see what's happening. You gotta build a canopy.' Over the course of several months, he convinced the owners to spend half a million dollars on building that canopy."

Phil has a real talent for seeing what's missing in a situation. His mind almost cannot help making the leap from what is to what could be. Marriott has an employee suggestion program, and Phil is a ceaseless suggester. It's not unusual for him to submit ten suggestions—handwritten—in a week; one January, he submitted sixty-three. He keeps the hotel's responses—he gets a reply to each suggestion—catalogued in three-ring binders at home.

WHEN QUANTITY IS MORE IMPORTANT THAN QUALITY

The closer an employee is to the customer, the more likely he or she will have good ideas for keeping the customer happy. The number of things the Cambridge Marriott has done based on suggestions from Phil is remarkable—from adding a vast glass awning over the main entrance to putting decals on the revolving doors so customers don't bump into the glass panels.

Of course, the number of Phil's suggestions the Marriott has rejected is probably ten times the number it has used. But all Phil's managers agree that the suggestions they used have brought benefits a thousand times greater than the effort required to say no to the less valuable ones. In fact, the quantity of Phil's suggestions is far more important than the quality of any individual suggestion. The suggestions show that he's thinking and watching—thinking about and watching out for the business. There's nothing wrong with a doorman who wants to tell you how to run the hotel—it shows he's not just doing time as an employee. Every business could use a few more minds thinking about how to make it better.

And employees like Phil may well know things about the way your business treats customers that you could never know.

The two critical aspects to any successful suggestion program are that the company respond in writing to every suggestion (Phil shows how important this is to him by cataloguing each response in three-ring binders) and that some suggestions are accepted and implemented.

One day Phil decided to visit the Marriott's presidential suite. "I just wanted to see what it was like, so I would know," he says. "It costs five hundred dollars a night. I went up. First of all, it doesn't face the Charles River. We've got a five-hundred-dollar-a-night presidential suite and it doesn't face the Charles River." Phil looks baffled by what kind of person would design a hotel whose most expensive room is denied a river view.

"Then I see this thing up there for $4.99 pizza—a little table advertisement. I said, 'Let's get rid of this $4.99 pizza and advertise wine instead.'" Marriott management responded that wine was available to the suite in the room service menu. But it did have the pizza advertisement promptly removed.

It's Hard to See the Big Picture Looking Through a Microscope

Employees can do their jobs better if they can see the big picture—but not all employees will take the kind of initiative Phil did to learn about the business. It's management's responsibility to make sure that everyone in the company has an opportunity to do so.

For example, cooks and dishwashers should have opportunities to eat in their restaurants with the customers—and managers should take the opportunity to work in the dish room and the kitchen.

People who work in manufacturing need to get out of the factory occasionally to see where their products are going and how they're used. Once people see how the customer uses their company's product or service, they will be in a position to make a bigger contribution to the company's success.

In some ways, the door at the Cambridge Marriott is merely the soapbox from which Phil expounds his philosophy.

"Am I too smart for my job? A lot of people say that. Some people would think, if I go to a wedding, that I'd be embarrassed. Everybody's saying, 'I'm a lawyer,' 'I'm a periodontist.' I'm a doorman. I love to say 'I'm a doorman.'"

PRIDE IS THE FIRST REQUIREMENT FOR PERFORMANCE

Phil doesn't just *do* his job, he revels in it, he's proud of it. If he were uncomfortable telling friends and acquaintances what he did, how likely would he be to do his job wonderfully? It is not likely that someone will be good at a job he or she isn't proud of. What's more, there is no way an employee can take pride in a job that companies and managers don't respect and value.

For managers, this means taking the time and effort necessary to make sure every employee understands just how critical he or she is to your enterprise.

All too often, businesses don't train new employees even in the simple mechanical aspects of their jobs, let alone explain the broader purposes and economics of the business. Both training and an explanation of the business should be part of new employee orientation—enough of both so your new employees feel comfortable with the equipment, the merchandise, the customers.

In service businesses, there is a chance to link quality and the economics of customer loyalty in vivid and understandable terms. In one take-out restaurant organization, the average walk-in customer spent $2.50 and visited an average of two and one half times a week. That's $6.25 worth of business a week, fifty weeks a year—or $312.50 a year from loyal customers. If you keep the customer for ten years, the person walking up to the counter for coffee and a muffin is worth $3,125.00—in the employee's view, that amount should seem to be stamped right on the customer's forehead. It just so happens that you get the $3,125.00 a little at a time—$2.50 at a time in this case.

But the real lesson here—for the business and its workers—is that when you are rude or dismissive or inattentive to a $2.50 customer, you're not blowing off $2.50, you're blowing off $3,125.00. Looked at another way, even the counter person at a take-out restaurant is routinely responsible for closing "deals" that are worth thousands of dollars over the life of the "contract."

It's not just important to give your employees a sense of how valuable they are to you and the business. It's also critical to make clear how valuable the customers are—to the employees and to the business.

THE PERFECT DOORMAN: NO EXPERIENCE AT ALL

Phil Adelman was, at best, a very unlikely candidate to become a doorman.

When Marriott hired him, he was fifty-nine years old and unemployed. He was a high school graduate who had been laid off after a career rising through the ranks of Lechmere, a New England discount department store chain where he'd started out as temporary summer sales help and ended up twenty-three years later as an assistant buyer. Phil had no hotel experience, no experience in the hospitality industry at all, and, by the time he saw the ad for a job fair to staff the newly opening Cambridge Marriott, he had been unemployed for the better part of three and a half years. He had long since given up hoping to find a job with the kind of responsibility, challenge, and pay he'd had at Lechmere. His application to the Marriott was sparse. He listed only his brief military service and his job at Lechmere. He didn't apply for any particular job at the Marriott; he was willing to take anything they considered appropriate.

And here's how Phil got a job at the Marriott: he went to the interview and told them how to run their hotel.

A job fair is an open call for applicants to come and be interviewed briefly by those doing the hiring. It resembles nothing so much as an open casting call—which is in fact precisely what it is. The point is to make a good impression in a very brief period, perhaps five minutes or less, to find a way to stand out from the nearly indistinguishable hundreds who also want a job.

"When I applied for the job, I used to go to the Marriott Essex House in New York City, and I had brochures from there," says Phil. "I took the brochures from this hotel with me to the interview. I said, 'We should have an escape weekend, we should have a seafood restaurant.'

"Who in the world ever applies for a job and tells the hotel how to make money before they even have a job?"

John Montano, now head of human resources at the hotel, was then front office manager and was one of those who met Phil during the mass interview held at a high school in Cambridge.

"He was my longest interview," says Montano. "We were doing thirty-five to forty interviews a day. He was my second interview, and it must have exceeded forty-five minutes.

"He just went all the way back, to his childhood, and gave me his whole life's picture of what he did." Phil Adelman made a powerful impression on Montano, who saw a man of perception, enthusiasm, and energy, even if he didn't have any actual experience.

WINNERS DON'T COME
IN PLAIN BROWN WRAPPING

Traditional hiring criteria often filter out people who could become service stars. Many interviewers would have dismissed Phil—fifty-nine years old, unemployed for three and a half years, no prior hotel experience—even before getting to the interview. But none of that was a good indicator of what kind of doorman Adelman would be. What counts is Phil's attitude, something difficult to ascertain from an application form.

At most companies, the application and hiring process is designed to screen out people like Phil. The question is not just whom a company is hiring—but whom is it missing? Dozens of companies to which Phil applied and where he would have been successful didn't even take the time to interview him.

Among other things, this example shows the value of meeting people in person, even briefly at the kind of mass interviews Marriott set up. From that group of hundreds of potential employees, Phil jumped out instantly in a way he could not have from a folder of written applications. To get the best service performers, you have to give them a forum to prove themselves to you. There's nothing wrong with bringing in five prospective employees—even for modest jobs—and meeting and talking with all of them in the space of half an hour or forty-five minutes. If you get one person even close to Phil Adelman's quality for every eight groups of people you meet (that is, one Phil for every forty people interviewed), you will have invested just a single workday in finding a Phil. That is a day well spent in almost any kind of business.

Phil celebrated getting the doorman's job at the Marriott by climbing in his car with his wife Helen and driving all over Cambridge and Boston, writing down step-by-step directions from the Marriott to places guests were most likely to want to go so he would be able to tell them. Eventually, the Marriott would print those directions on cards to distribute to guests.

ON STAGE

It is seven-thirty on an early May morning in Boston, and according to Phil Adelman's barometer/thermometer, it is forty-five degrees. Phil knows from having looked as he does each morning that 165 people will be checking out over the next several hours.

A group of three women comes out of the hotel. He hails them a cab, races up, takes the luggage from one of them, urges them all to "take your time," and loads them into the cab.

Phil spies a man in business clothes who is all but running

through the lobby, headed for the front doors. Phil snatches the door open, and the man doesn't even break stride. "He comes through a couple times a day," says Phil, who has no idea who the man is or why he is almost always running. "If I see him, I open the door so he doesn't have to stop."

The people come in waves from both directions—from inside the hotel, behind Phil, and from the driveway, in front of him.

Between the commuters who pass through the lobby on the way to the subway, the guests checking out, the business people heading off to meetings and others arriving for them, mornings at the door can be frenzied.

When the red carpet gets busy, Phil is a tornado of activity, grabbing doors, stowing luggage, maneuvering his brass-colored luggage cart with the skill and style of a drum major with his baton. Phil wants no one's needs to go unmet, and that is the first key element of great first impression service.

There is something theatrical about the relish Phil takes in the role. In his uniform with his feathered cap, he is as much a performer as a service worker—he has some dramatic ideal of the doorman in mind, and he tries to live up to that ideal. He enjoys being a doorman—he doesn't see it as a path to anything else; he takes pride and pleasure in the job itself.

There is something old-fashioned about the role—at least in part because a doorman does things that one can easily do for oneself, almost without thinking: open a door, raise a hand to flag a cab. The duties of the doorman seem so simple that when he isn't there to do them, no one even notices.

The talent and the charm of Phil Adelman's performance is that he does these small favors for people without the slightest suggestion that they are favors, with a graciousness and assurance that leave the hotel's customers with a feeling of well-being and confidence—and that is the second key element of great first impression service.

More than this, Phil never hangs around, waiting expectantly for a tip. He takes the luggage of guests who are checking in to the front desk on a cart and is often back out at the door before they can gather themselves to go inside. Not that the tip is unimportant to Phil—he earns $4.70 an hour, just 30 cents an hour more than he earned six years ago. Tips, though, add an average of $4.00 an hour to his pay.

But from Phil's point of view, waiting around for the tip spoils the ritual of providing the service for both him and the guest. And he's found that guests frequently track him down to give him a tip if they are so inclined.

GOOD SERVICE CAN BE SPOILED BY CALLING ATTENTION TO IT

Both service workers and management rely on tips to help compensate employees. And tipping is not just a matter between your customers and your employees. It is the responsibility of managers to make sure that service workers don't use good service as a kind of weapon to extract tips from customers. Phil concluded that waiting around at the front desk for guests to catch up with their luggage was just that: a way of saying, "I've delivered good service—now pay me."

Such an attitude on the part of workers takes all the pleasure out of good service for customers—it may even cause them to resent the service.

Bill Munck, the manager who opened the hotel, says a guest's arrival is the critical moment in the hotel experience.

"Most people, when they get here, are very confused. Where is the front entrance? Do I park my car? Do I tip them now? How do my bags get from the car to the hotel?

"The idea of someone greeting them, welcoming them, showing them how things work, that's key. If that first ten-minute experience is good, you've got 90 percent of the thing licked. Then, if something goes wrong, the guest just thinks it's an unusual thing.

"And Phil is also the last person they see. They think, 'Wasn't Phil Adelman a nice guy?' He wraps up that whole package in the end."

FIRST IMPRESSIONS ARE
LASTING IMPRESSIONS

To make sure that your customers are treated the way you want them to be treated right from the start, three things are essential. First, properly identify the person or people who first interact with the customer. Second, make sure their personalities and styles are consistent with the message you want to convey. And third, make sure they understand how critical they are to the success of your business. After you've done all that, make sure that the people who make the last impression (like the delivery people) know that what they do will have a great impact on whether or not the company gets a chance to make another impression.

THE MAKING OF AN OLD-FASHIONED
COMPANY MAN

Although Phil Adelman didn't become a doorman until after he had finished another whole career, and although he had never worked in a hotel before in his life, Marriott did not turn him into a doorman. He arrived at the Cambridge Marriott fully formed, with the skills, the attitude, the experience, and the personality to be a great doorman. The approach Phil brings to the door almost seems to be part of his grain.

Phil's father, Jack Adelman, was an immigrant and a small businessman, something of an entrepreneur, and a man whose style left a lasting impression on Phil. Jack Adelman started out in Boston wholesaling twenty-five-pound bags of wood and coal used for heating to stores. Then he bought a fuel oil truck and started delivering heating oil to individual homes. He lived with his family in Cambridge, in the same house Phil, his wife, and his mother still occupy. He kept the truck in another suburb, Dorchester, where the fuel oil was stored. He serviced customers around the Boston area.

"He would fill people up when they needed it," says Phil.

"My father would get into his car and head off to the truck when it was 15 degrees below zero with snow on the road.

"Sometimes, he'd have come home on Sunday, and with his work pants still on, still smelling of oil, he'd sit down to his dinner, his meat and his soup, and the phone rings. 'This is Mrs. Cohen in Newton, I'm out of oil.' And he'd say, 'Ada, gotta go.'

"And he'd leave his dinner, get in his car, drive to Dorchester, get the truck, drive to Newton, deliver the oil, back to Dorchester to drop the truck, then back home.

"He was concerned. Maybe Mrs. Cohen had a baby . . ."

What Phil Adelman has done is adapt his father's customer orientation—which is essential in a sole proprietorship—to the large corporate environment. Jack Adelman had to act as if his livelihood depended on how he treated each individual customer—because it did. At Marriott, Phil Adelman treats each customer as if his own performance determines whether that person comes back again.

The way Phil Adelman performs as a doorman, says John Montano, "You'd swear he had a hundred thousand shares of Marriott stock."

EVERYBODY HAS ROLE MODELS

Everybody has role models, people whose qualities and personalities they admire. Clearly, one of Phil's role models is his father—and all you have to do is hear Phil tell the story of his father rising from the Sunday dinner table to go deliver fuel to a customer to know some of what Phil absorbed from his father.

Ask job applicants who their role models are, what people they admire and why. It's not even a bad wild-card question on a written application—a way for applicants to begin to make an impression on you. If you find out whom an applicant admires and emulates, and why, you'll know something about the values they'd bring to your business.

IMPOSSIBLE TO MANAGE, A BOSS'S DREAM

Phil can be a pill.

The very qualities that make him a wonderful employee—his customer orientation, his passion for detail, his ability to see what's wrong, his insistence on follow-through and problem solving—can make him occasionally difficult to manage. If something becomes a priority for Phil, it also quickly becomes a priority for those around him. He can be impatient.

"Phil could be a pain," says his former general manager, Bill Munck. "Your freaking day would be going crazy, you're oversold, you don't have enough help—we never did back in the late eighties—you're about to blow your brains out, and Phil would be at the door bugging you about some little thing. 'Mr. Munck, do you have just one second?' And you'd have to say, 'Yes, Phil, what is it?' If he had one weakness, it was that he wouldn't know when to quit."

"He can be time-consuming," says Mike Wlodowski, who is now front office manager. "I can't say I'm always happy to see him. If I have fifteen minutes, I am."

Even Phil's wife, Helen, says his persistence can drive her crazy. "He says his biggest asset is follow-through, and he's right. He drives me nuts. If I lose something in the house, and he starts looking for it, he won't quit until he finds it, even if I say, 'Forget it!'"

But those comments are all in some sense out of context. Because everyone also has a story of Phil Adelman's thoughtfulness—a favor, an unexpected gift. And as Munck says of Phil, "What he brings to the table is that instantaneous I-want-to-please attitude. He comes to work thinking, What can I do to make the company better?"

WINNERS ARE NEVER HIGH-MAINTENANCE

Phil Adelman can be a little bit of a pest—and if you think as a manager that you don't have time for someone like Phil, imagine having ten Phils—which should be the goal of every great service organization.

But if you don't have time for Phil, you're thinking about your job as a manager backward. Time spent with Phil adds value that ripples throughout the hotel; he is exactly the opposite of a problem. Problem employees often soak up most of a line manager's time, and it is in fact that time that's wasted. All the manager is doing with problem employees is trying to maintain the status quo, or limit the amount that the standards slide.

That's why it's important to understand the difference between high-maintenance employees and low-maintenance employees. High-maintenance employees are perpetually late, don't have complete or clean uniforms, come to work tired or with a sour attitude, mistreat customers, colleagues, and your business. Just because Phil occasionally needs fifteen minutes to talk—and can't always pick the most convenient time—doesn't make him high-maintenance.

Think about the way you spend your time as a manager, especially with regard to staffing and personnel. If you had ten Phils on staff, you'd almost never have to deal with turnover, with discipline, with absenteeism or angry customers or irritated colleagues. And those are the things that are so time-consuming. There would be more than enough time to deal with a wealth of suggestions about how to make your business better.

Although Phil is a little unconventional, and Marriott is a big corporation, the company has done more than learn to accommodate Phil's personality. They've embraced it.

"We were just starting a new doorman," says Phil's supervisor, Marius Gallitano, "and I said to him, 'What you want to do is mold yourself on Phil.'"

The Marriott understands and tries to take advantage of the range of Phil's experience. "The customers have a real sense of security when he's out there," says John Montano. "I don't know if you've ever asked an eighteen-year-old for a restaurant recommendation, but . . . with Phil, there's a sense of maturity out there."

Says Bill Skoglund, the current general manager of the Cambridge Marriott, "Phil would be Phil, regardless of where he worked. Other places might suppress him. If we said, 'You're a doorman, concentrate on that,' he'd be devastated. He'd leave.

"What we do is encourage that in him. We nurture it, we enjoy it. We don't see him as a doorman."

But Phil, in fact, does see himself as a doorman. As Munck says, "He's proud to say, 'I run the door at the Cambridge Marriott.'"

WHAT'S PHIL ADELMAN WORTH?

Phil Adelman holds the door of the Cambridge Marriott with such grace and style that surely some percentage of the hotel's guests are impressed enough to choose Marriott over its competition.

What percent? Let's say just 1 percent. With an estimated average rate of $100 a night, corollary spending of $30, a 55 percent margin, 200 rooms, and a 70 percent occupancy rate, what is 1 percent worth to Marriott?

$130 per day

× 7 days per week

× 52 weeks (Phil can be an attraction even when he's not there because guests definitely don't know when he'll be on vacation)

× 200 rooms

× 70 percent (occupancy rate)

× 55 percent (margin)

× 1 percent

= $36,436 (per year)

The automatic door opener certainly can't touch that.

But think one step beyond that. What if the person in Phil's role does a bad job? If an outstanding doorman influences 1 percent of the guests positively, a bad doorman might influence 1 percent of the guests negatively—causing them to pick some other, more hospitable hotel, driving off $36,000 a year in business. So the difference between Phil and a bad doorman might be not $36,000, but $72,000.

HOW DO YOU FIND
PHIL ADELMAN?

At his first interview for a job at the Cambridge Marriott, Phil Adelman did two revealing things: he told John Montano what he thought the hotel should be like, and he told his personal history. In discussing these non-work-related topics, Phil showed an understanding of the customer perspective.

1. Even for the most ordinary jobs (perhaps especially for those jobs), applicants may not have specific, on-point experience—working the drive-through or the cash register or the front door. But almost everyone has eaten at a fast-food restaurant, or shopped at a clothing store, or stayed at a hotel. So as part of your interview, ask potential employees what kinds of experience they've had as customers in businesses like yours.

    Don't focus just on what experience the person has doing the job, providing the service; find out what experience they've had *receiving* the service. Instead of interviewing a potential employee, think of the meeting as a debriefing of a customer.

    You'll learn how the applicant thinks about the service you deliver, what's important to that person, and how he or she sees the customer-employee relationship. All those things are critical to the attitude that person will bring to taking care of your customers.

2. An all too rarely asked question of applicants is "Who are your role models?" Ask it. The answer will help reveal the values and work ethic of the applicant, and more than experience, that is what you're trying to hire.

3. Do not judge people too quickly, or simply on the basis of a written application. Phil's career doesn't look all that impressive reduced to the blanks on an application form. In person, though, Phil sparkles, which is exactly what you want in your doorman. If you're staffing a position for which personality and attitude are critical, give each applicant a chance to show you his or her personality and attitude.

CHAPTER 2

PERSONALIZED

SERVICE

photo by Marnieve

PAULA DORICCHI

TURNING CUSTOMERS INTO REGULARS

Sometimes the person performing a service is so powerful, so persuasive, that nothing else matters—not the company delivering the service, nor the setting in which it is delivered, nor sometimes even the quality of the product itself.

In such cases, the service provider actually becomes a service performer. And, much as you would with a favorite actor—it doesn't matter where the person is appearing, or in what context—you're going to see the person, for the performance, not for the plot or the producer.

Your first reaction to this idea may be to scoff, to say that such extraordinary service—service that transcends everything else—is the province of people who employ personal servants.

Not so. Almost everyone experiences service like this, without even realizing it.

Anyone who has ever had a favorite real estate agent knows the feeling. Do you care whether the agent works for Coldwell Banker or for Re/Max? Of course not. You care that when you beep her, she calls you back instantly. You care that she knows your taste and needs and doesn't spend a lot of time showing you houses she'd like to sell but that you have no interest in buying.

Independent insurance agents fall into the same category, as do stockbrokers. These are the kind of people you develop a relationship with—their service, in fact, is based on your willingness to trust them. Good insurance agents and stockbrokers don't have customers, they have a clientele.

If you find a stockbroker who understands your goals, your tolerance for risk, your willingness to experiment, and who also produces consistently good results, you don't care what company name appears at the top of your monthly statements. Indeed, should your stockbroker decide to jump from Smith Barney to Merrill Lynch, your account would most likely follow. Why not? It is your relationship to your stockbroker, not to the company, that matters.

There is an even more common example of this phenomenon: the hairstylist. A trusted hairstylist is as rare and precious as a trusted investment adviser. And if you can find someone who consistently cuts your hair in a way that lets you leave the chair with a smile on your face, the place where that stylist wields her scissors really is irrelevant (except perhaps in terms of travel time). And the intramural competition that goes on in most cities among haircutting salons for the best haircutters explicitly confirms that: all that matters is who is cutting the hair. When a really good hairstylist switches salons, she brings her customers with her to the new location. The customers are devoted to *her*—not to the place where she works.

To a somewhat lesser degree, the same is true of travel agents and car mechanics. These are all people you recommend to your friends, especially when they begin to crank about their hairstylist or real estate agent or financial adviser.

The critical element in all these service jobs is your relationship to the person delivering the service. Almost everything else is irrelevant—to the point where you might tolerate some slippage of overall satisfaction in order to maintain the relationship (the hairstylist may move to a salon ten minutes farther away from your home; the car mechanic may join a garage that is busier than the previous one, causing you to have to wait a little longer to get your car serviced).

The power of the connection between such outstanding service performers and their customers is illustrated by the frequency with which travel agents or car mechanics or hairstylists spin out on their own, relying on the loyalty of their customers to start their own businesses.

It is in this drawing power that you, as a manager, will find the great benefits of employing such people, and the great dangers.

If yours is the hair salon that has just hired the city's hottest stylist, you understand the benefits. You not only get someone of talent, skill, and proven ability to attract new customers, you get that person's existing customer base as well. But that hiring coup has also put your whole business at risk, because when you employ people whose skill inspires such loyalty, you don't have control. Your business's customers are not really yours—they belong to the great hairstylist. And should she decide to move on, much of your business (which is really *her* business) will move on with her. You can end up in competition with your own employees for the loyalty of your customers, and most often you'll lose.

You need to manage such service superstars with tremendous skill—they may need flexible hours or slightly better compensation, for instance. And while you have the luck to employ them, you must make every effort to see that the skills, attitude, and standards they set spread to the rest of your business. That way, when they leave, you have a business that is much better for their having been there, and you have a business that is much less at risk of losing all its customers.

The risk and difficulty involved in employing such powerful service performers is so great, in fact, that some organizations have structured their businesses to avoid it. They want the relationship to be strictly between customer and business, and they all but eliminate the chance for people to develop loyalty to a particular service provider.

The discount stock brokerages employ this technique—they advertise the fact that their brokers give no advice. You're unlikely ever to get the same broker twice, let alone follow a broker from one house to the next. The same is true for some national hair cutting chains, like SuperCuts. These places set a base standard for the quality of the haircut you'll get—the same at a mall in Richmond, Virginia, or Austin, Texas—and then they compete with all the other places to get hair done on the basis of things SuperCuts, the company, can control: price (cheap), hours (extensive), convenience (located where you're going anyway), waiting time (minimal). You might get the same stylist every time you get your hair cut for six or nine months, and then she might disappear. And you might feel a twinge of regret, because you liked her, because she did a good job. But you're unlikely to follow her. Your loyalty is to the convenience and the cost of SuperCuts, and that's not going to change just because the person with the clippers has changed.

Indeed, if anything has done more to reduce the extent of personalized service, it is the proliferation of national chains. All kinds of arenas that used to rely on personalized service—from clothing stores and stationery stores to restaurants and hotels—have now made a science of eliminating it.

What personality the chains do have often has the stale aftertaste of a training-manual script—as if the staff were trying to imitate the giddy actors in television commercials. These people don't know your name, and if they pick it up off your credit card and use it, they manage to sound like they're fishing for a tip. They don't know who you are, and likely don't care.

In the most dramatic cases of this kind of homogenization, you end up with indistinguishable products served up in indistinguishable environments. The fast-food companies are a good example of this, as are the car rental companies. But, in truth, renting a car should be an efficient process; car rental company employees should be helpful, but it's more important for them to be quick, and for the cars to be clean and well maintained. As several of the companies have discovered, the rental of a car can be handled virtually without the help of an actual person.

A more revealing example is the national chain restaurants, the ones that claim to offer friendliness and warmth no matter where you are in the country: Bennigan's, Houlihan's, Chili's Ruby Tuesday.

It's almost impossible to find anyone who has a strong preference for one of these bistros over another. Indeed, the fast-food restaurants inspire more passionate loyalty than the Bennigan's and the Chili's with their identical brass rails, fajitas, and grilled chicken Caesar salads. There's nothing wrong with any of them—indeed, they can be quite pleasant. But there also isn't any reason to go to any one of them in particular, except perhaps for convenience and predictability.

What they so sorely lack is *personality*; they lack magnetism. If one of these chains, or even one of the restaurants within a chain, could somehow capture a little of what Americans like most in a corner tavern—familiarity, a real sense of welcome, and the world's best coffee—it would have an insurmountable edge on all the others. Finding a way to have both a local feel—a little character—*and* national standards for service and quality is clearly the next stage of evolution for the chains. Personality—a real sense of a proprietorship on the part of the employees—has been seen as basically incompatible with chain restaurant management, and probably unnecessary. But as we discovered, it is anything but unnecessary, and it is certainly not incompatible.

■

We received perhaps a dozen nominations for the book for waiters and waitresses in the Morrison's restaurant group, which includes four separate national restaurant chains (Morrison's, L&N Seafood, Silver Spoon, and Ruby Tuesday). One nomination in particular, for a waitress at Ruby Tuesday, caught our eye because the form said, "People drive for miles . . . weekly just to enjoy [Paula's] company. Without her they might choose one of our competitors closer to home."

Here was a waitress who seemed to have the drawing power of a good hairstylist.

A supporting letter from a former manager included an equally astonishing claim. "My first weekend as a manager in Greenville," he wrote, "I was a bit perplexed when I walked to the hostess stand and saw two separate waiting lists being taken at the front door. I quizzed the hostess, thinking this might be a new system they were using. 'No,' she replied. 'This is the list for people waiting for the regular tables. The other list has people waiting for Paula's section.'

"In my year and a half working with her, it was not uncommon to have people willing to wait up to an hour to sit in her section—even if other tables were available."

This was our introduction to Paula Doricchi, who waits tables six nights a week at a typical Ruby Tuesday in a typical American shopping mall in Greenville, South Carolina. As we discovered, Paula's whole style revolves around trying to know the people she serves. She is doing what the best service performers do: establishing a relationship of trust with her customers. And she is doing it in a most unlikely setting, a chain restaurant, a place where you would expect *not* to find personalized service. Paula has developed powerful personal relationships in a business where the emphasis is on politeness and turning tables as quickly as possible, not on having people linger over their coffee for hours.

Paula's results are impressive on two counts: she has succeeded in completely transforming the character of the restaurant where she works, turning it into much the kind of place the television ads feature. And the economic benefit of that transformation is dramatic and measurable—Paula is among the chain's top-grossing waitresses.

She proves that it is possible to bring personality, charm, and sincerity back into the service industry, even a service industry dominated by conglomerates with thick books of service procedures and standards. And she proves that companies that learn to hire and nurture people with such attributes—places that do something as basic as serve good food at good prices *and* also find room to let the servers cultivate a sense of ownership—will reap tangible financial rewards.

She also illustrates the importance of recognizing whether your customers are loyal to your business or to your employees, and doing everything you can to keep employees like Paula Doricchi happy and challenged.

But before we found out much about Paula Doricchi, we were determined to get to the bottom of her nomination. We concluded that if there was even a nugget of truth in the claims in her nomination packet—if people were really willing to drive miles to be served by her, if people were really willing to wait for a table in her section when other tables were available—she must be someone very special.

Because, frankly, neither one of us had ever had a server so good that we would be willing to wait even ten minutes extra. When we're hungry, we're hungry.

JUST ANOTHER NIGHT AT PAULA'S PLACE

You have to venture to a corner of the Deep South to find Paula Doricchi, a thirty-five-year-old woman with luxuriant black hair and flashing green eyes, a woman around whom a certain folklore has grown up.

The word is that people are so devoted to her that if she is not working when they show up, they eat somewhere else. The word is that she remembers favorite drinks, favorite dishes, even the names of her customers' dogs.

The lore about Paula includes some real stretchers—that she got hired by accident, that sometimes she alone sells more food than the rest of the restaurant combined, that if she were to leave, her restaurant might collapse. What's more, it is whispered that this very embodiment of down-home Southern hospitality is an interloper—that part of her appeal is the sassy tongue of a New Jersey girl.

And then, of course, there is the kissing.

It is just before five o'clock on a busy Friday night, and Dixie and Carol Howell, an older couple, show up for dinner. Before they even get beyond the hostess stand, Paula kisses both of them on the cheek. "You smell good, do that again," Dixie says, and Paula does.

At seven forty-five Dora and Clyde Bigbee are summoned from their table by a phone call to the bedside of Dora's dying father. As they're leaving, Dora says, "Give me a big kiss." And Paula does.

Betty and Creighton Griggs, who have just finished their third dinner of the week at the restaurant, rise to leave and Paula kisses them both.

Jeff Dopkins, a regional manager of the company that owns the restaurant, leaves around eight-thirty, and Paula kisses him good-bye.

That's the kind of personality Paula Doricchi gives the restaurant where she works—the mood of a classic New Jersey diner or a small Southern café. Paula Doricchi is buoyant, she's exuberant. "People come in in a bad mood, they usually leave in a good mood," she says, just pointing out what's true.

What's really remarkable, though, is that Paula works in one of those national chain bistros where the sociability usually isn't any more authentic than the Tiffany lamps. She is a waitress at one of the 175 Ruby Tuesday restaurants across America—Ruby Tuesday #24, in Greenville, South Carolina. And although #24, like most of the others, is located in a fairly typical shopping mall, and although #24 has the same menu as every other Ruby Tuesday, and the same interior, Paula has transformed it into what is almost a neighborhood tavern, a place of warmth and amiability that manages to be comfortable for regulars and welcoming to those who just wander in.

"I never say, 'Hi, my name is Paula and I'll be your server,'" she says, assuming the artificially chirpy voice of a waitress from a television commercial. "That's phony baloney to me, it's not my style. I'd rather just be nice."

MAKING ORIGINAL COOKIES WITH A COOKIE CUTTER

The cookie cutter doesn't have anything to do with the way the cookies taste. The recipe and the way it's executed are what makes the cookies great. The cookie cutter simply ensures that they all look alike. And a chain is just a chain unless you have a Paula Doricchi. The bigger the chain, the more units, the more important it is to hire people who will give each outlet a unique personality and charm. The architecture certainly isn't going to do it.

You can't have a place with personality without hiring some personalities. You need to find characters and not be afraid to hire them.

Paula has her own unique style. From the kissing of the regulars to the personal greeting of first timers, the Doricchi approach to customer service can't be found in a Ruby Tuesday training manual. And we've got to give the company credit for encouraging Paula to be Paula. The recipe for great service at #24 is no different than anywhere else—it's the people.

The Ruby Tuesday where Paula Doricchi works has plenty of competition—across the way is the mall's food court, and also around the perimeter of the mall, where there are a handful of Ruby Tuesday clones—Cucos, O'Charley's, Bennigan's, Swensons, Applebee's. The challenge for the manager of Ruby Tuesday is somehow to distinguish his restaurant from this encirclement of competitors.

Once or twice someone has tried to hire Paula away—a prospect that makes her managers shudder.

"If she quit tomorrow and went to Applebee's," says Joe Lafferty, who was one of her managers, "we'd lose three thousand dollars a week in sales."

"Her leadership in that restaurant—she doesn't just impact her four or five tables," says Jeff Dopkins, area director for the region that includes #24, and a former manager there. "She makes the managers better—she's been with the company longer than most of them, and she knows what's right and wrong. She raises the entire level of performance in the restaurant. Every single person that works there was trained by her. If she pulled out, it would devastate that restaurant."

THE PLEASURES AND PERILS OF
SERVICE PERFORMERS

Jeff Dopkins has neatly summed up the benefits of having Paula on staff, and also the dangers. Not only does Paula generate all kinds of business, she sets the performance standards for the restaurant. The managers work up to her level, and she trains new staff, so they, too, work up to her level. As far as possible, Ruby Tuesday is using Paula to create a whole staff of Paulas.

But because so much of Paula's success is based on her personality, few of her colleagues actually have a clientele, as she does. And therein lies the danger. The people who come twice or three times a week to eat at Ruby Tuesday with Paula are Paula's customers, not Jeff Dopkins's customers. It is critical as a manager to understand the difference. Because if someone should make an effort to hire Paula away, you as a manager need to know just how valuable she is, so you can do what you should to keep her, and to keep her happy.

Given her importance to the restaurant, the story of Paula Doricchi's hiring is remarkable. One day in February 1983, Paula, who was twenty-five, was in the mall shopping and happened to walk past the yet-unopened Ruby Tuesday. The manager who opened the restaurant, Chip Thompson, was standing outside.

"He said, 'Hey, do you have a job?'" Paula says. "I said, 'Well, sort of.'" Paula was then waitressing at another local restaurant, Cork and Cleaver. "He said, 'Come on and fill out an application, we're hiring.'"

Something about Paula—something about her personality—clearly caught Thompson's attention. Part of it may simply have been her open, friendly response to his unconventional hiring gambit.

This random method of recruitment didn't strike Paula as particularly odd. "He was just a nice guy, as I found out after the fact. And I would talk to anybody, as you know. He took a chance, and here I am, and the rest is history."

Actually, not quite. After a week of training, before actually starting work, Paula had to take a test for food and liquor knowledge.

"I aced the food part, but I failed the liquor test so bad." Paula rolls her eyes. "I don't drink that much, I didn't know all that stuff." She almost seems to be still embarrassed about it, years later. "Chip said if it wasn't for my personality, I wouldn't have been hired."

PASSING THE PERSONALITY TEST

Imagine: If it wasn't for Paula's personality, she'd never have been hired. If it wasn't for her personality, she wouldn't be the best waitress in the Ruby Tuesday chain. If it wasn't for her personality, she wouldn't be a lesson for managers. When you think about it, after you get past a person's personality, there isn't much else that's important to consider when you're hiring a server for a Ruby Tuesday.

As a matter of fact, personality is probably the most important factor, when it's not the *only* factor, in making a good hiring decision for almost any service job. When you look at all the types of frontline service jobs in this world, there are relatively few that require skills that can't be easily taught. Prior experience is usually overrated. But the personality of the employee is something that management can't change.

So Chip Thompson may have been on to something very interesting. He approached Paula out of the blue, as a total stranger—just as a customer would—and he was instantly able to gauge her reaction, which was friendly, even welcoming. He might have approached a dozen different people in the mall before stumbling on someone who had Paula's easy response, but when he did, he knew he had found someone who would make customers feel as comfortable as she made him feel.

As a manager interviewing prospective employees, pay more attention to their personalities. Does she smile easily? Does he make eye contact when talking? Is she easy to like?

If prospective employees are going to be dealing with customers, the smile, the eye contact, the personality will be on
display every day.

Paula Doricchi works six nights a week and the income from
at least one night a week goes to pay for child care. She is working as hard as she can for around twenty thousand dollars a year.

Although she has only a high school diploma, Paula Doricchi
could choose to do something that pays more and is less exhausting. Even if she wanted to stick with waitressing, she could work
at a more expensive restaurant, the kind of place where the
tips—rather than the checks—are twenty-five dollars per table.

So what the heck is she doing at Ruby Tuesday?

The answer is as deceptively simple as Paula Doricchi sometimes seems to be. She's been at Rubys—as she sometimes calls
it—long enough so that she gets the schedule she wants. She likes
working in the evenings, because she's home when her two
daughters wake up in the morning, she gets to spend the day
with four-year-old Alycia, and she's home when eight-year-old
Danielle gets home from school. She never has to work on Sunday. Although there are no formal sick leaves, Ruby Tuesday #24
is appreciative enough of Paula that when she calls in sick, they
cover her shift. (She has called in sick two nights in ten years.) If
she needs a little extra money, there's almost always an extra
shift or two she can pick up.

"My life is set," she says. "I'm making four hundred and fifty
dollars a week, and I can shut the door and go home."

IT ISN'T JUST THE MONEY

There's much more to job satisfaction than money—and
there are ways to keep your best employees happy besides
pay. Paula could clearly go somewhere else and make more
money, but there would be a high cost to her in terms of
lifestyle—the convenience of her hours, the way Ruby Tuesday accommodates her desire to work particular days, the
chance to earn extra money as she needs to. Indeed, Paula's
seniority at Ruby Tuesday, the respect the company has for

her, and the way the job allows Paula to structure her family life clearly mean more to her than money.

It never hurts to ask employees what, besides money, would make their work and home lives better. There are many effective ways to find this out: informally, across the desk during a routine conversation, or over lunch; more formally (and sometimes more productively), in anonymous, division-wide or company-wide surveys that ask employees specifically what they like about their work environment, their company, their boss—and what they don't like. We work with a concept we call Internal Marketing that focuses on making sure employees are happy and have the tools they need to do their jobs. It focuses, in essence, on treating employees like customers. Nothing is lost by asking questions like "What can we do to enable you to be more effective in your job?"

The answers might surprise you, and the resulting requests are often surprisingly easy to implement. Most often, people want better basic communication about the goals of the company, and simple things that would let them do their jobs better—upgraded computers, more filing space, flexible schedules. The real surprise will be the payoff such low-cost changes provide in terms of morale, productivity, and retention.

Paula is petite, a little under five feet, and for work she wears khaki slacks, a white shirt, and the real essential: thick-soled, nonskid shoes. She also wears a Ruby Tuesday watch. In fact, one of Ruby Tuesday's trademark red-and-white-striped awnings hangs over her back porch—the restaurant was replacing it, and Paula gladly took the old one home. She is proud to be connected to Ruby Tuesday.

IDENTIFYING WITH THE COMPANY, PART I

Nothing says more about Paula Doricchi's attitude than her desire to wear a Ruby Tuesday watch and her desire to

have the company's trademark awning (even a slightly tattered version) hanging over her own deck.

That's the kind of goodwill and easy marketing that is
worth the price of a few logo watches and insignia sweatshirts. Put your company's name on stuff people like—mugs,
baseball caps, jackets, pullovers, pens, pads—and give this
merchandise to your employees. Or let them earn these
goods by achieving modest performance goals. You should
take advantage of every opportunity for people to identify
with the company. And you should allow people to express
their pride in where they work.

One caveat: buy good merchandise—invest in quality
sweatshirts, not cheap ones. The last thing you need is your
name adorning a shabby-looking sweatshirt.

More than simply a place of employment, Ruby Tuesday #24
is second only to Paula's home and family in terms of how she
identifies herself. In a way often portrayed romantically on television but rarely achieved in reality, Paula's restaurant and her
work are as comfortable, as entertaining, as energizing for her as
for her customers. Paula doesn't so much wait on tables as she
presides over them, the way Johnny Carson presided over "The
Tonight Show."

"I really enjoy my customers," she says. "That's what makes
my job. At a better restaurant, you can't talk with people, you
can't get close with your customers. It's not the type of place people frequent, you know? It would probably be better financially,
but it wouldn't be as much fun. I wouldn't love going to work
like I do."

IDENTIFYING WITH THE COMPANY,
PART II

It's not hard to see what Paula Doricchi gets out of her
work. She likes her customers, she likes talking to them, getting to know them, serving them, feeling as if she's an important part of their lives. If you can't see it, all you have to

do is ask Paula what she likes about her work—she'll tell you.

Tap in to what it is that makes your employees feel good about their jobs—ask them, ask their customers—and once you discover the source of their satisfaction, don't mess with it. It is that satisfaction that makes them feel part of the larger enterprise, that allows them to identify with not just the customers, but the goals of the company as well.

FRIDAY NIGHT AT PAULA'S PLACE

At four-thirty, when Paula comes on duty at the Ruby Tuesday in Haywood Mall, the Friday night crush is still a couple of hours away. The immediate concern at this evening's preshift meeting is the menu. Ruby Tuesday is grappling with a problem all kinds of businesses face—how to change the product lineup without alienating the customers. The company is phasing in a new menu a few units at a time, and #24 is only in its fifth day with the new one. The servers report that some of the customers—particularly the regulars—are sulky about the loss of their favorite items from the old menu. The most effective way to cope with such changes—whether the business is a restaurant or a line of cars—is to provide the frontline employees with plenty of information, and plenty of support.

Maggie Salemme, an assistant manager, tries both to warn and soothe the servers at the preshift meeting.

"Does anybody know the difference between the nacho pizza and the top-notch pizza?" Salemme asks. "Tues-tados," she continues. "Does anybody know what's under these?"

"Chips, chili, and cheese," comes the singsong response from the staff.

"Too much lettuce," adds one waitress.

"They don't have salsa," adds another.

Doricchi, who is left-handed, is sitting quietly, signing "Paula" on a stack of checks.

"People are liking the chicken alfredo," Salemme says brightly. "One woman did take the 800 number because the menu didn't have steak teriyaki anymore. I told her we have the top sirloin instead. She liked it. You just gotta turn the negative into a positive."

Says a waitress, "A man threw the menu on the table and said, 'Where's the beef chimichanga?'" It has gone the way of the popular steak teriyaki.

Doricchi, who has been through a couple of menu changes, who has seen the customer mood evolve from unhappiness to acceptance to enthusiasm, jumps in with a little counsel based on her own experience. She recommends two things to her fellow servers: learning the new menu thoroughly—both what the dishes are and how they taste—to be in a position to suggest alternatives. And she recommends patience.

"People don't like change," she tells her fellow servers, "but they'll get used to it."

THE ART OF SELLING CHANGE

Change is plenty hard on the customers, but what about its impact on the people who have to bring the news of change to the customers? The employees are the ones on the front lines—and it isn't always pleasant when change is afoot.

And you can't sell change to customers if you can't first sell it to your employees. They are the ones who can persuade customers to be adventurous, or at least open-minded. But your employees can't be working with you if they don't understand what you're trying to do, or what the change embodies.

When you need to change the product or service you deliver to customers, don't try to sugarcoat the process, or minimize it. Explain as much as possible to employees the reasons for the change, the details of how the new process will work, the advantages and, if necessary, the negatives. Suggest how best to explain the change to your customers.

And spend time reinforcing the material. A project like introducing a new menu can take a month or more, and the staff will need support during the entire time. Customers are often cranky about change because they care passionately about what your business provides them. Don't forget to remind your employees of that.

And take Paula's advice: provide as much information as possible, and be patient.

On this Friday, Paula has four regular tables, up on a small platform in the nonsmoking section: three booths along a wall and a table standing just off from them. She's also taking care of one table in the smoking section. This is the Bigbees—Clyde and Dora—who are Paula's longest-standing regulars. They started asking to sit in her section in 1984, when Paula was pregnant with her first child. This afternoon, they've already settled in, working on their cigarettes and waiting for Paula to come by and take their drink orders—blended seven and seven for him, rum and diet Coke for her.

"Clyde always changes his drink," Paula says at the bar. "Dora always orders the same thing. They only get a little ice in their drinks. With everyone else, it's ice up to the top."

KNOWING THE CUSTOMER IS GOOD BUSINESS

Paula knows a lot more than just her customers' names and food and beverage preferences. She also knows their kids' names, their occupations, even the health of their parents.

Research has shown a powerful connection between a customer's consistent business at a restaurant and the ability of a server to remember the customer's name on a subsequent visit. The connection between repeat business and recognition is so important that the Golden Corral Family Steak House chain has built an incentive program around this single issue—employees get pins for every hundred customers they recognize by name, and some employees now know and can greet a thousand customers on sight.

If you're staffing a position for which remembering people is an asset, don't hesitate to give memory tests. There are all kinds of sophisticated memory tests available, but there are simpler ways to evaluate an applicant. Introduce a prospective employee to a series of potential colleagues and see if the applicant remembers their names. Or use a set of pictures to which you have attached names.

Customer recognition is invaluable in every sort of retail business. It not only makes customers feel welcome, it makes them feel important—important enough to remember. Just look at how Paula treats her customers, and what it's done for Ruby Tuesday #24.

Paula delivers the drinks and then turns her attention to a new couple who have been seated in the middle one of her three booths. They both order "PhD" chicken sandwiches—chicken with melted cheese on top.

What is PhD? "It's 'pro-health dining,'" Paula says as she heads for the kitchen. But how can it be healthy—doesn't it have cheese melted on it? "Yes," says Paula, "but it's low-fat mozzarella and only one ounce."

KNOWING THE PRODUCT
IS GOOD BUSINESS

At times it seems to the customers that Paula Doricchi knows the contents of every dish on the menu. She does. Product knowledge is something Ruby Tuesday doesn't leave to chance. In addition to learning the basic menu when someone is first hired, whenever there's a menu change, those changes are reviewed at preshift meetings to make sure everyone knows them thoroughly.

You may feel that it's your employees' responsibility to know your products, but it's management's job to be sure they *do* know and that they stay current. Too often, product education ends after new-employee orientation. If you really want knowledgeable employees, product training should be an ongoing program.

The best way to do product training is to let the employees experience the product. Restaurant employees should eat the food on the menu; rental-car agents should drive the company's cars; retail clerks should wear the store's clothes.

Paula almost never heads into the kitchen or heads out from the kitchen empty-handed—she brings back dirty dishes from her tables, or from other tables, and she takes out a water pitcher or an iced tea pitcher.

"I don't hover," she says, "but I like my tea full when I eat out. I wait tables like I'd like to be treated."

Paula turns her attention to another pair of regulars. One lady orders a house salad. "Have you seen our Caesar salad?" Paula asks. "We have a Caesar salad that's wonderful—and a chicken Caesar as well."

"Okay," says the customer, instantly persuaded. "I'll have the Caesar."

Why did Paula bother to suggest the Caesar? "Because it's something different," she says, "and she'll love it. It's really good. It's sixty cents less than what she was going to order—and I want everybody to try out the new menu."

SELLING INSTEAD OF WAITRESSING

A waitress takes orders and delivers food. Paula is much more than a waitress—she's a menu consultant to her customers. And by being that, she often manages to sell more food and drinks than anyone else in the restaurant. Most successful salespeople are consultants to their customers.

Paula, though, doesn't think of herself as a salesperson, although she has enough experience in sales to know she is part salesperson. As a manager, make sure that anyone in contact with customers has the opportunity to make a sale. Help those people identify opportunities to make a sale.

The rental-car agent can suggest a more expensive but roomier car to a family; clerks at book or video stores can recommend titles similar to those a customer is buying.

As in Paula's case, selling may be as easy as suggesting a Caesar salad to a customer. This is selling as service.

Even though tips account for over half her income, Paula is matter-of-fact about tipping, as if it were a natural phenomenon over which she has no more control than the coming of night. "Some people have the mentality that they don't need to tip." She has only one rule about tipping: "I always go back to the table with the change. I would hate to ever assume."

GETTING TIPS ISN'T THE GOAL

Managers are being taught in the nineties that profits are the result of well-managed processes. Employees who work for tips need to understand that the same theory applies to them: tips aren't the goal of good service; they're the result of good service. Focusing on the service instead of the tips will ultimately yield larger tips.

Since bigger tips mean happier employees, managers should help educate their employees on this and other secrets of generating larger tips. Most companies ignore this entire issue, feeling that the employees' tips are their business. In fact, helping servers get bigger tips is management's business. For example, Ruby Tuesday spends time educating servers on the details of new menu items. That lets them make suggestions and answer questions—in short, deliver better service—that should lead to bigger tips.

The same logic applies to bonuses. Like tips, bonuses are the result of achievement, not the goal of achievement. There's nothing wrong with thinking about bonuses as incentives to perform. But if top performance depends on bonuses, you're not getting the best work out of your employees—even if they are "earning" their bonuses.

Paula doesn't neglect her walk-in customers for her regulars. Neither does she presume that she can take it easy with the regulars because they are inclined to view her indulgently. "The regulars are exhausting," she says. "I was so worn out last Friday. I had three hours of regulars. They take more work. They like to chat. And we have real customers, too. Sometimes they suffer."

When Customers Aren't Customers

The real secret to Paula's success is revealed when she describes newcomers as "real customers." Notice that Paula doesn't think of her "regulars" as "real customers"—they're her friends.

How many companies understand the power of relationship selling and train their frontline employees to build customer relationships? When Paula's regulars stay away for a few weeks, she calls them at home to see if everything is OK. Paula builds relationships by instinct, but managers can and should give employees the systems that allow them to build customer relationships.

At some hotels, when you check in for the second time, the clerk has access to information about your room preference, and perhaps even the precise room you stayed in last time, and can offer you that room, or at least that configuration, again. Pizza Hut's home-delivery operation keeps a record of what kind of pizza you ordered last time so the operator can offer you the same one again.

Such systems are effective selling tools, and they give the sense that even large corporations are trying to accommodate the customer's preferences. The systems should be transparent to the customer. The hungry caller doesn't need to know how Pizza Hut remembered the kind of pizza he ordered last time. The room service customer doesn't need to ponder how the person taking his order knows his name when he picks up the phone. But often such systems require little more than a personal computer and a good database program.

Paula delivers breadsticks to a table of just-arrived regulars. The breadsticks are deservedly popular, really miniature loaves of whole wheat bread. There was briefly a set-to about breadsticks a couple of years ago. Ruby Tuesday started charging for them—fifty cents for two, ninety-nine cents for four.

"For seven years, they gave away breadsticks, then they start charging for them," says Paula, with a little disdain. "My customers were just irate. I sat down with the area director. He said to me, 'You're approaching this the wrong way.' I said, 'No, I'm not. Bread is complimentary everywhere, it always has been.' Sure enough, two weeks later, they stopped charging."

HEADQUARTERS INTELLIGENCE IS AN OXYMORON

Sooner or later more companies will come to understand that decisions affecting customers must involve the people who deal with them every day. It is generally more important for information to flow up through the organization than down through the organization.

Many companies have customer advisory groups that help provide senior management with valuable input. More companies need to have employee advisory groups that are consulted before any issue affecting a customer is resolved. Such groups are easy enough to organize—just bring together a small group of employees and lay out the changes you are considering. Let them tell you what they think the reaction will be, what the strengths and weaknesses of the changes are. The employees may even suggest some changes that hadn't occurred to management.

AN EARLY TASTE FOR WORK

Paula, the middle of five children, started working early—at age twelve in a neighborhood clothing store—but only in part to earn money.

Although she did graduate from high school, Paula says she hated school. "I couldn't wait to get out. I got work so young, I got a taste for it."

WORKING IS HABIT-FORMING

Most employment applications and employee resumes assume that life begins with the completion of one's formal education. We even think of an applicant's "first real job" as the one he or she gets upon leaving school. While we know that personalities are mostly formed at a very early age, we fail to realize that work habits are learned early, too.

When interviewing prospective employees, have them talk about their first job—their *real* first job—not what *they* might call their first real job. Real first jobs can take you back to a child's preteen years. For real service stars, they almost always do. That's when work habits are formed, sales skills initially developed, and the thrill of victory first tasted.

With people who get formal jobs at an early age—right out of high school, even during high school—the key question is: why did you go to work? Watch for people like Paula Doricchi, who say that they couldn't wait to start working. Their enthusiasm is a signal of someone who may well turn out to be a devoted and diligent employee.

One of Paula's early jobs was as a manager and salesperson at a family-owned clothing store called The Garment Center. One of her sisters worked there with her.

"We were so competitive at the dress store," Paula says, "that my sister and I had a bank account at the corner bank and we'd run to the bank and take out money just to buy clothes to beat last year's sales total for the day. I still have those clothes, I still wear 'em."

A LITTLE SALES EXPERIENCE GOES A LONG WAY

Part of what makes Paula such a good waitress is her sales sense. You don't have to be hiring her for a commissioned sales job to realize that the competitive instincts that powered her during her early job at the dress store will also serve her well now—and your business, too.

An employee's experience doesn't all have to be precisely on-point to help her or him do a good job for you. Listen closely in an interview for clues about how seriously people performed in their other jobs. Just because
someone is changing fields or roles doesn't mean the previous job didn't work out. Sometimes it's just a sign of a wide-
ranging mind, and sometimes it's a chance to hire someone
who will bring skills you don't find in the people you normally hire.

Paula brought her ambition, her maturity, and her sense of
family to Ruby Tuesday, and the company embraced it. Jeff Dopkins, who came to the store as Paula's manager in 1988 and is
now her area director, says that when he arrived "the thing I remember most is that she introduced me to more customers than
any other person in that restaurant or in Greenville. I remember
how welcome she made me feel at the restaurant, and how welcome in general. I really believe that was the key to me being
successful at that restaurant."

Dopkins says Paula sets a high standard, not only for herself
and her fellow servers, but for management as well. "She's easy
to manage, unless you don't follow company standards. If you've
got a manager trainee or a new manager there, she will challenge
them. To me, as the general manager, I loved that. It was like
having another manager on the floor at times."

More than that, Dopkins says, although money is not Paula's
only motivation, "She understands the relationship between all
the things she's doing and putting money in her pocket. If more
people could understand that win-win relationship, we'd be a lot
more successful."

For Paula, her work ethic is unremarkable, just part of the
texture of her personality. "If I were digging ditches, I'd give 100
percent." The company, she says, "lets me be me."

Although her regulars require more attention than walk-ins,
they are the key not only to her success, but to her satisfaction. "I
think what keeps her going is the regulars," says Joe Lafferty,
Paula's manager in 1992. "She feeds off them and they feed off
her. She's like, 'Oh, the McClains are coming tonight, I'm so ex-
cited!'"

Paula is often asked to help open new restaurants—something she does less now because of her family—and has consistently refused management positions, both because of the time they take and because initially she'd make less money.

She does seem to have licked the liquor-knowledge problem that plagued her on her preemployment test. In 1988, there was a wine sales contest. Servers got points for selling various kinds of wine—one point for a glass of house, three points for chardonnay, five for premium, ten for a bottle; the points were based on the profitability of the item sold. Paula was averaging sixty or seventy points a night—amassing fifteen hundred points over four weeks. She not only won the contest, Paula herself actually sold more wine that month than the next two entire restaurants in her area sold combined.

As Friday night winds to a close, all three of Paula's booths are occupied by strangers, and the fourth table is empty. Trouble comes from the couple in the middle booth, where both the man and the woman have ordered the beef and bird, a twelve-dollar chicken and steak combination.

"She's really unhappy," says the man. "That doesn't taste good." He's indicating the steak.

"It's not marinated anymore," Paula says. "Can I get you something else?"

"No," the woman says, "it's just that it doesn't taste good . . ."

Paula comes back to their table with the couple's check—reduced from thirty-three dollars to twenty-three dollars by the removal of two steaks. "We charged you only for the chicken," Paula says. "And we'll marinate the steaks for you if you call us in the future. We'll do the chicken as well."

The woman wants to know if they can have a doggie bag—so they can take the steak they don't like and didn't pay for home with them. "Sure," says Paula, "I'll bring you a box."

Several weeks later, the couple actually returns to the restaurant for dinner.

TURNING UNHAPPY CUSTOMERS
INTO REGULARS

Glitches that happen while serving a customer are classic examples of problems that present great recovery opportunities. To recover, first the person delivering the service must realize that blame is irrelevant to the customer and the cause of the problem is best addressed at another time. Second, the server needs to empathize with the customer. Paula doesn't focus on excuses. Third, it is imperative that the offer to compensate for the customer's dissatisfaction be both instant and appropriate. No charge for the steaks in this case is appropriate, and the reaction by Paula was swift. Finally, some additional offer must be made to ensure that the customer doesn't leave feeling guilty, or worse, think that he or she is not wanted back again. Paula's offer to specially prepare the steaks in advance in the future certainly makes the customers feel important. All of the elements necessary for a service recovery are here. And it works.

There's an even more important lesson here, though. Bad service inevitably leaves a strong impression. But if a poor service performance is rescued with skill, you can actually impress a customer more than if you simply gave adequate service to begin with. Recovering swiftly from bad service leaves a far stronger impression than ordinary service—and can turn a casual customer into a disciple for your business. That's why recovery is so critical.

What Paula Doricchi does at Ruby Tuesday #24 is more than simply turning customers into regulars. She turns the regulars into friends.

First thing Saturday morning, Dora Bigbee—who left Ruby Tuesday abruptly Friday after a call from her father's nursing home—calls Paula at home to tell her that Dora's father died overnight.

"I was hysterical crying," says Paula. "She wasn't crying, but I was crying. I get torn up."

And Paula spends Saturday afternoon in her kitchen making a big pan of lasagna for the wake for Dora's dad the next day.

RECRUITING THE PAULAS
OF THE WORLD

The biggest obstacle facing most managers' ability to recruit proven talent is identifying the right people. Actually, it's not all that hard to do. When was the last time you shopped your competition to see who their best people were instead of simply analyzing their prices or quality? Shopping the competitor's people can pay much bigger dividends. In fact, it's the first step in building a championship team. You can't recruit the Paulas of the world if you don't know where to find them.

IS IT REALLY "PAULA'S PLACE"?

The answer to this critical question, and the implications of that answer, will ultimately decide the fate of Ruby Tuesday #24, Paula Doricchi, and the other restaurants in the neighborhood.

In acknowledging that Paula's departure would devastate the restaurant, Paula's area manager shows he understands that Paula's customers are really *her* customers, not the restaurant's. Paula obviously doesn't comprehend this, or the consequences. She says that her regulars are one of the things keeping her from going somewhere else. It's pretty obvious, however, that her regulars would follow her instantly. Right now, they don't come in if she's not there. So it's clear that, to a great extent, Ruby Tuesday is really Paula's Place—only Paula doesn't know it yet.

Indeed, Paula's manager is no different than the manager of a hair salon or a stock brokerage or an insurance agency. The question managers need to consider is: do our customers do business with us because of the services we provide, or because of the people who provide those services?

If anyone is ever able to convince Paula—or any good hairstylist, stockbroker, or insurance agent—to change allegiance, the new company must realize that its customers will still be Paula's. All she'll be doing is allowing her new employer to do business with her customers.

So employing people like Paula Doricchi involves a delicate balance—a business needs people like Paula for it to be as successful as it can, but managers must realize that employing people like Paula poses a critical challenge. You need to keep them happy, because should they leave, their departure can hurt business as much as their presence has helped it.

In the final analysis, Paula's Place is a traveling show. It is wherever Paula is.

WHAT'S PAULA DORICCHI WORTH?

Paula Doricchi is an easy example of what an employee is worth because her manager told us what business she could take away if she left. We can use the same figure ($3,000 per week) to estimate the business for which she is responsible.

If Paula's $3,000 per week disappeared, that would reduce total sales by $3,000 × 50 weeks (we will assume her customers don't stay when they find out she's away on vacation), or $150,000 a year. If those meals were not being served, the variable costs associated with them would disappear. This would include the food, Paula's labor, and some of the cooking labor. But other costs—rent, utilities, overhead—would still need to be paid. In light of those costs, we can be conservative and estimate a 25 percent profit margin on incremental sales of the type Paula is bringing in.

We can very safely argue that Paula is worth to Ruby Tuesday: $150,000 × 25 percent, or $37,500, per year.

And that doesn't begin to estimate her value to the organization as a motivator, a trainer, someone who sets standards and an example, someone who makes her restaurant an attractive place to eat and work.

HOW DO YOU FIND
PAULA DORICCHI?

Well, we can't say we recommend the method Paula's first boss used to find Paula—walking out into the middle of a shopping mall and picking her out at random. Except that there may have been a little method to his desperation. Even while she was just walking through the mall, that manager may have seen in Paula the kind of animation, the spark, he knew he wanted in the people who worked in his restaurant.

Because, ultimately, that is what Paula had to offer. There are several clues here to good hiring.

1. Keep in mind what you really need in the job you're hiring for. Yes, being a waitress involves knowing the menu and the liquor selection; but a far more critical quality is the intangible—verve, personality, charm. You can teach someone the menu, charm you have to hire.

2. You can minimize your own risk when you overlook test scores or lack of previous direct experience by talking to the applicant—or, more important, listening to the applicant. Given Paula's story about how she used her own money to beat sales records at the dress store where she worked as a young woman, it's quite likely she'll make a serious effort to learn the menu and the liquor selection.

As it turned out in this case, the risk was well worth taking. Not only has Paula's personality turned out to be one of the keys to the success of Ruby Tuesday #24, Paula is the one who wins the liquor sales contests. And her test scores notwithstanding, she's the one who seems to be able to remember everybody's name, their birthdays, anniversaries, kids, even the names of their pets.

And Paula Doricchi is another example of the importance of interviewing people in person. A restaurant manager or human resources professional evaluating her strictly on the basis of a written application and the liquor test (failed) would not necessarily have picked Paula as a good candidate for the job. But in person, it doesn't take ten minutes to realize how outgoing and personable she is, and how far that will go in a restaurant, especially one that needs personality.

3. Note how clearly Paula's attitude about work was conveyed by her stories about starting work early and being eager to leave school and work full-time. This shows a potent work ethic, a kind of discipline that a college degree cannot guarantee. Paula has worked six nights a week, from four-thirty to eleven-thirty, with only two weeks off a year, for ten years.

CHAPTER 3

SERVICE AS A PASSION FOR PROBLEM SOLVING

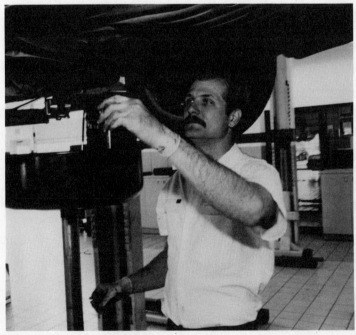

photo by Clint Grant

KEITH SPRING

PERFECTION IS THE ONLY STANDARD

In the first two chapters of this book, we have looked at service performers and kinds of service that are distinctive in large measure because of the personalities of the people involved. Both Phil Adelman and Paula Doricchi are people who make a powerful and lasting impression, and they do so precisely because of the charm and warmth and thoughtfulness they bring to their encounters with other people.

You would be unlikely to forget being taken care of by either one of them—and that is precisely why they are so good at what they do. They connect with people, they have the instincts and the experience to take care of people.

We turn now to the opposite end of the service spectrum—to a kind of service where the social skills of the service provider are almost completely irrelevant to the quality of the service delivered.

This is repair service.

When you need something fixed, there are only two real measures of the quality of the service: did the broken item get fixed, and did it get fixed on time?

With repair service, the outcomes are absolutely measurable. And unlike the kinds of service that Phil Adelman and Paula Doricchi deliver, the tangible performance of the provider of repair service is far more important than the intangible performance. One is perfectly willing to endure a shoe repair shop where the cobbler is quirky or indifferent or simply uncommunicative if the shoes are well resoled and ready in a couple of days. Likewise with a tailor or a plumber.

You can extend this idea to even a less obvious profession like cab driving. A cabbie with a wonderful personality, someone filled with trivia about the city and recommendations for the best restaurants, is grand; but it won't salvage the quality of the cab ride if he gets lost. There is an aphorism in the service industry that neatly sums this up: "A smile on the face of a limo driver is no substitute for a car."

Perhaps the best example of this genre is the one we've chosen as an illustration: a car mechanic. The thing that marks a truly extraordinary mechanic is not how he treats the customers, it's how he treats the cars. He treats the customers, in fact, only as well as he treats their cars.

Here is a job where what really matters are mechanical skill and problem solving. You don't want a mechanic who can bat the chat, you want a mechanic who can figure out what's wrong with your car and fix it. You want a mechanic with the integrity of a jurist and the single-minded passion for problem solving of a scientist pursuing the cure to a disease.

And you want your mechanic to work in an environment that acknowledges that problem solving is a five- or six- or seven-step process. Indeed, repair service is part of a whole genre of service delivery that requires systematic, rigorous problem-solving skills, where the right answer isn't always the first or most obvious answer, where the real solution may require several efforts and some serious thinking.

Even in the auto repair business, where this process of educated trial and error must be part of the routine, the industry is rarely structured to encourage a systematic problem-solving process. Most businesses require employees to respond instantly—mechanics have to book a certain amount of business per day, and their compensation is based on piece rate. In such a setup, thinking and problem solving are not only not encouraged, they are actively discouraged.

Looking for an example of a more sophisticated kind of mechanic, we turned to Carl Sewell, a businessman who is renowned for his insights about service, which are collected in his bestselling book, *Customers for Life*. Sewell has a string of car dealerships in Dallas: Sewell Buick, Sewell GMC, Sewell Hyundai, Sewell Village Cadillac, Sewell Lexus. He provides loaner cars for his service customers, he insists on delivering cars when they are promised, and he almost never charges more for repairs than was originally estimated. Every Lexus is washed and vacuumed before it is returned to the customer. The Cadillac dealership, Sewell's flagship operation, even has a restaurant on the premises. In a J. D. Power & Associates customer-satisfaction survey, the quality of service at Sewell's Cadillac dealership left the rest of the nation's Cadillac dealers in the dust—averaging 30 percent better than the national average, and Cadillac is routinely the top-rated domestic brand in service satisfaction.

When the Lexus first came on the market in 1989, Sewell immediately added it to his constellation of dealerships. The Lexus was quickly acknowledged to be one of the best-made, best-running cars in the world. Lexus has also redefined the car-sales process and the relationship between car dealership and customer. Not only was Sewell one of the first Lexus dealers in the world, he quickly became one of the nation's leading Lexus dealers. So we were curious: what would one of the nation's best car dealers, selling one of the world's best cars, recommend in the way of a car mechanic?

Sewell didn't hesitate. He pointed us in the direction of Keith Spring, the first mechanic he hired for Sewell Lexus.

In Keith Spring, we found a soft-spoken, deceptively easygoing man with an absolute obsession for making cars run perfectly. To Keith, the particular customer is in some sense irrelevant: he assumes that every customer wants his or her car to run perfectly, without a rattle or a hesitation or a vibration.

The way Keith treats the customers—and he has some contact with them—is irrelevant, really. It is the way he treats the cars that counts.

Keith musters awesome data-gathering and analytical skills—listening to a car, feeling how it handles, thinking constantly about what the source of a problem might be—in such a way that his talent has the air of intuition rather than problem solving. He regularly fixes cars that other Lexus mechanics—at his dealership or competing ones—have given up on.

And, as you'll see, Keith works in an environment that absolutely supports his passion and style. Lexus and Sewell want nothing more than for the cars to run perfectly—Lexus's slogan is, "The Relentless Pursuit of Perfection."

There is only one flaw in using Keith Spring as an exemplar of this style of service. It would be best if he were a cantankerous, eccentric, antisocial fellow. In fact, though, his people skills are as well-developed as those of Paula Doricchi (without the kissing). He is as unceasingly patient, thoughtful, and good-humored with Sewell's often demanding customers as he is with their cars.

PROBLEM CHILD, PART I

The four thousand pounds of taupe luxury sedan—a 1990 Lexus LS 400—are floating innocently at about shoulder height on the lift in the service bay. The car presents the worst type of automobile affliction, the kind of problem that slowly makes car owners crazy and gnaws at car mechanics until they plead for a long stint doing oil changes and wheel balancings.

This Lexus has a noise.

Not just any kind of a noise—an *intermittent* noise, a noise that appears and disappears with infuriating randomness.

The car, three years old, is on its fifth service visit this year just to track and eliminate this noise, and on the previous four visits, technician Keith Spring has only actually heard the noise once.

"I've taken it out twice this morning," Spring says. "I've driven it for twenty minutes, and it never did it. Then, as I was pulling in the driveway to the dealership, it popped." Spring thunks a socket wrench against the car's frame to give a sense of what the noise sounded like. It seems to be coming from somewhere around the right front wheel.

"Noises are the most difficult thing to fix on a car," says Spring. "Now I've heard it, unfortunately." He chuckles. "If I hear it, I have to fix it." Spring is mostly kidding. Even without being able to hear the noise, the car has had its front end ripped apart and rebuilt, with many parts replaced, trying to eradicate the noise by educated guessing and process of elimination. Since the noise won't cooperate—since it comes and goes according to its own mood—it's almost impossible for Spring to know whether any particular procedure has made it go away, until the woman who drives the car reports in that the noise has reappeared.

Spring is quite calm, almost matter-of-fact, about the noise, the car, and its owner. He doesn't particularly view the car as an evil being intent on defying him, he doesn't view the noise as some kind of malicious curse that haunts him, he doesn't view the owner as someone overly demanding who should just give up and learn to live with the noise—which everyone agrees isn't a sign of anything dangerous, and which isn't a problem most of the time. He and his colleagues were never taught—as so many dealership mechanics were—to make their customers feel like there's nothing really wrong with the car, that it's the *customer* who's a little off. Spring starts out believing that what his customers say is wrong really *is* wrong.

Believe in Your Customer

Keith Spring has faith in his customer. He hasn't been able to nail down the noise she's complaining about, but he believes she's hearing it—he believes it enough to have spent twenty fruitless minutes driving around in her car (a chore that was rewarded in the end), and he believes her enough to have done a lot of work trying to solve the problem based mostly on her description of it.

Trust is the foundation for building long-term relationships with customers. But you cannot expect customers to trust your company if the company doesn't first trust them.

Spring was one of the first mechanics in the nation to specialize in Lexuses when Toyota first introduced the cars in August 1989. He is an easygoing fellow, funny, relaxed, with a Texas-aw-shucks manner that disguises a sharp mind. Working on this car, he has the attitude of a scientist or a physician probing a problem he hasn't quite run to ground yet. Something's clearly going on, and with a little patience, a little intelligence, a little luck, and a methodical approach, Spring is pretty certain he can outmaneuver the noise.

This morning, he seems to have found something important. He's taken apart the brakes on the right side, just on a hunch. "We thought it was the steering rack," he says. "Nobody thought it was the brakes."

As soon as he dismantles the right front brakes, Spring finds a problem. The brake caliper—a cradle that holds the brake pads against the disk—is jammed on one side. The caliper should slide in and out freely, but only one end does. The other end is locked in position.

"That might be it," he says. "The brake pads might be popping around because the caliper holder isn't flexing to hold them in place."

He orders a fresh set of caliper holders for both front wheels—the left side turns out to have the same problem—and sets about the relatively simple business of swapping the old ones for the new ones.

THE ALL-IN-ONE TECHNICIAN

The guiding premise of service at Sewell Lexus is simple: you should always treat your customers as if you were trying to keep them as customers for a lifetime of car purchases.

This is where Keith Spring comes in. Spring was one of the first employees hired for the Lexus dealership—weeks before it opened. He was hired by the first service director, Mark Smith, who at one point had worked for Spring. Smith wanted to run his service department differently than Sewell ran his others—he wanted technicians to be able "to fix anything and everything they could lay their hands on."

The tradition, at least at dealerships, is for mechanics to specialize. But from studies of job design and worker satisfaction, it's clear that employees much prefer handling complete jobs, not specialized ones. Spring prefers to do everything to take care of a car—not just doing the transmission work, then handing the car off to someone else who does the brakes.

"They had never met a technician with those [broad] kinds of qualities," says Smith. "They didn't understand this kind of person. They said, 'Go hire one.'"

Spring was then working at a Ford dealership almost two hundred miles south of Dallas, and he jumped at the chance to work on high-end luxury cars—even though it meant literally starting out as a one-man service department. He went to Lexus school in Atlanta before there was a single Lexus on the streets.

SOMEDAY YOU MAY GET TO HIRE YOUR BOSS

It pays to keep track of impressive associates you've worked with. And you never know when you might have an opportunity to hire someone who's worked for you before. But if you really want to keep all your possibilities open, think about the people you currently work *for*. Mark Smith couldn't possibly have guessed when he was working for Keith Spring as a college student that just a few years later he'd be in charge of service and parts at a new luxury car dealership—but he knew just where to find Spring when he needed him.

And might you treat the people who report to you differently if you thought that someday they might be in a position to offer you a better job than the one you have now? Stranger things have happened!

Lexus was so popular right from the beginning that for months the cars were sold before they arrived on trucks at Sewell's dealership. "Every customer was waiting, every salesman was waiting," says Barry Pryor, general manager of Sewell Lexus. "We'd get two trucks in on Friday afternoon, and everyone was promising them by Saturday afternoon or Sunday afternoon—and it never occurred to us to tell Keith they were coming, or to ask if he was going to be here this weekend. We just assumed he'd be here."

Pryor says the hope was that early on, the new dealership (right next door to Sewell Village Cadillac) would sell sixty-four cars per month. But immediately it was selling a hundred per month. During the first seven or eight months, Mark Smith says, "Keith didn't take a day off, other than Christmas, and that's because we were closed on Christmas. He was up here working late Christmas Eve, though, making people's Christmas presents ready."

And to start out, Spring was the dealership's only service technician. "We relied on him for everything," says Pryor, "including taking care of the trade-ins. The number-one trade-in was Mercedes. But we did everything: BMW, Jaguar. We did our reconditioning in-house. He was immediately ready to do anything."

Pryor says that more than just helping get the dealership up and running, "Keith set the tone for the service department—this is a place where everybody does what Keith does. He was like the chairman of the board back there."

Carl Sewell has learned a lot from Keith Spring. He was so impressed with some of the innovations of service director Smith and Spring—the car washing, the technicians who fix the total car—that he is now using these procedures in his other dealerships.

ALWAYS DRAFT THE BEST AVAILABLE PLAYER FIRST

It starts when we first choose up teams at recess in grade school and continues when professional sports teams gather to pick their new players: you try to build your team by picking the best players first. Sewell Lexus's service department grew from a single employee in August 1989 to twenty-five employees by the end of 1992. It's far wiser to start out hiring the kind of people who set the standards you want than to hire frantically, thinking you'll impose the standards later. Sewell built a first-class team by starting with a first-class player.

GOOD TEACHERS LEARN FROM THEIR STUDENTS

One of the reasons Carl Sewell is so successful, and one of the reasons he's renowned for the service at his dealerships, is that he's never satisfied with the service he delivers. What could a twenty-seven-year-old mechanic from southern Texas teach one of the largest luxury-car dealers in the nation? A thing or two, as it turns out. And Sewell wasn't just willing to listen—he was eager to listen. He's always looking for new ideas to improve his relationship to his customers, and he's unashamed to steal good ones from other people.

This is a book about what managers can learn from world-class employees. The point is that the really successful managers have been learning from their employees for a long time.

"There's a lot of technicians—because of the fact they work on commission—who care more about making money than anything else," says Mark Smith. "Keith cares more about making the customer happy.

"He had a guy who had a back problem, every car he'd ever had, it hurt his back to drive it, and Lexus was no exception. Keith just said, 'Let's fix it.'

"He custom fit the foam, custom cut the leather, he built the guy a seat. It still hurt. So Keith had him describe where it hurt, he'd mark the seat, tear the seat down, take out a little foam, add a little foam, change the pressure points. The car went back and forth three or four times until it didn't hurt anymore.

"The guy came back, he said to me, 'Not only doesn't my back hurt when I drive now, it doesn't hurt at all anymore.'

"And we own that guy for life now."

Problem Child, Part II

Benny Rutledge, the technician who works next to Keith Spring and is a member of the team of mechanics he leads, is replacing the transmission on an LS 400. Rutledge is wearing surgical gloves as he works. He takes some ribbing for his slightly prissy insistence on cleanliness in a job as messy as swapping out a transmission. But as Spring reassembles the front brakes on his car with the noise, he too is wearing surgical gloves.

In the context of the Sewell Lexus service department, there doesn't seem anything all that odd about the surgical gloves. Stylistically, the service area resembles a hospital operating room more than a car garage. The floor is cream-colored ceramic tile that is polished each night, and after three years it is virtually stain free. When cars roll in and out, their wide tires make the same kind of squeaking sound as sneakers on a freshly waxed kitchen floor. The service area is brightly lit—skylights run down the middle of the ceiling—and at each service bay there is a live tree and a ceiling fan.

Says Rutledge, "This is the shiniest place I've ever worked."

As Spring works on the brakes of the car with the mysterious noise, it is possible to kneel in business clothes on the floor beneath the car to watch him and not get dirty.

"It's an easy fix," Spring says of the brakes. "It's finding them that's hard." This car has had such persistent problems—Spring calls it "my problem child"—that Spring has talked to the regional Lexus representative and has permission to do whatever is necessary to make the noise go away. The owner has a loaner vehicle, and the car is still under warranty. Almost all of the work Spring and his colleagues do is warranty work—Lexus pays the dealership for doing the work, the customer pays nothing. And unlike the stereotypically irritable attitude from dealerships about warranty work, Lexus and Sewell are generous with car owners in deciding what falls within the terms of the warranty. The woman who owns this LS 400 didn't even buy the car from Sewell.

The cars range in cost from thirty to sixty thousand dollars, and Lexus seems far more acutely aware than most car companies that an owner will actually associate any problem with the car immediately with the company that made it. Lexuses are aimed specifically at the demanding luxury market—it is the rare Lexus that comes to Keith Spring for service that doesn't have a car phone—and they are marketed in large part on the quality and quiet of the ride they offer.

Lexus is so eager to have its cars perfect that when the service department is slow, Spring will roam the new car lot, looking over the cars waiting to be sold, trying to find problems with them that need fixing—before they get into the hands of buyers. "Lexus encourages us to go out and find things wrong," says Spring. "They like it. They want 'em right."

Great Surgeons Don't Operate in Alleys

These elements—a squeaky clean service department, the unhesitating attitude of Sewell and Lexus toward warranty repairs, and Lexus's insistence that technicians do whatever is necessary to make cars perfect—all focus on the same thing: creating an environment that fosters the best possible work and the best possible service. All these things allow Spring to do the best job for his customers. They also set a tone that raises the performance standards of technicians who might not have Spring's instincts for quality and service, but who can be taught to perform similarly.

The same types of factors are relevant in offices, where the influence of the work environment may not be as obvious but is no less critical. Do workers get tired and cranky as the day unfolds because their chairs are poorly designed or the lighting is inadequate? or because the office is too hot or too cold and there is no one who can adjust the temperature? Are people too close together to be able to get quiet work done? or too far apart to communicate effectively? Do they work with equipment that is up-to-date and enhances their productivity? or are they burdened with antiquated technology?

All these things not only influence the quality of the work and the mood of the workers, they send subtle signals about how you value employees. It is remarkable how even something simple like a copier that is constantly on the blink can corrode office morale and productivity.

Managers have no right to expect that the quality of the work being done will be any better than the quality of the environment it's being done in.

Spring gets the brake calipers changed, but he doesn't have time to test-drive the car until the next morning to see if that has solved the problem. When he does, he starts out driving in the wedge-shaped parking area behind the dealership, driving slowly, braking sharply, rocking the steering wheel back and forth to try to persuade the car to make the noise.

He drives over to the Cadillac dealership, he drives around the block. Silence. Spring's technique with difficult cars involves patience, persistence, and intuition. To track noises, for instance, Spring won't hesitate to put the hood of a car up and lie across the engine while someone else drives, trying to hear where a noise is coming from. "I've found suspension noises that way," he says. "They're harder to hear from inside [the car]."

He wheels the taupe car back into the parking lot and begins the weaving and braking calisthenics again, and suddenly there's a pop. Spring can't help smiling. The car pops again. It pops even when he's not braking or weaving. The noise is pronounced—and it's appearing with a sudden frequency that makes it clear why the owner is unhappy when it starts happening. "It's gotten louder," says Spring. "It's almost a rattle now. It was more subtle before, more muffled."

He wheels the car back into the garage and into his service bay. He's about ready to put in a new steering rack, but he has another idea he wants to try first.

He raises the car well above his head, unscrews the splash shield that covers the forward undercarriage, then takes his air wrench and starts loosening the bolts that hold the suspension and the front end together.

"They've been tightened and retightened in desperate attempts to find that noise," he says. "I'm gonna loosen everything up and then go drive it around—and we'll let all the suspension pieces settle in. Then I'll tighten it back up." He loosens a dozen large bolts, then it's back in the car for some more driving. For the first few minutes, the noise is even more pronounced and regular than before, and Spring says he can feel the looseness in the front end. Then the noise fades away, and Spring brings the car back into the service area to tighten up all the bolts.

WHERE THE MONEY IS AND WHERE THE FUN IS

Keith Spring makes well over fifty thousand dollars per year as a service technician at Lexus. But he doesn't make the hundred thousand dollars per year he could make, and the reason is that making a hundred thousand dollars would be boring.

Like most mechanics, Spring is paid piece rate: an hourly rate for each job, based on how many hours a typical technician should need to do the job. If he can replace the brakes more quickly than the rated time, so much the better for him. He gets paid the same amount for the job no matter how much time it actually takes him to do it.

The car service jobs that pay best relative to the time invested are simple jobs—a good mechanic can whip through a tune-up, an oil change, a tire rotation in little more than half the rated time, and Spring could book a lot of job hours at sixteen dollars each.

"All the stuff that really pays money is boring," says Spring. He explains this problem while doing a routine service—oil change, tire rotation, air and fuel filters—on an almond-colored 1990 Lexus ES 250. After the old oil has drained, Spring sprays a solvent along the frame and the underside of the car, to make sure all the oil drips are cleaned away. "I don't want her to get home and have any oil drip on her driveway," he says. "She wouldn't be happy."

More important, of course, Spring wouldn't be happy. It is his sense of perfection that demands he spray away the oil drips, not the demands of his customer.

"A lot of people would much rather be changing oil, rotating tires, changing spark plugs," he says. "I'd much rather work on an electrical problem. I like doing the complicated stuff. I get tired of the mindless stuff. It's like having to mow yards."

Spring isn't nearly as interested in the amount of money he can make as he is in having interesting problems to solve.

"I get cars all the time that someone else has already tried to fix, and they couldn't, and they said, 'We know someone already tried, but would you take a run at it?'

"I like the challenge. I know the people at Lexus will back me. So I don't have any problem. It's not my fault there's a broken spot-weld on the inside of the frame that only pops at thirty-two degrees—but we'll find it. We'll find it.

"I have confidence in myself that way. Everything on a car— it can be fixed. It's all man-made. It's just the amount of time it will take." Because of his skill and his reputation, Spring has credibility with the technical support staff at Lexus. The taupe LS 400 that is making the noise had reached the point where Lexus was ready to send out the district engineer to try to find the problem. By giving Spring free rein under the warranty, Lexus can only save money and trouble.

"If I get to a point where I would throw up my hands, I would just call the engineers and they'd be flying in," he says. "I've got a whole dealership behind me, and a whole factory behind me, so I don't have any reason to be scared of it."

SOMETIMES WORK IS A HOBBY

There is far more to work than simply pay. To do the job he does as well as he does it, Keith Spring has to be smart. Successfully employing people as bright and as good as Spring means realizing that money is not the only thing they draw from their work, sometimes not even the most important thing. Smart people want challenging work. Sewell Lexus takes advantage of Spring's intellect by making sure he gets a good mix of work—including the kinds of challenging problems no one else seems to be able to solve.

If Keith Spring weren't doing what he's doing for a living, he'd be doing it for fun—and he does. Anytime you can find people whose hobbies are similar to the job you're looking to fill, snatch them up. People are usually pretty good at their hobbies.

Spring gets two completely different sorts of pleasure from cars. One is a visceral pleasure—the excitement of showing what the four-liter engine in a Lexus coupe will do on city streets, of showing how the car's antilock brakes handle stops in the middle of a sharp turn in a driving rainstorm.

The other sort of pleasure Spring gets from cars is cerebral. He can talk for five minutes about the elegance and simplicity of the interior of a Lexus sedan: "I like the big armrest, that says solidity. I like the center console being raised and forward a bit, that makes it accessible. I like the key on the dashboard instead of the steering column—you can see where to put the key that way."

Working in the trunk of a Lexus to replace a failed light bulb, he points out the steel framing piece across the back of the trunk. "That's to keep the body rigid, to keep it from flexing," Spring says. "The metal is not cut out for weight, like you see on most cars these days, it's solid all the way across. It gives it a better ride, keeps down the rattles."

The Pleasures of Perfection

It is misleading to think that Keith Spring's personality is irrelevant to his work. His *personability* may be irrelevant—but his personality is critical.

Spring routinely reveals precisely the sort of character you'd want in a person doing a job for which perfection is the standard. He is not only obsessive about fixing the cars and manic about returning them to their customers in spotless, showroom condition, he gets great pleasure in the tiniest details of the way the Lexus is designed and put together. Nothing the designers have done eludes him.

That complete appreciation for the Lexus's engineering is critical to Spring's performance, and it is something to look for in hiring people for jobs like Spring's.

Keith Spring's fascination with cars started not only before he could drive, but before he could read. "I've been a fanatic from the time I was little," he says, "since before I went to school. I was building models even before I was in kindergarten. My dad helped me. Me and my brothers all like cars. We had tons and tons of car models.

"What I really love to do is build a model—just work on it all day long, not even talk to anybody."

Spring grew up in Wharton County, southwest of Houston. Both his parents work. His father, a chemist, was a professor at a local junior college and is now staff chemist for a sulfur mine. His mother was a caseworker for a social-service agency, and now owns a Hallmark card shop.

"My dad took care of our cars," says Spring. "He never took a car in to be serviced. My dad is a very smart man, very well educated, very patient. He loves organic chemistry. He happens to have the book smarts."

After high school, Spring went to junior college for a year, "to make my parents happy. They didn't want me to be a mechanic."

But after that first year, Spring transferred to Texas State Technical Institute in Waco—a technically oriented junior college where he spent two years learning to fix cars. "People learn different ways," he says. "Some people, like my dad, learn really easily in lectures. Some, like me, are kinesthetic. I learn by doing things, and by seeing people do things."

Spring thrived at TSTI. "I loved it. My grades went up immediately."

Between years at the school, he worked at a shop that repaired almost exclusively imported cars. "That's where I got my taste for working on foreign cars." When he graduated, he got a job at a nearby Mazda/BMW dealership. Six years later, the owner bought a Ford dealership and asked Spring to be the service manager, which is where Mark Smith and Carl Sewell found him.

He had by that time earned an excellent reputation, especially because of his six years working on BMWs. When Smith and Sewell were in California on business, Spring says, "They were visiting a big BMW dealership out there, they mentioned my name to the manager. He knew me. He said, 'How'd you ever get him away from BMW?' That was nice."

PROBLEM CHILD, PART III

The taupe LS 400 has had its front end retightened. Spring wheels the car through the wealthy neighborhood behind Sewell Lexus, trying to get the car to make its noise. Along the way he points out a home designed by Frank Lloyd Wright, another that belongs to a customer, and a house where the lawn is sprinkled with sculptures by Henry Moore and Alexander Calder. The simplest of solutions seems to have worked. In forty minutes of test-driving, there's not a sound from the front end.

"The way it was clunking when it was loosened," Spring says, "you know it was shifting. But it's fooled me before. I hate to give it back—I don't want to declare victory too soon."

Spring's skill, and his attitude, make the jobs of many of the people at Sewell Lexus easier. It's not just that he sets the tone in the service department, or that he is good at training new mechanics.

Every mechanic at a dealership has a service adviser—the person who deals with the customer, who takes the complaint, writes the service order, and decides how long it will take the mechanic to fix the car. Spring's service adviser, Bill Van Tassel, is young and has only been at Sewell Lexus six months, but has quickly learned how valuable a technician like Spring is. "There are a couple crucial points in satisfying and delighting the customer," Van Tassel says. "You gotta do what you say you're gonna do, and you have to have it ready when you say. And Keith has to make that happen. He's a whiz. I haven't run into anything he can't fix.

"He gives me a lot of information about what exactly has been done to the cars. And the more specific I can be, the more the customer will relate to what we're doing."

When there's a problem that can't immediately be solved, Van Tassel doesn't hesitate to bring the customer back to talk to Spring directly. "Customers like that," he says. "And Keith knows if he's talking to a customer, he's not making any money. But he's sensitive to the customers. He's so long-term customer oriented."

Spring makes a particular effort to see that cars go out fixed right the first time, so irritating second trips are kept to a minimum. "I've got people who produce two times as many hours as him," says Wayne Pritchard, the current service manager at Sewell Lexus and Spring's direct supervisor, "but I'll take a whole shopful of him. He has so few callbacks—everybody is going to have *some*. But a good technician won't have them because of a stupid mistake. If Keith has one, it'll be because of something out of his control."

Sewell Lexus is one of those rare dealerships where customers are welcome in the garage. "We encourage the customer to go back and talk to the technicians if they're confused or curious," says general manager Barry Pryor. "We know the customers who go talk to Keith understand better. We're proud to have customers talk to him. He has a great bedside manner."

GOOD SERVICE IS CONTAGIOUS

Good service breeds good service—from one end of a company to another. That Spring does his job well, that he takes responsibility for work and takes responsibility for personally trying to make customers happy, makes the jobs of his service writer and his service manager easier. It makes those people more likely to do a good job. It also reflects well on the dealership. By the same token, because Sewell and Lexus are determined to see customers satisfied, it is possible for Keith Spring to do his job. Indeed, without the kind of support he gets from Lexus, it would be difficult for him to do the job he does at the level he does it.

Spring has the taupe LS 400 back in the service bay for one more job. The owner has complained about another noise: the air conditioning blower is making more noise than it used to, especially at the highest fan speed. There *is* a distinct *Brrr*-ing on high, but it doesn't sound excessive. Spring isn't so sure. He goes and tries the blower in another LS 400. He claims to hear a little difference. "It might be a balance problem in the fan motor," he says, "or it might be a bearing."

He shrugs, settles in with his tools in front of the glove compartment, and starts doing the dismantling necessary to get at the blower motor. It takes more than twenty minutes before the motor is even in view—it is buried behind the dashboard on the right side. He removes a cover panel, dismantles the glove compartment, removes the computer for the antilock brakes and, behind that, the larger computer that controls the engine, and sets aside the wiring nets for both. He removes the plastic door guard that runs along the right side of the car, he removes a cooling duct, and finally the blower motor housing is visible, looking like a tiny version of a nuclear reactor's containment building.

"I've never put one of these in before," Spring says. "I have the confidence to tear stuff down, though. I know I can get it back together." By the time he gets the housing apart and the motor out, there are nineteen multiline electrical connectors hanging loose.

And once again, Spring's faith that the customer has noticed something wrong is vindicated. In the basket-shaped fan blower, Spring finds four dried-out leaves. "At least we found something positive," he says. "She'll like that." Spring decides that he might as well replace the motor anyway, just in case the faint rumble was caused by something other than the leaves. "There's no need to take a chance," he says. "It's covered by the warranty."

It takes Spring a little longer to get everything screwed and plugged back together than it did to take it apart, but a little more than an hour after he started, he is ready to test the fix. The motor is distinctly quieter on the low speeds, and Spring says he thinks it's also a little quieter on high.

He isn't the least bit bothered by the trouble involved in what was essentially a minor aesthetic improvement.

"This is nothing," he says, chuckling. "I put a new motor in this car." A whole new engine? "Yup. Earlier this year. She said it was burning oil, but we couldn't ever document it. But we replaced it. Lexus paid for it [under warranty]." The new engine, installed in February, required fourteen hours of labor and cost $13,500. "All to make her happy!" says Spring.

WHAT HAPPENS WHEN IT ALL COMES TOGETHER?

What happens when you take an employee who is world-class—Keith Spring, for instance—couple him with a business owner who is thoughtful and imaginative the way Carl Sewell is, then add a car company that is totally focused on quality?

You get the situation you have here: the business equivalent of nirvana—for customers, employees, managers, and the company as a whole. It's actually just people working to their full potential. When you hear Keith Spring's story, you see how he embodies the Lexus slogan: "The Relentless Pursuit of Perfection."

WHAT'S KEITH SPRING WORTH?

We can use Carl Sewell's own numbers to help figure out what Keith Spring is worth.

Sewell's Cadillac division estimated a customer to be worth over $300,000 in sales and service during a lifetime. We'll be modest and assume that a Lexus customer is also worth $300,000.

So what role does a Keith Spring have in retaining that customer? A huge one! Unless the sales department or someone else in service really messes up, once a car owner has found a mechanic he or she likes (and everyone likes Keith Spring), they stay with a dealership. So in many ways Keith is the guardian of that $300,000.

Given that he is zealously protecting that handsome sum, how many such sums do you suppose he can guard? Well, let's be really conservative and say that he works on 4 cars per week that need his particular, extraordinary talents, 50 weeks per year. Let's also say that while a customer may be worth $300,000, half of the customers will move away, so the average realizable value drops to $150,000. Further, 75 percent of his business is from repeat customers (we shouldn't double count).

$150,000 per customer

× 4 customers per week

× 50 weeks per year

× 25 percent (new customers)

= $7,500,000

The $7,500,000 kind of justifies the live tree in the garage, and maybe even the ceiling fan, don't you think?

HOW DO YOU FIND
KEITH SPRING?

Finding Keith Spring is a little different from finding many of the other people you'll meet in this book, because his job requires a certain amount of seasoning and training.

1. In the case of a car mechanic—or anything but the simplest sort of repair person—experience matters. Not necessarily the extent of the experience, but certainly the quality and character of it. Ask for references and check them out. Better yet, when you're looking for a person like Spring, ask around at local competitors who do similar work. Invariably, people know about technicians of Keith's skill and integrity.

2. The key to Keith Spring's performance is that he's a perfectionist. When hiring for a job that requires virtual perfection, look for people with obsessive personalities. Keith's is somewhat shrouded—until you start asking him about cars. Then his absolute passion for understanding how they work, and how they break, is quickly revealed. What's more, Spring would rather work on aggravating and elusive electrical system problems than change oil and do tuneups. That's exactly what you want in a car mechanic.

3. If you're going to hire a repair person, one of the most revealing things you can do during an interview is take the candidate back to the shop and let him do two things. Show him something in need of repair, and let him talk about how he'd go about fixing it. And explain to him how your repair system works and let him critique it. Even before he was hired, Keith Spring changed the way Sewell thought about car mechanics. Spring works on the whole car—not just the brakes or the transmission—and he wanted a garage organized that way. Sewell was smart enough to listen.

CHAPTER 4

SERVICE BY PHONE

photo by Mark Hobson

MARIE WILLIAMS

WORKING WITHOUT A SCRIPT

Without question, the service Americans experience most commonly now is delivered over the telephone. No matter how much you travel, eat out, do business, or shop, it is hard to imagine anyone who doesn't have more service encounters by telephone than in any other way. Telephone service is so common, we don't even notice it.

When you leave town and need to suspend delivery of your newspaper, that's a telephone service experience. When the air-conditioning breaks midsummer and you call to invoke your service contract, that's a telephone service experience. When you call a local department store to find out how late it's open; when you call the dentist's office to make a routine cleaning appointment; when you call room service from your hotel room; when you send flowers to your mother on her birthday using an 800 number—all of these are telephone service experiences.

Indeed, it may be the advent of the 800 number—really just a way of placing collect calls without the intervention of an operator—that has cemented the telephone as the nation's premier service-delivery device. You can now use 800 numbers to do everything from buying stocks to getting technical advice when your hard drive crashes. Often, with telephone service, you don't even have to talk to a person.

And that is the problem. The phone has supplanted all kinds of relationships that once took place in person, relationships that are no longer cost-effective to conduct face-to-face (for either business or customer). But what is the quality of this substitute?

Often it is aggravating. The person taking the room service order says yes to several modest requests, but the salad still comes drenched in dressing, instead of with the dressing on the side. The credit card "service center" is open "for your convenience" on Saturdays, but when you call to get a billing problem resolved, the customer service representative can't answer your questions, doesn't have the authority to solve the problem, and recommends you call back during the week when a supervisor will be available, at which point you have to begin your explanations all over again.

Perhaps the most irritating experience is when you call someone with a request that seems to be "off the script." Heaven help you if the person on the phone doesn't have a scripted set of responses for your problem.

Customer-service representatives, operators, receptionists, even people taking sales calls, are harried, distracted, and often react to what must be very routine requests ("I want to talk about this annual service fee on my credit card bill," "Can I leave a message?") with dumbfoundedness or irritation. The whole experience of taking a message or answering a question is made to seem an imposition.

And we haven't even considered the most notorious class of telephone "service"—provided by the people who call *us*, trying to sell something or take a poll. (Nor do we consider that other most hip and successful telephone service—sex by telephone, one area where we confess that the value of convenience seems to have supplanted the value of the experience itself.)

If, as the saying goes, long distance is the next best thing to being there, it often is a very distant runner-up.

But sometimes, it works beautifully. Everyone has had the kind of lively, satisfying telephone experience that does two things: it reminds you how effective "remote control" service can be with people who have some empathy, who are paying attention, and it makes you want to do business with the company again.

There are people in catalog sales who actually know the merchandise, and can gently guide you to the right item and the right size. There are customer-service representatives who simply remove a disputed interest charge from your credit card without first trying to extract your four most recent federal tax returns.

Such people are successful for a couple of very specific, very clear reasons. First, they have the power to handle the complaints or requests they are likely to encounter. Sometimes that power comes from autonomy given by the company, sometimes it comes from extensive knowledge of the products or services the company provides. Most often, the power is a combination of those things.

Second, great phone service representatives have the ability to read people's emotions over the telephone, without the clues of body language and facial expression that most of us are so dependent on. Really valuable phone service workers know how to listen; they can sense the frustration level of their customers. Like the best service workers who operate in person, the best phone service workers can tell what's really bothering a customer—which sometimes has nothing to do with the problem the customer claims to have.

Finally, great phone service representatives have the ability to convey their personality over the phone—their competence, assuredness, and empathy come shining through over the telephone.

Even a brief conversation with such a person leaves you thinking, Hmm, that's somebody it would have been fun to deal with face-to-face.

The key to having phone service reps with all these traits is very simple: careful hiring and careful training.

At General Electric's Answer Center in Louisville, Kentucky (which the company itself has made famous with its television ads), teams of customer-service people are trained together using role playing. Some employees are customers, calling in, some are customer-service representatives. And the training is conducted in such a way that the reps and the customers can see each other during the call—to help the reps visualize the frustration of being the customer calling in.

The other thing such team training does is emphasize the need for people using the telephone to listen. There is no script—you must hear what the person calling needs, and use your own intelligence and the resources of your company to solve the problem.

The telephone, especially in combination with the 800 number, is clearly a piece of technology that can make service more accessible and more responsive. The real challenge, as phone service becomes even more widespread (and it will), will be for business not to allow the telephone to depersonalize the service experience. The goal should be to use the telephone to develop as strong a relationship as you would in person.

While Bill Fromm's company was doing some preliminary work for a mail-service pharmacy named Stadtlanders, we literally stumbled over one of the most remarkable telephone customer-service people we have ever found, a woman whose only script is fifty years of making her way in the world.

Stadtlanders specializes in providing drugs to chronically or terminally ill patients—in all cases, people who rely on their medicine for the quality of their lives, if not for life itself. Dealing with such patients over the phone clearly requires extraordinary skill, patience, and creativity.

One of the Stadtlanders employees that Fromm's staff interviewed was a woman named Marie Williams. Marie related a story that demonstrated her extraordinary ability to work without a script. One of Marie's clients, an AIDS patient who had gone on vacation to Florida, somehow forgot some of his medicine. This didn't phase Marie in the least. She simply had the medicine delivered to the tee of a golf course where the customer was going to be playing.

And this is not exceptional behavior for Marie Williams. If anything, it is routine. She has a knack for thinking her way through problems; more than that, she has the ability to win people's confidence and trust over the phone. That skill serves her in soothing anxious patients and their families, in calming them enough to find out what she needs to know to solve their problems. It also serves her in dealing with bureaucrats at what we believe are the nation's two most unyielding, unhelpful kinds of organizations: government health-care agencies and private health-insurance companies.

Marie's skill also serves Stadtlanders at what is probably the company's most critical service point (except for actually getting the medicine right). Stadtlanders is trying to have its customers do by phone and Federal Express what most people are used to doing in person—getting medicine from a pharmacist, and feeling confident that the medicine will do what it should.

HASSLE-FREE WITH MARIE

When you clear it all away, what Marie Williams does for a living is talk on the telephone, and she is a champion talker. It isn't so much the speed or the style of her conversation that is so impressive—it's the sheer quantity. Marie knows how to talk a problem through, and will stick with it until the solution to something that had just moments before seemed heartbreakingly insoluble suddenly appears, surprising everyone, even Marie, like a chunk of precious metal appearing after panning through a lot of conversational sand.

For all the talk, one of Marie Williams's secrets is that she's also listening. Her voice is a little loud, a little spirited, so Marie can sometimes give the impression she's *all* talk. But the talk is a strategy, a disarming cover Marie uses to put people at ease, so she can slip in and find out what she needs to know to take the most effective action.

The kind of comfort, competence, and steadiness that Marie provides over the phone is the only way Stadtlanders can be successful. It not only means satisfied customers, it means customers who provide Stadtlanders with the best sort of word-of-mouth advertising it could want.

Stadtlanders specializes in providing drugs to people who have to take medication routinely, month after month. Its patients have cancer or diabetes or AIDS, or they have had an organ transplant of some kind. Stadtlanders sends out each client's drugs a month's supply at a time, by Federal Express. The key to the service is that it is designed to be completely "hassle-free," as Stadtlanders's creator puts it. The patients are presumed to have enough to worry about besides whether their medicines are going to show up on time, so the company does whatever it takes to get drugs to patients—from refusing to be stymied by delivery difficulties to routinely wrestling for reimbursement with insurance companies.

Stadtlanders has dispatched Federal Express couriers to all kinds of places, including airport gates. Sometimes even Federal Express isn't good enough. Just recently, Marie Williams had a patient who couldn't wait until the next day for Federal Express delivery of medicine. Marie talked a corner pharmacist in Minnesota into delivering the drugs to the patient's home. She told the pharmacist to bill Stadtlanders whatever he thought fair for the delivery. He charged fifteen dollars.

TURNING A PROMISE INTO REALITY

Stadtlanders sells service, not medication. The company frees its customers from the hassle of dealing with insurance companies, and it provides dependable, door-to-door delivery of the drugs. The company's practice of sending out all the drugs by Federal Express is important symbolically: it defines the minimum standard for hassle-free.

Symbols, though, are only the beginning. Empowerment is the key ingredient for Stadtlanders to deliver on its promise, and empowerment isn't a symbol—it is a corporate way of life.

Marie Williams is empowered by her employer to make decisions that deviate from normal company routine when dealing with both customers and suppliers, and those decisions often involve spending the company's money. If she only had the authority to accelerate a shipping date but couldn't engage a competitive pharmacy to take care of a customer, the company's service promise would be an empty one.

It is much easier to talk about empowerment than it is to actually make it happen. There are two critical elements to success here. First is to train new employees by example—to put them with people like Marie Williams, so they can see how to treat customers, and see that the service guarantee is more than a marketing slogan. It is the minimum performance standard.

The second important element is to give employees a guideline they can fall back on, so they don't have to worry about being "wrong." In the case of Stadtlanders, the customer should get the medicine, and the customer should end up happy. Federal Express, a company itself widely known for service and responsiveness, has a similar kind of standard. Every Federal Express telephone customer-service representative is authorized to satisfy a customer's complaint up to a cost of $250.

In both cases, even if something is done "wrong," if it's done within the broad guidelines, and in the service of the customer, it can't be too far wrong.

Stadtlanders's reputation for hassle-free service has fueled tremendous growth. In five years, the company has gone from being a neighborhood drugstore to an outfit that employs thirty-five full-time pharmacists. In 1989, the mail-service part of Stadtlanders filled one hundred prescriptions per day. By the end of 1993, Stadtlanders was writing thirty-five hundred prescriptions per day—most for a month's worth of the kind of exotic drugs many neighborhood and hospital pharmacies don't routinely stock.

Marie Williams spends her days enrolling new patients and solving the problems of existing patients. The folks she talks to fall into two broad groups, groups most people find it difficult to relate to. The first are patients and the relatives of patients, people who are desperately ill and often, by the time they reach Marie, also simply desperate. Marie always seems perfectly happy to hear from them—and some of her regulars are so devoted that they call Stadtlanders's 800 number just to chat with her.

The other group Marie spends time talking to are people who work for health-insurance companies. Marie deals with the same kind of bureaucracies as the rest of the world, and she often has to apply a conversational two-by-four to get insurance companies to do what she thinks they should for their patients—who also happen to be *her* patients.

In early 1992, a young girl from New Jersey came to Pittsburgh's Children's Hospital for a liver transplant, and Stadtlanders was engaged to supply a special feeding formula for her, along with post-transplant drugs. New Jersey state officials balked at paying. "I went nuts," says Marie. "I called every agency there is in New Jersey. The New Jersey people asked, 'What is the girl doing in Pennsylvania?'

"I said, 'Well, where do you give liver transplants in New Jersey?' They said, 'We don't.'"

While New Jersey mulled over whether to pay for the girl's medications, Stadtlanders went ahead and started supplying them. The bill for the first six weeks of medicine was twenty-five hundred dollars. Ultimately, New Jersey Medicare was persuaded to pay.

TRUSTING CUSTOMERS IS GOOD BUSINESS

From time to time Marie and the other customer-service representatives decide to send drugs to a patient without knowing if Stadtlanders will get paid. Although that might seem high-risk, the fact is that write-offs from these actions occur in less than 10 percent of such cases.

No company can successfully attract and keep customers if

it operates with a philosophy that most customers can't be trusted.

A New York–based retail sporting goods chain replaced uniformed guards at the entrances of some of its stores with greeters. The company saw shoplifting decrease and sales increase. Shoplifters are less likely to steal from a store if they feel they are recognized and acknowledged as they come and go. And customers are more likely to buy when they're greeted at the front door, à la Wal-Mart. There is fifteen years of evidence that shows that, on average, 1 to 1.5 percent of American consumers are systematic cheaters: build that into your economic assumptions and be done with it.

This same issue of trusting customers carries over into other areas of a business. If when developing special sales programs—contests and other promotions—management attempts to design programs that are impervious to customer cheating, the chances are the program will not be very attractive to anyone, especially honest customers.

Marie Williams actually takes this a step further. She sometimes falls into the role of representing not her employer, but her customer. This too may seem risky in the short term, but it can only be good business in the long term.

The company that starts out not trusting customers will usually end up without any customers to trust.

WHAT THEY KNOW THEY DON'T KNOW

It's just a few minutes past nine in the morning when Marie begins what is for her a typical battle. Her phone rings.

It's Clay Lombard,* whose wife Julie has recently had a kidney transplant. There is a panicky edge in Clay's voice. His wife is a young woman, not quite thirty years old, and to safeguard her new kidney she is reliant on an array of powerful drugs, in-

---

* The names of all patients in this chapter have been changed to protect their identities.

cluding Imuran, cyclosporine, and prednisone. The drugs cost $350 per month.

Julie Lombard is covered by Medicare and a private policy from a state Blue Cross/Blue Shield organization. Blue Cross has been happily paying for her drugs, until just recently, when Blue Cross decided it will no longer pay; it doesn't pay for drugs when a patient also has Medicare. Unfortunately, Medicare doesn't pay for the drugs either. The ridiculousness of this—two insurance policies, yet no coverage for essential drugs that cost almost as much as the rent—is what has Clay Lombard in a panic, not to mention his feeling of powerlessness and his fear for his wife's health.

Marie is soothing, and the first thing she does is order overnight delivery of a three-day supply of drugs—without any assurance that her company will be paid by anyone for them. "I'm not going to let the woman *die*," Marie says.

Then Marie dials up Blue Cross, where she reaches a Mrs. Green, who confirms that if a patient has Medicare, Blue Cross won't reimburse drug costs. "If he submits it to Medicare and is rejected, will you take it then?" Marie asks. Mrs. Green says no.

Mrs. Green does say something interesting, though. She says it's not clear why Blue Cross has suddenly declined to pay Stadtlanders for future drugs, because the company has *no record* that Julie Lombard has Medicare.

Marie assures Mrs. Green she'll be back in touch, then she calls Clay Lombard to tell him what she's learned, and to pass on Mrs. Green's name and phone number.

Moments later, Mrs. Green calls Marie back.

"I just talked to him," Mrs. Green says. "The man was almost hysterical. I really feel sorry for him. He's almost in tears."

Marie clucks sympathetically—customer-service person to customer-service person—but she points out that the man's wife loses her kidney without her drugs, which explains his tears.

Marie does a little musing out loud. "You say you don't actually *know* that Julie Lombard has Medicare," she says. It is both statement and question—a verbal habit of Marie's, her voice rising just a little at the end of the sentence. Marie is trying to see whether Mrs. Green might come to the conclusion Marie herself has already come to.

"No . . . ," Mrs. Green says, "technically, we don't know she's on Medicare. So . . . I guess we could reimburse him. Sure, we'll pay his claims."

It is a remarkable moment: an insurance company in retreat before the combined forces of Marie Williams, a little humanity, and the kind of logic usually used *against* patients.

PROBLEM SOLVING REQUIRES PERSISTENCE

Customer-service representatives are often the last line of defense in preserving customer satisfaction. If they can't satisfy a customer, the customer is probably lost forever. And most of the time customer-service representatives are dealing with problems that, while not unique, fall outside the routine situations covered in the training manual.

Solving these problems usually means cutting red tape or circumventing established procedure. People who can do this effectively are persistent. They rarely take no from anyone and are single-minded in accomplishing their goal. Managers need to identify those instances when persistence is a job requirement and look for it in the people they hire.

One of the easiest ways to test for persistence is to set up some very modest obstacles to hiring. Don't return the first phone calls of job candidates, for instance, and see if they are aggressive in following up. Really persistent people cannot suppress this part of their personalities.

THE PATIENCE AND THE PAYOFF

At fifty-seven years old, Marie Williams is a little loud, a little brassy, unceasingly frank and friendly. She has a husky voice and is easy to like.

Although Marie is outgoing and enthusiastic, she isn't particularly excitable. She has the kind of self-possession that comes from having lost one child and raised two others, from having lived around the world, survived two marriages and half a dozen jobs.

Marie Williams's personality translates wonderfully over the telephone, whether she's talking to confused patients or resistant bureaucrats. Her patience is nearly unlimited. The fumbling, vagueness, and inadequate information she gets would send most people off into a temper tantrum. Marie just works around the problems.

A woman named Suzy Singer calls; she's heard about Stadtlanders and she wants to sign up. Suzy sounds tired on the phone. Marie explains one of Stadtlanders's services: "You pay nothing up front. We send you a thirty-day supply of drugs—we'll send it out in twenty-four hours."

"Wow!" says Suzy.

Marie slowly takes medical and insurance information from Suzy, who is thirty-eight. She's had a pancreas transplant, but she can't quite remember when, about four weeks ago she thinks. Suzy gets the name and phone number of her insurance company—one Marie knows by reputation is not the most generous—and the name of Suzy's doctors, so Stadtlanders's pharmacists can get the details of her medications. Marie assures Suzy she'll call her back that afternoon to tell her if she's been accepted.

"What if I'm in the tub when you call?" Suzy wants to know.

"I'll call back," says Marie, "or you can call on the 800 number."

The first thing Marie discovers after she's hung up is that the phone number Suzy has provided for her insurance company is wrong. Marie makes a couple of calls to the employer of Suzy's husband to get the right office and phone number of the insurance company, so Suzy's benefits can be verified.

Later that day, Suzy is approved, and she promptly recommends Stadtlanders to her mother, her sister, and a close friend, all also seriously ill.

How to Turn Customers into Apostles

Marie Williams is recruiting apostles. Her job title may be customer-service representative, but she's really an extension of Stadtlanders's marketing department.

She could easily have called Suzy back and told her to get the correct insurance information and call back with it. Instead, Marie made the calls herself and tracked the information down—probably more quickly and simply than Suzy would have done it.

There is a tremendous economic multiplier effect to turning customers into your advertisers. Few companies take the time to work out this multiplier effect, and to reward employees with incentives based on it.

When your frontline employees go above and beyond what is normally expected of them by customers, they turn those customers into apostles for your business. The business reaps rewards, and you should build in some incentives so your employees reap some of the rewards as well. The incentives can be as simple as a modest bonus—a hundred dollars—for unusual recruiting efforts. Or there can be a more elaborate system of bonuses and rewards for bringing in new business.

One of the most gratifying ways of making clear how important your employees are is to create opportunities for your customers to praise them. You can do this with customer surveys or reaction cards, particularly ones that request the name of particularly outstanding employees and examples of great service performances. Such surveys and comment cards have a remarkably tonic effect on employee morale: they show employees that they affect real people, that they do not labor in unappreciated anonymity.

Such efforts remind employees that the value of a company is not just in its customers, but in how those customers think about and talk about the company.

In rapid succession Marie hears from several of Suzy's relatives, and has to gently nurse each one through what is, in fact, not a very complicated process.

Suzy's mother, Janine, has cancer. When she talks to Marie, she has just one day's worth of medicines left. Marie asks if she has insurance. "No, I have Medicare," Janine says. "I pay for my medicine."

"You're not reimbursed?" Marie asks.

THE REAL HEROES OF BUSINESS

"No. What's that mean, 'reimbursed'? Oh, yeah, I send in the receipt and I get back 75 or 80 percent."

UNEDUCATED CUSTOMERS ARE THE LIFEBLOOD OF A BUSINESS

Marie Williams understands that if her customers had all the answers they wouldn't need her.

There is a relationship between the amount of knowledge a customer has about your product or service and the price he or she is willing to pay for it. The more knowledge the customer has, the less that customer will usually pay. For example, someone with no prior experience with computers, looking to buy a personal computer, will probably shop at a retail store that offers the added value of knowledgeable sales people and installation specialists. For this, the customer will pay more than someone with a lot of knowledge, who may buy a computer by mail order.

The hardest part of customer service can be the customer. Many customers are confused, uninformed, and need a lot of hand-holding. But these are the very customers for whom many companies exist. And it's these customers that make up most of a typical day for a customer-service representative. Stadtlanders's management knows that solving customer problems is how the company got into business in the first place.

Your customer-service people should look at customers with questions as people who can be converted to customers forever.

Marie's patients realize just how valuable she is to them, and often take pains to show her. "They are wonderful to me," she says. "They make me cry."

She has had patients passing through Pittsburgh take her to lunch or dinner—including a truck driver who'd had a heart transplant and insisted on Marie and a colleague meeting him at an interstate exit ramp.

One patient, Lou DiMineo, recipient of a new kidney, was so

happy with Marie's intervention on his behalf in an argument
over benefits between his insurance agent and his insurance company that he called her up one day.

She explains: "He said, 'Hi, Marie, hold on!' I hear this mu-
sic. It sounds like a funeral home in the background. He's playing 'And Then There Was You' or some romantic thing on his organ for me." She smiles and shakes her head.

When Marie encounters someone who helps her do her job,
she is similarly appreciative. A woman from Maryland Blue Cross
helped her disentangle the benefits of an AIDS patient who had
run up a ten-thousand-dollar medication bill only to be told he
had a five-hundred-dollar coverage limit. Ultimately, Blue Cross
paid. "The woman [from Blue Cross] was so nice, I sent her a
Stadtlanders mug," says Marie.

TREATING SUPPLIERS AS CUSTOMERS

In most businesses, you can't deliver outstanding customer
service without the cooperation of outstanding suppliers.
Not only does Stadtlanders's service image start with an outside supplier, Federal Express, but it ultimately also needs the
cooperation of third parties like insurance companies.

It wasn't the mug that Marie sent the woman at Maryland
Blue Cross that was important—it was the thought behind
the mug that will enable Marie to be able to count on her
the next time. Just as employee-recognition programs are an
important part of motivating people, a supplier-recognition
program will help you harness the energy of other companies and use it in achieving your own goals.

If a company strives to be the favorite supplier to a customer, it should start by becoming the favorite customer of
its suppliers.

Marie does get her share of abuse. One patient insisted that
his thirty-pill shipment was five pills short. "He called up and
screamed at me, 'You goddammed don't know how to count!'"
Marie Williams, of course, never sees any pills, and the count-

ing—which is checked three times—takes place two floors below her. "I just pretended I couldn't count," says Marie.

THE CUSTOMER IS NOT ALWAYS RIGHT—BUT THE CUSTOMER IS NEVER WRONG

You cannot win arguments with customers. The best result you can get from arguing with customers is that they will leave you. The worst result is that they'll leave you and tell their friends.

Marie understands this, so she ends the discussion with the customer as quickly as possible by accepting the customer's count. Although the customer may not always be right, it's important to remember that the customer is never wrong.

Much of Marie's ability to solve problems comes from Stadtlanders's policy of giving its people discretion to do what's necessary to take care of patients. But, as her boss Phyllis Huber says, training and support only go so far. The instinct for doing the right thing plays an important part. "It has to come from within," says Huber. "It's just the type of person Marie is—it goes beyond taking responsibility, she really wants to help."

Precisely because it's hard to envision what might arise, Stadtlanders does not believe in giving its people scripts for dealing with customers. "You can't do that here," says Huber. "You may take thirty calls a day, and they may all be different."

YOU CAN'T TEACH PERSONALITY

Have you ever gotten good service from a company that has phone-mail answering its telephone? For some reason, the management mentality that opts for computerized call answering has trouble staying focused on outstanding customer service. In the same way, you rarely get caring, personalized service from people who are operating from a script—whether the script is delivered over the phone or in person.

Home Depot makes a big point of having its salespeople instantly greet customers when they walk into the store. Home Depot also emphasizes that the greeting needs to be something that each individual employee is comfortable with and can deliver with sincerity and energy. The greeting is not something written by the training department.

Great customer service is delivered by people who genuinely like people. And liking people is a personality trait developed long before an applicant tries to hire on with your company. Through both testing and interviewing, it is relatively easy to determine if someone likes interacting with people. If an applicant doesn't, your training department can't do anything about it. So once you hire people, don't try to script their personalities. Set clear, simple goals for your employees, then let them use their own styles in achieving them.

And don't be afraid to make sure the standards you set are upheld. Mystery shopping—hiring people to anonymously patronize your company and check the levels of service—is a vital part of monitoring what kind of service your company is actually delivering.

One Saturday, Marie received a call from a woman. "She said, 'I've got a box of medicine here, and my kids opened it up, but it's for a guy who's across the courtyard. If you get me the address, I'll take it to him.'" Marie didn't think that was such a great idea.

"Who wants that?" she asks. "The neighbor coming over with the medication that the kids had been at. We can't do that.

"I called the man and said, 'Are you all right? Do you have enough medicine for the weekend? I'll send it out again for Monday delivery.'

"Then I had Federal Express go pick the first one up."

The medicine was discarded when it arrived back at Stadtlanders.

There's No Substitute for Common Sense

Judgment is probably the most important intangible quality employees can bring to their jobs. If you give people the goals you want them to achieve and the resources to do the job, you then have to step back and let them exercise their own judgment as each new crisis occurs.

Management can never develop enough rules for handling the myriad customer situations that come up daily. Your best chance for resolving a customer problem is to have someone dealing with the customer who has good judgment and the freedom to use it.

Marie Williams says that although working for Stadtlanders is not the job where she's had the most responsibility, the problems of the patients and the bureaucracy of the insurance companies absolutely absorb her, and she easily recalls the details of incidents that happened two years ago.

"I've enjoyed practically every job I've ever had," she says. "I like it here because I have so much freedom to talk. I love to talk."

What's Marie Williams Worth?

As with Paula Doricchi, let's consider how Marie's employer, Stadtlanders, benefits from her extraordinary service level. For the sake of argument, let's say Marie is able to work her magic with an insurance company often enough that once a week (on average), someone who might not have been a devoted Stadtlanders customer becomes one. We know that these people buy about $700 in drugs per month (remember, these patients are very ill), and we'll guess that Stadtlanders has a 30 percent profit margin, given that these are incremental customers. We'll give each customer a four-year relationship with Stadtlanders.

The numbers, then, are:

1 incremental customer (per week)

× 50 weeks (per year)

× $700 per customer (per month)

× 12 months (per year)

× 30 percent (profit margin)

× 4 years

= $504,000 (over four years)

Over a year, she would produce a quarter of that amount, or $126,000. Remember, this is incremental, above and beyond what she produces for the company at normal "production" levels.

Casts a whole new light on the value of a good telephone manner.

HOW DO YOU FIND MARIE WILLIAMS?

1. There's really only one key question when hiring people for jobs like Marie's: how do they handle themselves over the phone? That said, there's really only one effective way to hire them: interview them over the phone.

    When looking for good telephone representatives, tell prospective applicants the truth. That all things being equal (reasonable work history and work habits, reasonable references), the only thing that matters is their ability to sell their personality over the telephone. Because that's what the job is all about. So interview such candidates over the phone, and see how they do.

    If you actually want to meet them after talking to them over the phone, you know you've got a strong candidate. That's when you bring them in for a personal interview.

2. By the same token, if you're considering as a new receptionist someone who already works in that job somewhere else, call her up at her current job and see how she sounds. What you hear when you call is, if you hire her, what your customers will hear when they call your business.

CHAPTER 5

CONSULTING

AS SERVICE

photo by Professional Photographic Services—Gregg H. Owen

DAVID GREENE

THE SALESMAN WHO DOESN'T SELL

More and more, we live in a world in which consumers choose products based on service quality, not out of brand loyalty, or even because of differences in quality. With the spread of technology and modern management techniques, new quality standards quickly spread even to generic products. The evidence of this is everywhere. How do you pick a laundry detergent? or a long-distance service? or a brand of cigarettes? or a personal computer with 486 power? Most often, we'd guess, not by brand.

So what is there for the self-respecting, growth-oriented company to compete on?

Well, there is price. And price can be effective, but it is a very tough strategy to compete on. It requires single-minded focus on being the low-cost producer.

You need look no further than two of America's powerhouse industries to see this. Airlines are a critical element of the American economy. They fly more and more people as time passes, and it should certainly be possible to make money flying people from one place to another. But because of an almost cannibalistic pricing policy, America's great, globe-circling air carriers keep going into bankruptcy—or out of business altogether.

The personal-computer industry is an equally vivid example of both the value of competing on price, and the peril. Personal computers get more powerful every three months—computers sold in mid-1993 were twenty times quicker and more potent than those sold eighteen months earlier, and they also get cheaper every three months. Not just cheaper in terms of how much computing power you can get for a dollar, but cheaper per unit. In terms of computing power for the dollar, personal computers are beginning to live up to the types of claims made long-ago by proponents of nuclear power. Computers are approaching the point where absolutely astronomical power is available for very modest cost.

What's more, the nation's great personal computer companies are selling PCs at record rates, generating huge sales volumes. And as a group, this success has brought them to the edge of financial catastrophe. Computers have become just one more commodity, like pasta or gasoline. The quality is pretty uniform, and pretty high, so people buy on price, and the prices keep crashing.

One way to be a leader, clearly, is to be one of the lowest-cost producers. But that is a risky life.

Another way to be a leader in a commodity industry is to compete on marketing and quality of service. If you can't count on differentiating yourself on the basis of your product itself (and if IBM couldn't, what company is safe?), the way to differentiate yourself is by your service.

Many businesses instinctively understand this. Banks are so heavily regulated these days that the "products" they offer are virtually indistinguishable. The only ways to compete are marketing and quality of service. Provide a bank with friendly, knowledgeable employees who can tackle any problem, get the statements right, and accommodate equally people who want direct deposit of their pay and those who want to come chat with the branch manager every day—and customers will come.

In the airline business, the upstart British carrier Virgin Atlantic is making serious in-roads against British Airways based on the philosophy of its creator, Richard Branson. He got fed up with the quality of service on most airlines and said to himself, "It can't be hard to do a better job than what's being done now."

Independent insurance agents sell exactly the same products at exactly the same prices. They can compete only on service, on the quality of the agent-customer relationship, and on their expertise in insurance, which is itself an aspect of service (product knowledge). In truth, they compete on something a little more subtle than simply service. They compete on their ability to be consultants—to figure out what you as an insurance buyer need, and sell you that, in a way that you end up feeling you've gotten just what you need. And there must be something to this technique, because we know wildly successful independent agents, and ones who only do okay.

In an interesting twist, the big department stores like Bloomingdale's and Nordstrom are battling back against the discounters like Wal-Mart and Kmart—not on price, but on the quality of the service they deliver. They use exactly the same technique as the insurance agents: the department stores want you to use their salespeople as consultants—fashion consultants, decorating consultants, wedding consultants, gift consultants. Service is being sold almost as a new discovery, as a perk! (My how the world has changed.)

In each of these instances, service, provided by the salespeople, is a vital part of the product. And in most of these instances, the key is for the salesperson to act like someone working not on his or her own behalf, but on the customer's behalf. It is the salesperson as consultant.

The most striking example we found of this idea in practice involved a man who looks, at least at first glance, as if he labors under a lot of disadvantages. He sells the paper rolls that go in cash registers and the ribbons used to print on that paper—items in which there is very little variance in quality. And because of what he sells, the service opportunities seem severely limited. What kind of consultative service does a company with cash registers need? It simply needs ribbons and cash register rolls—here are the sizes, here are the delivery dates, what's your price? It's the kind of product that could be sold without a human being, via computer, and probably will be within a few years.

We almost didn't bother to visit David Greene for precisely those reasons. The only thing that caught our eye in his nomination form was a story about him racing to supply a large customer in a bind, a customer he'd been wooing for months without success. But what salesman wouldn't do that? The potential for almost half a million dollars in sales per year would bring even the most ordinary salespeople up out of their chairs.

But there was something intriguing about David Greene's nomination story. We checked him out.

What we found was anything but ordinary. Greene sells products that are very similar to those of his competitors. But he managed to quintuple sales in his territory after taking it over. And he did that by being the quintessential consultant. He listens carefully to his customers, and his potential customers, and figures out ways to help them.

If a man with such limited options in terms of product and service can put consulting techniques to work as a sales tool, virtually anybody with any sales opportunities—from car salespeople to airline reservations agents—can use consultative service as a powerful tool. Watching David Greene work, you know you're in the presence of not just an intuitive salesman (although he is that) but an intuitive expert on human nature.

SELLING SMART

Anyone who has ever attended a college football game on a sunny fall afternoon knows that by the time the guy selling sodas gets up into the stands, the drinks have become watery and warm, with only tiny motes of ice floating at the top of the cup.

David Greene knows this too. When he was growing up in Raleigh, North Carolina, he often spent his Saturdays at Carter-Finley Stadium, selling sodas during North Carolina State football games.

He was fourteen years old and it was his first job. David quickly took stock of the customers and came up with what he thought was a prudent business strategy: He secured the hip-flask trade, the folks who smuggled in their own alcohol.

"They used up a lot more drinks than anybody else," says Greene. "What they were wanting was a lot of ice, because when you pour the liquor in, it melts the ice. They would say, 'Just get me ice, that's all I really need is ice.'"

So when David would go get his tray of drinks, he would tell the guy filling the cups to give him mostly ice, with just a splash of Coke. Then he'd head for the sections filled with alumni. The drinks sold themselves. And sometimes David received more than the fifteen cents per cup he earned. "If I could find a group of friendly drunks, I would get a nice tip in the process."

ONCE A SALESMAN,
ALWAYS A SALESMAN

Few great salespeople first start selling as adults. When you find a great salesperson, you'll usually discover that early in life he or she experienced success in selling. It may have been something as simple as selling Girl Scout cookies door-to-door. One of the first questions you should ask prospective salespeople is when they first started selling. If someone can't think of anything before the completion of his formal education, buyer beware.

Fourteen years later, David Greene has graduated from college, moved to Charlotte, put on a suit, polished up his style a bit, and is selling business supplies for NCR Corporation. But he hasn't had to do too much tinkering to the basic technique that worked so well at N.C. State football games. He used it to take over a territory that was doing $300,000 per year worth of business and in five years turn it into a territory that is doing $1.5 million per year.

One September day, for example, Greene got a call from a man at Food Lion, one of the nation's fastest-growing grocery store chains. The man had for months refused even to talk to Greene on the phone. But this day, the guy was out of paper rolls. Not just any paper rolls, but those for the adding machines at Food Lion headquarters. He wondered if Greene could help him out. Greene knew if he moved fast, he could get the paper rolls overnight. The man was delighted. Then David Greene had another thought: he might be able to scare up an emergency supply that very afternoon from some of his current customers. A quick phone call, a little wangling, a mad dash to a rural barbershop, and Greene had five cases of paper rolls in his Subaru station wagon and was traveling the sixty miles to Food Lion headquarters to deliver them. Until that moment Greene had been unable to get in the door at Food Lion. That day he walked off with purchase orders for $40,000 worth of business. Within twenty-four hours, Food Lion had signed up for $600,000 worth of business. David Greene's quota for the whole year was $750,000.

WHEN IN DOUBT, WOW 'EM

Greene had told the prospect he could get the rolls to him overnight and the man was happy with that response. The critical moment, however, is when David decides to do more than please him: he's going to wow him. That's what turned the prospect into a long-term customer.

Meeting customer expectations has become the service slogan of the nineties. But in many instances, meeting expectations really requires exceeding them. David Greene had already exceeded the prospect's expectations when he said he'd have the order the next day. When he showed up the same day he exceeded their expectations again.

Research at the Xerox Corporation indicates that a customer who is "extremely" satisfied is six times more likely to purchase from you next time than a customer who is "merely" satisfied. In today's competitive service environment, good service is increasingly the minimum. It takes extraordinary service to get noticed.

THE UN-SALESMAN

Part of David Greene's charm, frankly, is that he's a bit awkward. He's tall, with long arms and long legs, and he always seems a little puzzled about where exactly he's supposed to put his limbs when he's not using them.

For a man so large, Greene is anything but intimidating—he has impeccable manners, and on first meeting, he gives the impression of friendly hesitancy. He always seems to have a nagging doubt that he might be imposing.

Greene is a bit of a dandy—he has a weakness for stylish suits and exotic ties, and he wears his clothes well. But he doesn't wear them with any sort of swagger. If anything, with his cheerful baby face and his slight gawkiness, he looks a little as if he sneaked into his father's closet and put on the neatest clothes he could find.

CAN YOU REALLY SPOT A SALESMAN A MILE AWAY?

Maybe you can spot a bad salesman from a distance. But the great ones are hard to pick out. That's because, very often, much of their success is predicated on not looking or sounding like a salesperson.

When trying to find great salespeople, don't search for men and women who fit the stereotype—that is, someone who is a smooth talker.

Talking is not the key to great salesmanship—listening is.

If there is one quality that all great salespeople share, it is the ability to listen to customers, to discover what they want or need, and supply that.

David Greene feels just about the same way most people do about salespeople: he hates them.

"I think a lot of people are fed up with salespeople," he says. "I know I am."

He doesn't like their pestering, their pushiness, the way their focus on their commission seems to crowd out his needs as a customer.

And Greene is self-conscious enough to have thought about his distaste for salespeople and his own selling style. "I look at those qualities that are turnoffs for me," he says. "I don't think people want to buy from a salesperson. They don't trust salespeople. They always think you're holding something back, that you're selling them something they don't need and don't want. They always leave feeling ripped off."

Greene, in contrast, tries to act much more like a consultant than a salesman. He has an advantage being in business-to-business sales because most of his pitches, unlike those on a car lot or the selling floor of an appliance store, are more like presentations: he has an appointment, he has plenty of preparation time, he knows what his potential customers are interested in, and it is Greene's style to arrive armed with plenty of information. He seems to follow the lawyer's credo that the surest path to success is to know not only your own case, but your opposition's case as well—the defenses and objections you're likely to encounter.

He is in some ways the exact opposite of the stereotypical salesman who bulls forward, undiscouraged by and almost unconscious of hesitation or discomfort on the part of his mark. Even when he's talking, Greene watches his customers carefully, and he seems to have a keen perception of when to push a little and when to back off. It is a watchfulness he applies to himself, as well.

"I hate it," he says, "when I'm feeling salesy."

The Difference Between Buying and Selling

David Greene's customers are mostly large companies, or more specifically, the purchasing managers and operations managers at large companies, and they are a particular and demanding lot. Moreover, much of what Greene sells is indistinguishable or nearly indistinguishable from what his competition is selling.

A roll of cash register paper is 200 or 220 feet long. The inner end may or may not be attached to the core. These are not matters on which quarterly dividends rise or fall, nor matters on which companies can afford to spend a lot of time. As for price, as Greene himself said to a customer whose business he was bidding for: "You could barely buy lunch with the difference between us and the people who came in second." Indeed, the price of a roll of cash register paper depends mostly on something companies like NCR have little control over: the prevailing price of paper.

To woo customers and keep them, to give companies a reason to buy from him, Greene has evolved a variation on the ice-in-the-stadium method. He does something salespeople often seem too impatient to do: he listens to his customers. He figures out what's important to a company, and then he delivers it. One of his favorite one-line descriptions of a client begins "Their issue is . . ."

Selling Begins with Listening

Listening plays a critical role in selling. You need to listen to what the customer wants to buy. That is often different than what you think you're selling. People believe that ultimate success in salesmanship is the proverbial ability to sell ice to Eskimos. In fact, ultimate success in salesmanship is exactly the opposite: not selling people what they don't need, but figuring out what they do need and selling them that.

Sales training programs should concentrate less on traditional sales skills and more on critical listening skills.

One of Greene's clients is the local Coca-Cola distributorship, the second largest in the nation. Greene read in the newspaper that the company was trying to become more environmentally conscious. His contact at the company was quoted in the article. After reading the story, Greene called and offered her paper rolls made of recycled paper for use in the small computer printers in the company's trucks. Although the recycled paper cost 5 percent more, the company switched over immediately.

When Greene learned that world paper prices were falling, he immediately called Food Lion, which now buys over two million rolls of paper per year from NCR. The company is very cost sensitive. "When paper prices are dropping, you don't wait for someone else to tell them," says Greene. "You call and say, 'Paper prices are dropping, and I'm checking to see what we can do for you.'" Ultimately, Greene was able to lower the price of Food Lion's paper rolls dramatically, in line with the drop in world paper prices.

KNOW A CUSTOMER'S HOT BUTTON

When senior management of a company decides to take a public stand on a major issue, you can be sure that the line managers of that company know it. David Greene's buyer at the Coca-Cola distributorship was one of the people quoted in the story about the company's commitment to become more environmentally conscious, so Greene knew if he could offer her a product that was more environmentally sound, she might well be interested.

There are really two lessons here. First, if you're trying to sell or service a company, find out as much as you can about seemingly unrelated issues or positions that could have an effect on your success. This isn't just true for prospective customers—the Coca-Cola distributorship was *already* a customer of Greene's. The recycled paper rolls allowed him to keep current with the company's strategy and approach. Second, and maybe more important, if you're a senior official of a company, be assured that any stands you take in public will have an impact on how the people in your company act.

Make sure the actions they take are the ones you antici-
pated.

The senior management of the Coca-Cola distributorship
knew the environmentally conscious stance would mean increased costs in some areas. But make sure you as a manager
have thought through all the possible consequences of any
new programs or positions you outline.

THE BEST DEFENSE IS
A GOOD OFFENSE

In football, it is often asserted that the best offense is a
good defense. In selling, it's often the other way around. If
one of David's competitors goes in with a lower price because of a drop in paper prices, David will be on the defensive with that customer. On the other hand, if he gets there
first with a new quote, as he did, he can further cement the
relationship.

In business, it is quite common to have increases in price.
And management usually spends a lot of time thinking
about the best strategy for informing the customers and im-
plementing a price increase. Price decreases are much less
common. However, the strategy for communicating and im-
plementing a price decrease can often be more critical than
for an increase. If your competitor gets there first, you'll either have an unhappy customer or a new prospect that was
recently a customer.

LEARNING THE MOVES THAT
WORK FOR YOU

David Greene has the kind of accommodating manner that can
sometimes be mistaken for weakness or vacillation. But Greene's
even temper shrouds a surprising determination. Greene, for instance, keeps a list of written goals on his desk, and unlike some
people's New Year's resolutions, he worries about fulfilling his
goals on a weekly and monthly basis. "You can put them off each

day," he says, "but if you actually write them down, then you can look back and say, 'Six months ago, I wanted to do this.' "

Greene grew up in Raleigh, one of three brothers. His father Hilliard, now vice president of a commercial printing company, played basketball for the University of North Carolina at Chapel Hill, as did David's younger brother. David's older brother played varsity tennis for N.C. State. But David, the middle boy, was anything but an athlete.

"As a kid, I didn't have a whole lot of confidence in myself," he says. "I was uncoordinated and had a weight problem. I was 215 pounds when I was five nine or five ten. I never excelled in school."

Greene had to find an area where he was comfortable. His experience hawking soft drinks at N.C. State football games whetted his appetite for selling, more because of the sense of accomplishment and the chance to take care of people than for the rush of excitement some salespeople enjoy.

"You know, those candy sale things in junior high and high school—I was always trying to come up with some strategy to win some tacky little prize for selling the most candy bars."

CONTESTS ARE FOR WINNERS

David may call it a "tacky little prize," but he still remembers it today, and he still likes to talk about it. Great salespeople are very competitive and they love contests because they usually win.

The challenge for management is to have enough contests to satisfy the thirst of the habitual winners while being creative enough to keep everyone's interest in the game.

You can have contests for new salespeople. You can have a special category for salespeople in new territories. You can have contests for largest percentage increase as well as total sales. You have to create a lot of ways to win if you want to have a lot of winners.

The job Greene really wanted as a teenager was working at the local Belk's, an outlet of the regional department store chain, and he hounded them until he was hired. "I really did like working at Belk's," he says. "I didn't sit behind a cash register and wait for people to bring me a sweater to ring up. I really helped people pick things out."

The job meant not only selling and a salary, it came with a clothing discount, and even in high school, Greene liked to dress fashionably. "That was when preppy was the thing," he says. "My folks wouldn't buy that for me. They said, 'Son, if you want that horse, if you want that alligator, you're going to have to pay for that stuff yourself.' "

Greene went off to college at Appalachian State, in Boone, North Carolina, where he not only grew up, he became comfortable with his own rhythms. "When I got to college, on my own, that's when I got my act together," he says. "I met a great group of friends, who are still my best friends. And I gained a lot of confidence in myself.

"It's given me inspiration to do whatever I wanted. Now I have the confidence to try—where before I might not have because I might fail."

College is also where Greene developed his unconventional work habits. It's common these days to find him at the office at six in the morning—something he does so he can leave promptly at five-thirty in the afternoon to be with his wife and children. "In school," he says, "when I had exams, I used to go to bed at 10 P.M. and wake up at 3 A.M. to study. My mind clicks better that way."

"THE EARLY BIRD GETS THE WORM" IS NOT JUST A TRITE TRUISM

Good salespeople, as a general rule, get up early in the morning. Obviously this is not true without exception, but it is true more than you would ever imagine, and it is one more question to ask potential salespeople.

If you are interviewing and hiring college students, or those recently out of college, one way to get at this information is to ask about their class schedule in school. College students can decide when their day starts; pay special attention to those who went after the classes that started at eight and nine in the morning.

Greene went to work for NCR straight out of college—it's the only company he's worked for since graduating in 1985. His first assignment was in Savannah, Georgia. And although that's where he met his wife Holly—a schoolteacher and, at the time, the roommate of an NCR colleague—Greene wasn't all that happy in the beginning, either selling or being in Savannah.

Laurie Gullickson, who is his current district manager and a major Greene booster, was still a salesperson when they first met, just about to become Greene's district manager. "When I met David," she says, "he was a little disenchanted . . . The district manager prior to my taking over—she knew she was going to be moving, and David didn't get a lot of attention to start off. He had to learn a lot on his own—that can be pretty discouraging."

SELLING IS A LONELY LIFE

Being a salesperson is an emotional roller coaster. When things are going well, a salesperson needs almost no supervision or support. But when things are going poorly, a salesperson needs a combination of mother, psychiatrist, and friend. Gauging those moods, and providing encouragement at the right moment, is what managing salespeople is all about. Says Greene of his boss, Laurie Gullickson: "Laurie always knows when I need a boost. She's a big reason I'm still here, a big reason I'm still successful."

District managers, regional managers, and sales managers usually end up in those positions because they were the most successful salespeople. Unfortunately, success as a salesperson is no guarantee that an individual will be a successful mentor. In fact, the skills necessary to succeed in these two areas are often mutually exclusive. Many companies would do better if they'd keep their best salespeople in front of customers and find their sales managers some other way.

Greene himself now regularly leads selling seminars for NCR—particularly in the somewhat obscure area of bar-coding products, on which he's become an expert—but his own early training at NCR only confused him. "They trained you as though you didn't know how to sell. They had scripts and scenarios, lines like"—Greene's voice takes on a wheedling whine—" 'If I can do this for you, Mr. Customer, will you buy from me?'

"I felt like I was the vacuum salesman who goes into the house with a cup of dirt and throws it on the carpet and gets the vacuum out . . .

"I did horribly at first because I did what they told me. I got in there and I would just feel so cheesy. I ended up coming up with my own style and being myself. That's when I started to do well."

TRAIN SUBSTANCE INSTEAD OF STYLE

Successful salespeople either come to a job with their own style or they develop a unique style on the job. In either case, they'll be successful. Important as it is, though, management can't train style.

You can educate people so they can be more successful, but you can't program them. Enthusiasm sells, but it's got to be genuine.

THE REAL SERVICE:
LETTING CUSTOMERS BE PROUD
OF THEIR PURCHASES

One of David Greene's cardinal rules of selling is that he never specifically bad-mouths his competition.

"Customers distrust you if you bash the competition, because you sound like a salesman, and they think you're a shark and will do anything to get the job," he says. Greene tries to keep the focus on his customers' needs. "If I think there's some quality problems, I'll say something like, 'I've had another account tell me this has been a problem. Do you see that?' "

Greene has found that asking questions—and listening carefully to the answers—can be the most important strategy for both winning an account and servicing it. As approachable as Greene is, he's found people are leery of confrontation, and often don't want to say no or talk about problems they're having.

"So many people out there just nice you to death, but you can't get any business," he says. "Or there really is a problem and they won't tell you about it. I never assume everything's okay with a customer. I just ask lots of questions."

IF YOU DON'T WANT TO KNOW, DON'T ASK

Most people don't ask questions for which they won't like the answers. Some doctors, for instance, judge what they tell terminally ill patients by the questions the patients ask—the doctors usually only tell them what their questions indicate they want to know.

In business, it's the questions that you *don't* ask that can eventually kill you. David Greene, like most successful salespeople, knows that getting the bad news from a customer is a lot more important than hearing the good news. The problem is that customers generally don't like giving bad news any more than salespeople or management like hearing it. It's important that you keep digging for bad news when you don't get it at first.

If you probe and dig, you may find a problem that needs attention. If you've been probing and digging and finding nothing, there's always one last question you can ask that will either uncover a potential problem or put your mind at ease. Just ask the customer what you do best and what you do worst. If they don't have an answer for the second half of the question, then you can finally be comfortable that no news is good news.

Greene also tries to make it as easy as possible for his customers to tell him when something goes wrong, so they won't feel like they are imposing on him by complaining.

When Greene wins an account, he gives the purchasing person a "Commitment to Service" certificate, something he created.

"As your representative," the certificate reads, "David Greene encourages your feedback so that he can continually mold our program to your changing needs. I guarantee . . . same-day response to any questions, concerns or inquiries you may experience . . ."

The certificate is a little hokey, but it has important symbolic value, and it includes the phone numbers of several people in addition to Greene, so if customers have an emergency, they can reach a live person, not Greene's phone mail.

For an account the size and complexity of Food Lion, Greene goes one step farther: he prepares a quarterly report. He uses it to remind a customer of the things he and NCR have been able to do for a company during the previous quarter (consistent on-time performance, for instance), and he includes in the report a kind of scorecard, on which he asks the Food Lion buyer to rate NCR's performance in each of several areas. The report not only gives Greene the chance to remind a service-conscious customer how well things have gone, it gives the customer a low-pressure way to raise simmering problems. It gives Greene one more opportunity to learn about and solve those problems before they hurt his business.

"Customers know if you're listening to them," he says. "They can also tell if you're *really* listening"—not just nodding to indulge them. "I'm motivated by the challenge. I want to win somebody's trust."

Greene tries to set up a situation where the very act of buying from him seems like the savvy thing to do, leaving the buyer feeling smart rather than ripped off.

"I present the facts and I let them sell themselves," he says. "Then they're gonna be proud of their decision."

HOW CAN NCR HAVE MORE DAVID GREENES?

The techniques and systems that David Greene has developed to make himself a successful NCR salesman are impressive. And NCR has a mechanism—an in-house newsletter—that lets David and his supervisors share his ideas with other NCR salespeople, and also allows David to crib good ideas from his colleagues.

Do you know what innovations your employees have come up with to make their work more effective and efficient?

If you're managing a group that contains highly innovative and successful people, you can be sure they will come up with creative ideas just like David did. Your challenge as a manager is to take those ideas, give proper credit and recognition to the innovator, and then make them available to everyone in the organization. Successful people are important in helping companies achieve success. But successful companies have figured out how to help their people be successful.

WHAT'S DAVID GREENE WORTH?

David Greene sells paper—cash register rolls and other total-commodity papers. The profit margins are thin on that type of product, perhaps 5 to 10 percent. Although the production of paper is a high fixed-cost endeavor, the demand swings widely due to cyclical usage, while output is remarkably flat (except when a major plant starts up or shuts down). So it's hard to estimate a gross margin. As usual, lets err on the conservative side and say that the profit on an incremental dollar sold is about 7.5 cents.

David told us that he increased the sales in his district (by improving service levels to his customers) from $300,000 to $1.5 million. In doing so, he added an incremental $1.2 million in business to NCR's revenues. Using our conservative estimate of 7.5 percent margin on incremental sales, those sales are worth $90,000 per year to NCR in pure profit—that is, after you account for the cost of David Greene himself!

Of course, this estimate completely ignores the fact that

customers tend to become less price sensitive when they become accustomed to receiving great service. While this doesn't mean that David can gouge his customers, he may be able to maintain a reasonable price when a particular competitor lowballs prices in his market in an effort to gain market share. Needless to say, that improves the margin on David's total basket of business and may push it above the 7.5 percent level we have estimated for the entire country. With total sales of $1.5 million, an increase of a single percentage point in profitability is worth $15,000—nothing to sneeze at.

HOW DO YOU FIND DAVID GREENE?

1. If you're looking for King Kong salespeople, the truth is, you can't train them. You've basically got to hire them. Very few great salespeople first discover sales in their mid-forties.

   So the first clue to hiring David Greenes is to ask about their earliest sales experience. The key to finding David Greene himself, of course, is his story about selling drinks with lots of ice at the N.C. State football stadium as a kid. Greene had the instincts of a salesperson before he was fifteen.

2. We've said it before, but you can't hear it too often: don't decide in advance what someone doing a particular job should be like. David Greene had almost no formal sales experience (NCR hired him straight out of college—and must be pretty happy they did, too), and he is not a classic salesperson in demeanor or approach. But he is a classic salesperson in results.

3. Don't always judge people on their first three months of work. It took David Greene a while to find his groove, to find a style he was comfortable with. For months, he stumbled along, not doing a particularly

impressive job in Savannah. But once he found a selling approach that felt good to him (because it was *his* approach), he took off. Can you imagine if David had been fired by NCR during his early months—and hired by a competitor? Have a little faith and a little patience with smart, inexperienced employees—and give them support. They may just need some settling-in time before they knock your socks off.

CHAPTER 6

SERVICE

SYSTEMS

photo by Jim Graham/GSI

RICH CIOTTI

The Customers Are in the Cards

We can't emphasize enough that hiring is the most important element in finding the right kind of people to take care of your customers. But there are ways to increase the quality of service your company delivers—and ways to guarantee all your customers a basic level of service—that don't depend on making perfect hiring decisions. Indeed, such service systems work almost regardless of the attitude or motivation of any particular employee.

Let's start with a very basic example of how service systems work. Everyone these days receives calls from telemarketers trying to sell merchandise and services over the phone, everything from time-shares to aluminum siding. In the most sophisticated of these telemarketing organizations, the salespeople are polite and brisk and don't argue with people who are irritated at being cold-called. There is a reason for this briskness, a system. The salespeople know that for every hundred calls they make, they will get, say, three sales. They know the numbers, and the numbers have held up over months and years and tens of thousands of calls. So someone hanging up on them is no particular cause for concern: it just means being one call closer to a sale.

This basic principle is at work all over.

In the last few years, quick oil-change businesses have proliferated across the country. Several of the big national chains in this business put a small, clear sticker inside the upper corner of the windshield of each car after changing the oil. The sticker suggests the date (typically three months later) and the mileage (typically three thousand miles later) when the customer should bring the car back for the next oil change. It's a sales tool, certainly. But it also happens to be one that provides a service. How many people can actually remember when they last had their oil changed? This way, all you have to do is glance at the sticker. It may be grandiose to call such a sticker a *system*, but that's exactly what it is. The companies know that for every hundred stickers put in the upper corner of a windshield, a certain number of people will come back for an oil change. And many people are most assuredly grateful for the subtle reminder.

There is a national mail-order florist that uses a version of the same system. The company will call you in anticipation of important dates—birthdays, wedding anniversaries, Valentine's Day, Mother's Day—to remind you of the upcoming event and see if you need to send some flowers. The florist will even keep records of what kind of flowers each person on your list likes. It's a sales gimmick, sure, but it's one that works wonders for both the florist and the absent-minded customers. And it's as simple as keeping a database in a personal computer. Anyone who works for the florist can work with this system. It doesn't require a lot of training or the right attitude (although the person who does the actual calling to notify customers should be someone who enjoys that work). Using what has come to be known as database marketing, the florist has managed to systematize *thoughtfulness*—and it benefits not only the florist and the customers, but the recipients of the flowers as well.

Such tools and techniques lend themselves most easily to selling situations, and they are probably not used nearly enough by big companies, considering their modest cost and potential payoff.

We found a person who has perfected this kind of systematized service almost exclusively on his own. Rich Ciotti works for JCPenney, but the system he uses to keep track of customers—their buying histories, their tastes, what pieces of furniture they may still need to complete a particular set—is one he's put together himself.

What first attracted us to Ciotti was a story in his nomination packet about a customer who was so pleased with his help that she anonymously arranged to pay for his lunches at a restaurant in the mall where he works. Ciotti would move through the cafeteria line, and the cashier would smile and tell him his meal was paid for.

We were surprised to find a commission salesperson who could inspire that kind of gratitude. And the funny thing is that Ciotti turned out to be cut from the very traditional salesperson's cloth: aggressive, eager, not particularly subtle. He remembers your name, and uses it often. He knows how to close.

But he is also, as you'll see, remarkably focused on service. He has enough knowledge about the furniture his department stocks to be considered a furniture expert. He knows styles, colors, variations, optional features, manufacturing methods, and the schedule for upcoming discounts. He knows about credit and delivery, and he knows about people, too. He calls to remind his customers when something goes on sale, and to tell them when a coveted piece has come back in stock.

And for a salesman with an almost stereotypical style, he is careful about one very interesting thing: he listens, and he never tries to sell his customers something they don't want.

There is no question that for Ciotti, service is simply a selling tool. His goal is to move furniture, and he has figured out the techniques that will help him do just that. There is no question that his techniques work: Ciotti sells more furniture than any other JCPenney salesperson.

But there is also no question that the motivation for Ciotti's approach is irrelevant: the result is outstanding service for his customers. They clearly love it. Ciotti has refined the *sell* to the point that the act itself is very often a service.

SELLING AS SPORT

It's a spring Sunday morning, about an hour before Rich Ciotti will take the floor in the furniture department at the JCPenney in Oxford Valley Mall, outside Philadelphia. Ciotti, trim at fifty years old, is dressed for work in a sharp black pinstriped suit. On his left hand Ciotti is wearing an onyx and gold ring, a reward for his sales in 1989. His watch is also a gift from JCPenney, in honor of his 1986 sales. On his right hand he wears a diamond pinkie ring he bought himself.

Ciotti is sitting in a booth in one of the mall's coffee shops, and when he's done with breakfast he pushes aside the dishes and, like some kind of magician, starts to pull customers out of his pockets. He's got customers in his back pants pocket, he's got some in his shirt pocket, he's got a few tucked in one of his inside coat pockets, he's got a couple in each of his outside coat pockets. He fans the customers out on the table before him. "These," he says of the ones retrieved last, from the outside coat pockets, "are a little more current"—as if this explains the filing system.

The customers are in the form of three-by-five cards, each preprinted to allow JCPenney sales associates to keep track of potential sales. This is what Ciotti uses the cards for, after a fashion. Each card has blanks for the customer's name, phone number, and the kind of merchandise in which the person is interested.

Ciotti has all this information, but he completely ignores the blanks. He's got names, phone numbers, furniture styles scribbled every which way on the cards. Some cards have just a single person on them, some have two or three, some have customers on just one side, some have customers on both sides.

It is chaotic, not the sort of system Ciotti could hand off to a colleague, but it is the chaos of a virtuoso.

DON'T CONFUSE RECOGNITION AND COMPENSATION

High-powered salespeople have as great a need for trophies as they do for commission checks. You can't display a commission check—but Ciotti proudly wears the jewelry he has received as premiums for his sales achievements. He enjoys meeting the JCPenney CEO each year that he's the company's leading salesperson, and he talks about that meeting for weeks after he returns from Dallas. For Ciotti, and for most great salespeople, the recognition of his sales prowess by others is very nearly as important an incentive for his performance as the money he makes.

THE SYSTEM ONLY WORKS FOR CIOTTI

JCPenney may have provided Rich Ciotti with the cards, but the system is clearly his. And therein lie the problems. First, it's rather obvious that if and when Rich leaves JCPenney, his customers could easily leave with him. Second, only those few salespeople with Ciotti's focus and sense of mission will actually have the customer files that he has. But it doesn't have to be that way.

Database management systems are inexpensive and easily accessible for any company. JCPenney should take Ciotti's mechanical system and adapt it to computer technology. Then the company should have all the salespeople turn in customer information so it can be recorded for the company as well as given back to the salespeople in a form that will make them more effective. It's nice that Rich can remember when to call a customer, but it would be even better if all JCPenney salespeople could.

It might be difficult for Rich to get used to using a computer. But once he saw the things a computer could do for him, like keeping a tickler file of customers he needs to call on any given day, he'd never switch back.

The JCPenney store where Ciotti works does about $24 million worth of business per year. Although he is just one of the store's 250 salespeople, Ciotti typically sells $1 million of that $24 million himself. Working on a straight 7 percent commission, Ciotti earns more than anyone in his store except the store manager, and his pay exceeds that of some of the chain's store managers. He is, in fact, number one out of all JCPenney's sixty-thousand-odd salespeople in the world—in each of the last seven years.

For Ciotti, the money is in the sales, the sales are in the customers, and the customers are in the cards.

Here, for instance, are Julia and Olga, two older sisters from Philadelphia who had been in two weeks previously, looking at a sofa and a recliner. Ciotti called them yesterday at home, to give them his Sunday hours. "Let's hope this happens today," Ciotti says, and crosses himself.

Ciotti picks out another card. "This is Mrs. Vatter. She lives in New York, but she always buys from me. She's interested in a rocker." On another card is a Russian couple, the Nemirovskys. "They bought a bedroom set," he says. "They're interested in a garment bag."

Ciotti shrugs, reshuffles the cards, and parcels them out among his pockets. The movements and moods of customers are a fluky business, hard to make sense of, like the weather, sometimes even dependent on the weather.

This Sunday is turning out to be sunny and warm, and walking to the store Ciotti eyes the blue sky a little dubiously. "Yesterday was damp and rainy," he says, "a good day in the mall."

In the furniture department just before the store opens at eleven in the morning, one of Ciotti's fellow salesmen, Lou Beckett, is looking irritably for his desk chair, a comfortable burgundy leather one Lou particularly liked.

"Where's my desk chair?" Lou asks a little accusingly.

Ciotti grins. "I sold it Saturday," he says. "For five hundred and fifty dollars."

So who knows what Sunday will bring?

NOBODY GETS PAST CIOTTI

Sunday morning gets off to a slow start, with all three salesmen on duty—Ciotti, Lou, and Dave Evanetz, an eleven-year veteran of the department—talking idly while their eyes scan the horizon near the escalators for possible incoming customers.

There are two basic ways to run a commission sales floor: the up system, in which each salesperson gets a crack at walk-in customers on a rotating basis; and the free-floor system, in which walk-ins belong to whichever salesperson gets to them first.

This furniture department runs on the free-floor system, although the free-for-all system might be a better description. Since all three men stand in the same place when they don't have a customer, the free-floor system literally means that the guy who spots first, is fastest off the mark, and fastest in pursuit gets the customer. This occasionally creates the somewhat ludicrous spectacle of grown men chasing after customers, although in practice the trailing salesman rapidly breaks off and returns to the scanning position.

Ciotti is clearly the most keyed-up of the three men. If he is actually standing in one place—more often he paces in a small oval—he rocks a little on the balls of his feet, his hands clasping each other behind his back, his eyes working back and forth like powerful target-acquisition radar. He looks just barely fastened down, as if the slightest suggestion of interest will launch him in a customer's direction.

This is what Ciotti thinks of as his low-key mode. "I'm low-key," he says, never allowing his conversation to distract his eyes. "I want to be low-key. I'm intense, okay, but I don't like to project that. I don't want them to think I'm coming in for the kill. I don't want to bark.

"If you jump on people right away, you can back 'em off. I do go in, then I back off." That, of course, is the way the free-floor system works. Once Ciotti has talked to a customer, the customer is his. "Nobody gets past Ciotti," he says.

FAIRER ISN'T NECESSARILY BETTER

The up system, which is most commonly associated with car dealerships, gives everybody a fair chance. Everybody, that is, but the company. What the up system does is guarantee that your worst salesperson will get as many chances to sell as your best salesperson. It's a great way to keep the poorer salespeople happy, but it's also a great way to ensure that the company will not maximize its sales opportunities.

The free-floor system actually tends to shake out the lazy or ineffective salespeople, because it is an arrangement that gives them very little selling opportunity.

JCPenney would not be getting the results it is getting in that furniture department if every salesperson took turns. And, in all probability, Rich would be working for a competitor by the time his turn came.

The furniture department of the Oxford Valley JCPenney is on the second floor of the store, just beyond the escalators, squeezed in between the optical shop and the luggage department.

Like most department-store furniture departments, the furniture here is jammed in close together—the Southwest living room, the traditional dining room, the country kitchen table, the Queen Anne end tables, the recliners, bedrooms, and bare mattresses. Despite the effort to arrange the furniture into coherent "rooms," it is hard to distinguish one setting from another. The customer has to focus, to tune out the background clamor all the rest of the furniture creates and concentrate on his or her own taste, needs, and budget. Rich Ciotti stands ready to help.

Occasionally, Ciotti leaves his post to scout through the department to make sure no unattended customers have slipped in. This time he finds a woman in one of the crannies.

"I'm looking for a TV table," she says.

"What kind of wood?" Ciotti asks.

"Dark," she says.

Finding something like a television table in the furniture department almost *requires* a salesperson, because smaller accessories like that are sprinkled among two dozen room groupings. Ciotti knows the stock cold, not only where every piece is, but what colors it comes in, what its regular price is, and what its sale price is.

"We have one here," he shows the woman. "It's really pretty. You put the VCR here, the tapes here. It's two hundred and seventy-five dollars."

The woman examines it, but is unenthusiastic. "Anything else?" she asks.

"Everything else is bigger," Ciotti says. He senses that she is not going to buy today. The woman tells him she wants to talk it over with her husband, perhaps bring him by.

Ciotti hands over his card. "Your name, please?" he asks.

"Jeanette Rineholt," the woman replies.

"Okay, Mrs. Rineholt," Ciotti says, "my name's Rich. My pleasure." She walks off and Ciotti says to himself, under his breath, "We'll see what the husband says. We'll see. She'll bring the husband back. Yes. Mrs. Rineholt." He's committing her— her face, her name, her VCR table—to memory.

A large, overweight man comes walking along the aisle in front of Ciotti's scanning post. "How are you doing?" Ciotti says to him with familiarity.

"Good," the man says, looking at Ciotti a little skeptically and not slowing down.

"How's the insurance business?" Ciotti asks.

The man's pace slows half a notch. "Good. Picking up, actually. The first three months of this year were horrible, but it's picking up."

"Prudential, wasn't it?" Ciotti asks.

"Yeah," the man says, now moving beyond Ciotti.

"Well, good," Ciotti says, flashing a big smile. "Take care."

This moment is vintage Ciotti. He's met the man once or twice in the store, can't recall his name off the bat, but remembers enough about him to make contact, to treat him as a person, not just a mark. This has been one of the keys to Ciotti's tremendous success. He woos the walk-ins, and they become customers for life, coming back to him whenever they need more furniture. In some families, Ciotti sells furniture to three generations.

WHEN SALES AND SERVICE ARE ONE

Rich Ciotti is not a sales theorist. He practices his trade, he doesn't analyze it. And for him, sales and service are in essence one and the same. He operates on instinct.

"A fella once asked me, when did I become a salesman?" he says. "I was *born* a salesman."

Ciotti's father was a chef at an Italian restaurant in Philadelphia. "My dad couldn't give me no allowance," Ciotti says, but "I've always been blessed. I've been a hustler since I was seven or eight years old."

That's when Ciotti's first scheme occurred to him. He was walking home from school, he says, when he stopped to ask "some of the older people in the neighborhood who couldn't go out if they needed anything." The result, Ciotti says: "I did their food shopping for them."

Ciotti, who is not a particularly reflective fellow, briefly gets a far-away look in his eye. "Mrs. Walker," he says. "Mrs. Keenan— God rest her soul." He can still remember their names.

"They would send me out with a list and the money, and I would bring back the groceries from the A & P." His pay, often as not, was the deposits on the bottles he returned for the women.

PUTTING SERVICE FIRST

As a young boy, Ciotti saw a service opportunity. He helped people, and money followed. He didn't charge his grocery customers; he provided good service and they rewarded him. (Obviously, if they had not, Ciotti would likely have stopped providing the service.)

Ciotti has never lost that core idea (one shared by most great service providers), even now when the monetary part of his job is far more obvious. He provides service to his furniture customers, he helps them figure out what kind of furniture they need and want, and they reward him by buying furniture.

Ciotti also delivered newspapers and cut lawns. "I built up a customer following whose lawns I'd cut," he says. "In them days, a dollar-fifty or two dollars for cutting a lawn was a big deal."

From his teenage enterprises, Ciotti says, "I learned to treat people right and give 'em good service and they give you a bigger tip."

Actually, he learned something more subtle and more valuable than the good-service, good-tip connection. He discovered the importance of the regular, repeat customer. It was simpler, more efficient, and far more lucrative to keep his established grocery, newspaper, and lawn customers happy than it was to constantly find new ones. Particularly in a service business, Ciotti discovered, building a clientele was the road to prosperity.

It is a lesson that goes a long way toward explaining his nineteen years of success in JCPenney's furniture department. Catherine Raupp, Ciotti's current supervisor, tells people considering going to work in the furniture department, "Of ten customers who come in, eight ask for Rich. One asks for Dave. And the last one is yours—if you can get him.

"I don't believe in giving people an unrealistic view of the job."

CUSTOMER RETENTION CAN BE THE KEY TO PROFITABILITY

Research that's been well-documented and reported several times in the *Harvard Business Review* indicates that a 5-percentage-point increase in customer retention creates a minimum of a 25 percent increase in net profits. Just imagine for a moment if you and your company had never lost a customer. Your sales would be larger than they are, but your profits would be astronomical. When you consider the cost of acquiring them, new customers are rarely profitable, while older customers become increasingly profitable over time.

That's because with established customers, the acquisition costs have long since been paid. Old customers know how to do business with you, so your employees don't have to invest time and energy teaching them how to buy from you. Because of their familiarity with you, studies show, established customers tend to buy more, and because of their level of satisfaction, they tend to make word-of-mouth referrals, generating fresh business for you at no cost. Finally, because your employees and your organization know these established customers so well, you can consistently deliver the goods and services they need, even as those needs change, adding value to your relationship with them without adding any costs.

Many companies could take a lesson from Rich Ciotti, spending more time on the potential of the customers they have and less time looking for new ones (often at the expense of the existing ones!). In fact, many successful companies use various forms of direct marketing to accomplish what Rich does with his cards. Fishing for new customers is time-consuming and expensive. After you've finally caught them, it doesn't make a lot of sense to throw them back.

Don't Promise Them a Rose Garden

If you want to avoid excessive employee turnover, start by reducing your hiring mistakes. Catherine Raupp has done herself and prospective furniture salespeople a big favor by telling them up front exactly what they can expect. Most applicants will pass—which means that she saves the expense and disruption of hiring, training, and then losing them. But, best of all, she is giving herself a chance to find someone with enough self-confidence to perhaps be the next Rich Ciotti.

Closing with Olga and Julia

Just after one in the afternoon, Rich Ciotti finds a pair of cheerful older women browsing in a grouping of sofas and chairs. One of the women is sitting on a Nantucket-striped couch, bouncing a little, testing it out.

It is Olga and her sister Julia, who have come in as they promised when Ciotti called them yesterday, perhaps to buy the sofa and a matching wing-backed recliner. The couch is soft and comfortable, the fabric classy, with little pleats in the skirt.

"What is this?" Olga asks, patting the cushion.

"Fabric on polyurethane," Ciotti says.

"Does this already have Scotchgard?" she asks.

"Yes," Ciotti says, "Penney's does it with the fabric."

And that's it. Julia and Olga have really come back just to make sure the couch and the recliner are as nice as they remember. They are ready to buy, and Ciotti takes them over to his desk to do the paperwork.

It is when Ciotti brings customers who are ready to buy back to his desk to do the sale that you really sense the pleasure he takes in his business. For him, the paperwork, the closing, is a moment of visceral satisfaction, the equivalent of spiking a football after a touchdown—although he reins in his excitement.

"I like to do it where it's more of a low-key thing," Ciotti says. "Not so they think they're buying something. Not like I'm forcing them. Like they're making the decision, not me. Not like it's a commissioned salesman."

He makes the process into a small ritual, with the customers sitting near him in chairs, savoring their purchase while he savors his sale. He is noticeably calmer, his face relaxing into a gentle smile as he runs the ticket through the register and arranges delivery.

"We were in two weeks ago," says Julia. "He made a good presentation, he didn't pressure us when we were looking around. His attitude was good. And he called yesterday because we wanted to know his hours this Sunday. He said, 'Hi, this is Rich from Penney's.' "

And what caused them to think of JCPenney for furniture?

"We went to Penney's, Wanamaker's, Sears," says Julia. "We came to Penney's first. We looked around, we still came back to the one we're buying today."

Together, the couch and recliner come to $1,092, including tax and delivery. Ciotti's commission: $70.

GAMES AREN'T WON ON GAME DAY

Ask the winning coaches and they'll all tell you the same thing—it's the practices and the preparation that spell the difference between success and failure. Selling is no different.

Sunday's effortless transaction makes the sale look a lot simpler than it was. When Olga and Julia first came in, Ciotti not only had to handle them with the right touch, he had to make sure he got their names and phone number, and using his card system he had to remember to call them with his hours, as they requested. He also had to survive the subsequent competition.

The casual observer wouldn't know all this. An effective aspect of sales training is to chronicle the history of various sales. By understanding all the unseen steps it can take to make a sale, other salespeople can begin to develop the habits of success.

Too many salespeople think that their fate is decided when they come face-to-face with the customer. Managers must make sure their salespeople understand that by the time they see the customer, the outcome is almost preordained.

That's why doorman Phil Adelman has his cards ready to go with traveling directions to locations in Boston. That's why Ruby Tuesday spends so much time and energy going over the new menu with its servers. That's why JCPenney takes its furniture salespeople out of the store twice a year for seminars on the furniture being sold. And that's why Ciotti takes those seminars so seriously. Preparation is much of the key to success.

Money, of course, is the real measure of Ciotti's performance, and he keeps meticulous track of his sales. Among the items he brings to work every day are two calendar books, one from last year, one for this year. He keeps them in one of his inside coat pockets, and in the block of every day that he works he writes the dollar amount of the furniture he sells that day. He carries last year's calendar so he can compare his performance day by day.

"What motivates me? A lot of things motivate me. I'm a self-motivator, I self-motivate. Money motivates me. If I took it easy, that's less money I'm going to make. Money, making sales, self-satisfaction. When I make a sale, I feel good about myself.

"If I could make 16 percent selling sewing machines, I'd be out selling them."

THERE'S NO POINT IN PLAYING IF YOU DON'T KEEP SCORE

There are plenty of people who don't subscribe to this philosophy—who are content simply playing the game—but they aren't world-class salespeople. Champions like to keep score because that's how they know they've won. For winning salespeople, their biggest competitor is themselves. Past performance is the standard by which they judge themselves.

What's missing here is that JCPenney isn't providing all the necessary tools. It doesn't matter to Rich—he buys the calendars himself. But there are probably some potential Riches out there who could be motivated if they were given the calendars and the systems.

WATCHING THE PROS

Rich Ciotti has an ample ego—he is not shy about his ability or his achievements—but it has not changed the way he handles customers. He will often run out to a customer's home to show a fabric sample or pick up a check for payment. He also routinely attends the funerals of customers, "Just to pay my respects. I think it's very good will. They appreciate that. If you bought something from me, I always try to pay you the respect."

Rich Ciotti was twenty-two, with a wife, two kids, and a mortgage, before he discovered furniture, and it wasn't exactly love at first sight. He was already working three different jobs, including checking out customers at A & P.

He had no interest in college. "I was making the money, so I didn't want to go. I hadn't thought about my career too hard."

Through the A & P, he met Nick Visalli, now retired from Macy's, who was then managing the huge furniture department at Korvette's.

"I went and saw him, we talked. It was a full-time job, straight commission." Ciotti shrugs. "It looked like a new challenge. They had good benefits, paid for your glasses, and your prescriptions were only fifty cents."

Visalli remembers a kid who was as green as he was eager. "When Ciotti came in, he was pretty sincere, well-dressed, nice looking," says Visalli. "He told me he had no experience, nothing whatsoever."

EXPERIENCE COMES IN MANY SHAPES AND SIZES

It's lucky Nick Visalli didn't believe everything he heard. Rather than rely on luck, understand that previous selling experience can come disguised as a lot of different things. And the job candidate you're talking to may be just like Rich Ciotti and not realize all the selling experience he or she has already had.

Rich Ciotti's selling experience goes back to when he was seven years old. During a job interview, it's important to help the candidate sell himself. To do that often means you have to get him to start at the beginning. Ask a sales candidate, "What was the first thing you ever sold anybody?"

Ciotti took the job, but stayed on at the A&P just in case. Visalli had a philosophy for his new salesmen—he started them all off with thirty days in the warehouse. "He'd be moving furniture, unloading trucks, learning styles. I said, 'The first thirty days are going to be tough, I'm not gonna kid you. After thirty days, I'm going to interview you.' That's how I find out how fast they pick it up."

IF YOU WANT TO LEARN THE
MERCHANDISE, GO TO THE STOCKROOM

Product knowledge is sales power, and the best place to get that knowledge is in the plant, warehouse, or stockroom. A person not only becomes familiar with the products, but can also have a better grasp of how the systems work that help get the products to the customer.

Before putting salespeople on the road or behind a counter, give them an opportunity to understand how the business works. It will provide an education that can be applied every day.

And, as we've said in other instances, the ultimate customer service is knowledge. Empathy or a smile come and go, but stupidity (which causes frustration) is forever.

Ciotti picked it up pretty fast, Visalli says, "but he came to me after two weeks, he told me he didn't think he could take it. It was killing him. He said, 'The thing is, I'm not interested in this, going up and down ramps with this heavy stuff.' I said, 'Stick with it.'"

Visalli put Ciotti out on the floor after thirty days, and prodded him to become a real salesman. "He taught me about the furniture," Ciotti says, "how to follow up, how to treat people. If I ever got discouraged, Nicholas Visalli was the one to keep pushing and encouraging me."

Visalli recalls that in the beginning, "Ciotti would sit down after he left his customer, waiting his turn. I used to tell him, up on your feet! Keep on the floor. Even though you drop a customer, go to the other ones. If no one is touching a customer, go up to them. If you don't talk to people, you don't make any money. And these guys he was working with, they would take the eyes from their own grandmother."

Visalli schooled Ciotti in the art of the close, drilling into him the notion that people come to a furniture store for a reason: to buy furniture. "I told him, you ask the customer questions. You never know what's bugging the customer. Find out what it is that's holding them up. They came to buy, they're buyers. You have to overcome their objections."

Behind Every Great Salesman . . .

More important than the role of the sales manager or sales trainer is the impact of the mentor in the development of every great salesperson. Young, inexperienced salespeople need someone they can watch, mimic, and learn from. That person may or may not have the appropriate title or responsibility. Find the mentors in your company and then make sure that the new salespeople get some time to shadow them.

Ciotti made ten thousand dollars his first year at Korvette's, and stayed eight and a half years, until the store closed its furniture department in September 1973. By then, Ciotti had developed a stable of customers and had become the department's number-two salesman.

Korvette's offered Ciotti a job at a store in another city, but he wanted to stay in the area. He heard that the JCPenney soon to open in the Oxford Valley Mall was hiring.

When he showed up at the mall, he discovered the store was still under construction. "It was just painters, carpenters, construction men, so I went up in the freight elevator with the painters." Ciotti asked around, and someone pointed him toward the makeshift office of the personnel manager, whose first question was "How'd you get up here?"

Selling is Not for the Faint of Heart

Aggressiveness is easy to spot. And for many jobs, like selling, it's a prerequisite. Ciotti's aggressive approach was instantly noticed and the personnel manager reacted instantly. Unfortunately, there are too many times when a Rich Ciotti would be told to come back at the appropriate time or be told to "go to the back of the line."

He was hired almost immediately, to help set up before the store opened. And when it did open, says James Goetcheus, now manager of a JCPenney in Ohio and then assistant manager of the Oxford Valley store, "It was like a gun going off. He immediately became the number-one salesman, from the day the store opened."

The biggest day Ciotti has ever had at JCPenney is twelve or thirteen thousand dollars in sales. And JCPenney helps him do his job.

"They stock good furniture, they give you the best customer service—they'll exchange an item twenty times until the customer is satisfied," Ciotti says. "This is what Penney's can do for you. This is how you can build up repeat business."

GREAT SALESPEOPLE DON'T DO IT ALONE

If a company won't stand behind its products, salespeople can't be expected to stand in front of them. Salespeople like Ciotti simply won't work for companies that don't support them—or their customers. Ciotti realizes the importance of the quality of the furniture he sells, the quality of service JCPenney provides, and the reliability of the JCPenney return and exchange policy. These are things that make it possible for Ciotti to do what he does—sell furniture, keep the customers happy, and keep the customers coming back.

No company that provides less than ideal sales and customer support can expect to attract and retain ideal salespeople.

THE NICE CUSTOMERS AND THE TOUGH ONES: ALL THE SAME TO CIOTTI

Rich Ciotti starts trying to sell you a second piece of furniture the day after you take delivery of the first one.

Since Michael and Erina Nemirovsky bought a bedroom set for one of their daughters from him a week or so earlier, Ciotti has called them twice. Once he called to tell them a garment bag they expressed interest in was in stock. And he called just yesterday, to tell them they could get 25 percent off any non-sale merchandise if they brought in canned food for a food drive JCPenney is sponsoring.

It is nearly four in the afternoon when the Nemirovskys show up. They are young, successful Russian immigrants, and they have two young daughters in tow. As soon as they arrive, Ciotti jogs to a back room, where he has put aside the garment bag. When he comes out, he finds the parents looking at a three-hundred-dollar mattress and box spring that will fit the bedroom set they've ordered for their older daughter, Fallon.

"You said if we bring in the canned food," says Michael, "we get 25 percent off anything."

Ciotti tries to explain that the canned food discount does not apply to the mattress set, which is already on sale. Michael is insistent. "If you want, I'll ask the manager," says Ciotti. "You are good customers." Ciotti is trapped between wanting to keep the Nemirovskys happy and knowing that they simply can't have the mattress for 25 percent off. He's worried they'll storm out without the garment bag too. He goes to page Catherine Raupp, muttering under his breath, "They're busting my chops."

When Raupp arrives, he explains the confusion to her. She has no trouble being firm.

"If it says 'Smart Value,'" she says, showing Michael Nemirovsky the price tag, "we can't give you the 25 percent. That's still a good value."

Michael sputters. "Well, considering that I've bought a seventeen-hundred-dollar bedroom set, can I do better?"

"Sir," Raupp says, "I don't make the rules. I don't own this. If it's a floor model, I can negotiate, but this is just a sample."

Nemirovsky dismisses them both with a wave of his hand, and he and his wife Erina begin talking heatedly in Russian. Ciotti moves back to the front of the department.

And then, suddenly, as quickly as the storm arrived, it passes. Erina and Michael Nemirovsky catch up with Ciotti, and they are all sunshine. They'll take the garment bag *and* the mattress set.

"Back in Russia, we never believed we could have afforded a bed like that," says Erina. "Fallon just fell in love with it."

Ciotti rings up the sale. "He was great," Michael says. "He

called me back to tell me the bag went on sale. He told me about the can of food and the 25 percent off. This was really exceptional service."

Ciotti promises to check to see if the mattress can be delivered with the bedroom set, and sends the Nemirovskys on their way.

He is jubilant. "You're seeing a little vintage Ciotti," he says. "They're nice people."

Nice people? Wasn't he muttering about them busting his chops just minutes ago?

"You put up with it," Ciotti says, laughing. "He just wants to squeeze me. That's okay."

Going to Bat for the Customer

Ciotti's determination to sell is legendary. Says Catherine Raupp, his boss: "If he has a prospect, he will find any angle. Credit? Floor sample? Negotiate the price? If I can't help him, he'll go to my boss."

As a manager, you need to realize that when salespeople go to bat for their customers, they're usually also going to bat for themselves, and for your company.

"We are constantly preaching customer service," says Phillip Rohr, the current manager of the Oxford Valley store, "but he's one of the first people I've ever met who follows through on these preachings. He knows what it can do for him personally."

The bottom line on this particular Sunday for Rich Ciotti: $6,580 in sales, $460 in commissions—which would be a good week for some people.

"When I come in tomorrow, I'll forget what I did today," Ciotti says. "You gotta keep pushing. Never let up."

WHAT'S RICH CIOTTI WORTH?

Rich Ciotti sells approximately $1 million worth of furniture per year. The average furniture salesperson sells perhaps $350,000 worth of merchandise per year. What does the difference mean for JCPenney?

If we guess at an average markup of 100 percent, we know that JCPenney makes 50 cents (gross) on every $1 of sales. If we subtract salesperson commission and a few variable expenses, the incremental sales dollar probably brings in 35 cents in profit. Now let's compare Rich to his fellow salespeople. Rich sells about $650,000 more than each of his typical fellow salespeople. That means $650,000 in extra sales he produces multiplied by 35 percent is the incremental profit he brings to JCPenney, because—and only because—he is so good.

$650,000

× 35 percent (incremental profit)

= $227,500

Think about what it would mean to JCPenney if all its salespeople were that good.

HOW DO YOU FIND RICH CIOTTI?

1. JCPenney didn't have to try to find Ciotti—he came to the company, before the store he works in was even open. But JCPenney was smart enough to overlook the fact that Ciotti actually showed up before the hiring had begun, by wiggling his way into the store while it was under construction. Some people would have irritably turned Ciotti away. The person who hired him saw that Ciotti's determination was just the kind of signal you look for in a good salesperson.

   So that's one hint: pay attention to precisely the things that might first drive you crazy about a potential employee, and see if those aren't exactly the reasons to hire that person.

2. With a salesperson of the caliber of Ciotti, it doesn't really matter what he's selling. Ciotti himself started out selling his grocery-delivery services, and says today that if he could make 16 percent commission (instead of 7 percent), he'd happily sell sewing machines. What a salesperson has been selling is often irrelevant. It's the fact that he's been selling that is important, and the manner in which he approaches selling. If you're running a clothing store, don't pass up the chance to hire a real estate salesperson. Sales success is a lot more important than product experience.

3. Don't worry so much about finding Rich Ciotti—pirate his most important technique instead: set up systems to help the employees you already have. Use computers (and relatively inexpensive personal computers are more than enough) to keep track of customers, their likes and dislikes, their birthdays, their jobs, their kids, their buying history. Give your employees the opportunity to send cards on important dates, to notify their regular customers of sales a little bit in advance, to remind customers when an item they want comes in. Give your employees daily or weekly summaries of their performance—not only in dollar figures, but information about how they're doing compared to last year, number of items sold, merchandise they are not selling, even lists of customers who haven't visited in a while.

If you put strong, helpful systems in place, you won't be in such desperate need for superstars like Ciotti. Your ordinary employees will end up doing a much better job.

And when someone like Ciotti comes along, you'll be ready with the support systems he needs to really excel.

CHAPTER 7

WHEN SERVICE
CAN'T WAIT

photo by Scott Rosenberg at Harvey Dresner Studios, Inc.

ALAN WILK

TAKING CONTROL IN A CRISIS

It's Sunday night. You've just had your in-laws over for a dinner party. The dishwasher is full and your kitchen counter is still littered with dirty dishes. The sink fills up with water. No problem. You run the disposal to clear it. Works fine, except that dirty brown water with bits of lettuce and rice backs up into your bathtub—about two inches worth. Your spouse screams. You don't need a plumber; you need a super-hero.

Actually, you need an expert at clearing drains to solve the problem, and an expert in human nature to soothe your nerves and assuage your fears. You need them both at the same time, and in the same person. If you're lucky, you might get one or the other. If you live in New York City and call Roto-Rooter, though, you might well get both—in the person of Alan Wilk.

Wilk is an expert at clearing drains and sewers. He is unquestionably the best Roto-Rooter man in New York City, according to the company, and he may well be the best in the nation. Wilk's personal philosophy is that there is not a pipe in New York that can outsmart him. But the real magic of a service call from Wilk is not in fact the technical performance. It's the emotional performance. Because Alan Wilk knows as much about handling distraught people as he does about handling distressed drains.

As we discussed in the chapter about Keith Spring, simple technical competence is rare enough these days, even in professions that require it. And there is one way in which Wilk is like Spring: he knows that a clogged drain or sewer pipe is not possessed by some evil sprite, but has a problem that he can solve once he figures it out. Wilk shares Keith Spring's patience, determination, and quiet confidence about his diagnostic and technical skills.

But unlike Keith, Alan Wilk must do his work in the presence of his customers, and his customers are rarely calm and cheerful. There is no convenient time or place for the toilet to back up. Alan's perceptiveness about people, his calm, unhurried, methodical approach, his outgoing manner, all combine to soothe his customers. There is about Alan a clear sense that your problem is not unusual, that he can fix it, that he will restore order to your home.

When you watch Alan Wilk work, in fact, what is so striking is how unusual a combination of skills he has. From airline reservation agents to university professors, people in all kinds of professions seem to think good enough is good enough. (And we do admit that often enough just getting the reservations right these days seems worthy of celebration.) Brusqueness seems to be the order of the day. And when you're treated as an obligation—by the airline reservation agent or the surgeon—it can sour the service experience, even if you get exactly what you want in technical terms.

This intuitive feeling about what service should be is supported by research performed by Len Berry and Parsu Parasuraman at Texas A&M University. They concluded that great service (and consequently a service superhero) has five specific qualities: reliability, responsiveness, tangibles, assurance, and empathy.

Reliability simply means doing what is promised, when it's promised. Without even thinking about it, Alan Wilk has made reliability part of his personality. And when you see him at work, you will see how Roto-Rooter has used systems to build reliability into its performance, for the many employees who aren't quite up to Alan's standards.

Responsiveness for Alan means much what it means for Keith Spring. It means listening to the customer, it means not shrugging in bafflement at the problem and giving up. Alan, though, is also responsive to the customer at an emotional level.

Tangibles are the telltale evidence that service has been performed. They are important because without them, it is possible to spend a great deal of time and effort on behalf of a customer and have the customer forget, or never realize, what was done. In hotel bathrooms, the old-fashioned strip of paper across the toilet was a signal that the toilet had been cleaned. These days, hotel housekeepers make the same point by folding the end of the toilet paper into a triangle.

Alan Wilk actually cleans up not only from himself, but helps clean up the mess that caused him to be summoned in the first place. Most people would weep with gratitude simply to have a plumber who cleaned up after himself—let alone one who also cleaned up after them.

With assurance and empathy, we move from those qualities of service that are part of performing the service to those qualities that are more psychological. These psychological elements of service are very important, at times as important as the performance elements. An example: on a recent airline flight, a friend was "beveraged" by the flight attendant. He requested a sparkling water with lemon and an aspirin. Without a moment's hesitation, the flight attendant advised that there was no aspirin.

He was then handed a club soda and told that there was only lime—and the flight attendant dropped a wedge in his glass. Thus ended the man's service encounter—the flight attendant moved on down the aisle.

What's wrong with that picture? Given that the friend drinks club soda and not just sparkling water, and likes lime and not just lemon, the performance elements of the service encounter were not good, but hardly tragic. The psychological elements, however, were a disaster.

There was no "I'm sorry you have a headache" (empathy), nor "I don't have any aspirin, but let me ask the other flight attendants if there is any on board" (assurance). There was no question as to whether club soda was a satisfactory substitute for sparkling water, or lime for lemon. In short, the service delivered fell well short of adequate, and the manner in which it was delivered was totally unacceptable. Our friend just chalked it up to yet another bad airline experience, but you can bet if he has a choice in the future, he will avoid that airline.

Alan, on the other hand, delivers assurance by his confident demeanor, and by bringing his customers into the repair process and telling them what he's doing. Alan understands that there is a psychological side to a customer's problems. He knows that a little empathy can go a long way, particularly when things go wrong that are even out of the control of the service worker.

Empathy's greatest enemies are arrogance and indifference. A service provider who believes it is beneath him or her to acknowledge a customer's concern, or who simply doesn't care how the customer feels, will never be empathetic. He or she will also never deliver truly good service—because treating the customer is as important as treating the problem. Empathy is something that cannot be trained into a service worker (although it can be encouraged). Empathy is either present or not in an individual, and management must include it in the list of qualities they look for in selecting new employees.

A caution: neither side of these service elements (performance or psychology) is adequate alone, and too much of one with none or too little of the other is frustrating to customers. If Alan Wilk were friendly, concerned, confident, and empathetic, but couldn't clean drains worth a darn, he would simply be a glorious incompetent, of no value in the field. Service providers must strike a balance, and deliver some combination of them all.

What first tipped us off that Alan Wilk might be something more than the average Roto-Rooter man was the number of letters in his personnel file from people he had helped who weren't Roto-Rooter customers—mostly people who had broken down on one of New York City's highways. Wilk makes a habit of helping "rescue" them. Here, surely, was the kind of person you would want rescuing you from a backed-up sewer.

Alan Wilk faces a particularly unusual psychological challenge with his customers in that, unlike most of the situations we've encountered to this point in the book, his customers start out angry and frustrated (not at him, but upset nonetheless). His job is as much to take care of them as to take care of their problems.

THERE ARE A MILLION CLOGGED DRAINS IN THE NAKED CITY, AND ONE MAN CAN CLEAN THEM ALL

When Alan Wilk showed up at Charlie Mihulka's house in the Glendale section of Queens one winter night in 1985, his chances of success seemed remote. The pipe connecting Mihulka's house to the main sewer was plugged, and four sewer-and-drain companies had come out over several days, each cockier than the last, only to be defeated by the pipe. They left behind plenty of advice—a couple of them said only an expensive, high-pressure jet truck could clear the clog, one told Mihulka the pipe was broken and had to be dug up and replaced—and they left behind their bills.

It was just the kind of situation Alan relishes: an exasperated customer, a devilishly difficult pipe for an opponent—a pipe that had already amassed an unbeaten 4–0 record against the professional pipe cleaners. Now it was time for Alan Wilk of Roto-Rooter to step up to the sewer trap.

Roto-Rooter keeps very careful statistics, and they reveal that Alan Wilk almost never meets a pipe problem he can't solve. His way with balky plumbing is second only to his ability to calm the people who are being victimized by their pipes and drains.

Alan showed up at the Mihulkas' in his truck and settled in. The pipe was indeed a nasty one. Working in the basement, Alan was eventually able to determine—mostly by the noises his snake made as it traveled down the pipe—that it had a deep sag in it. The ground had settled beneath the pipe, giving it a broad V shape as it carried its cargo from the house to the sewer main running beneath the street. In the bottom of the V had collected what Alan describes as "sludge—stuff the consistency of oatmeal and tar."

Alan consumed several hours and broke one snake figuring this much out. The problem was simple: the sludge was blocking the pipe, but all the multibladed head on his snake did was slice through the sludge, it didn't clear it away. The snake's tip— which looks like a combination of a hand-mixer and a food-processor blade—was designed to cut away root blockages (hence "Roto-Rooter") and solidified clogs. It was all but useless against the sludge.

Alan Wilk pondered the problem—not unlike a surgeon contemplating a badly clogged artery—and conceived a new technique. "Technique sometimes gets you more than brute strength," he says. From the ample stock of implements in his customized van, Alan picked a wire-brush disk, which he attached to the end of the snake. The spinning disk would present a nearly solid face to the sludge. With a little help from water pumped into the pipe to make things flow out in the right direction, the spinning wire brush whisked the tarry sludge right out of the pipe. Who needed a jet truck, at six hundred dollars per visit? Who needed a new pipe, at two thousand dollars a throw? All Charlie Mihulka needed was Alan Wilk.

By everyone's recollection, this pipe-clearing operation took fully a tenth as long as the Persian Gulf War: Alan Wilk was in the basement for ten hours, maybe twelve.

He charged Charlie Mihulka $140 for the cleaning of the main line, plus $65 for one hour of extra time. And Alan didn't get a tip.

But you can bet he got Charlie Mihulka's attention, and his future business.

WHAT'S THE VALUE OF A CUSTOMER?

Charlie Mihulka spent $205 with Alan Wilk in 1985, and as we'll see a little later on, that service call made a deep and valuable impression on Mihulka in terms of his repeat business.

Do you know the value of your company's customers? Their value is not just in the business they bring you on a particular visit. It's not even in the money they might spend with you over a lifetime. Their value includes all the people—friends, neighbors, coworkers—that a very satisfied customer like Charlie Mihulka refers to your business. Particularly in service-intensive businesses like plumbing, word-of-mouth advertising is better than any commercial advertising you could do.

Once you understand the value of your customers, it may change the way you think about them. It may effect what you'll pay to get new ones and what you'll do to keep your current ones happy.

PREPARING TO MEET JUST ABOUT ANYTHING

Alan Wilk is so unassuming that it's easy at first to pass off the occasional signals of idiosyncratic genius.

There are his flashlights, for instance. A Roto-Rooter man, constantly peering under sinks, into drains, and at tangles of old plumbing, needs reliable, powerful flashlights, and can spend a fair sum keeping them supplied with batteries. The flashlight problem didn't occupy Alan Wilk very long. He strapped a car headlight to a motorcycle battery, and he had a better flashlight than he could ever buy. He's wired up his van with two big truck batteries and appropriate electrical outlets—both alternate current and direct current—and he just plugs in his flashlights between calls and charges them as he drives around the city.

That's exactly the way Alan's brain works—he is constantly searching for less costly, more convenient ways to do everything. He puts enormous thought and energy into reconfiguring his world so that when an emergency is at hand, or when something comes up that he hasn't encountered before, he has exactly what he needs to do the job.

The truck is kind of an oversized Swiss Army knife on wheels. Behind the passenger seat, he has rigged up a glove dryer using an old car air-conditioning blower and some plastic pipe punched with holes. The gloves fit over the pipes, and the blower forces air through the pipes and through the gloves. Alan rarely has to endure the discomfort of pulling on a pair of cold, wet work gloves.

The two principal Roto-Rooter machines Alan uses weigh 110 and 260 pounds. The big machines—metal frames with a motor and a round cage at one end, in which the snake is loaded like a well-coiled aluminum garden hose—come with wheels. Alan has modified the wheels on both: he replaced the small ones on the junior machine with big baby-carriage wheels so it moves more easily; and he replaced the big ones on the 260-pound machine with smaller ones, and moved them inside the frame, because the original wheels made the machine too wide to get in a lot of places.

But the really interesting thing is how Alan gets the unwieldy machines in and out of his truck: he has installed a winch and a crane at both the back door and the side door. The winches, of course, run off the truck's electrical system.

Although Roto-Rooter employees are responsible for equipping their own trucks, Alan, as far as he knows, is the only one who has the simple winch and crane arrangement. Every other Roto-Rooter worker muscles his machines in and out of the truck, often several times a day. Alan has mentioned that he'd be happy to rig up winches when his curious, admiring colleagues ask about his. He's never had any takers.

Alan has been pondering the tougher question of how to get the machines easily up and down basement stairs for sixteen years. He's got a little item in development now that will actually allow the machines to crawl up and down the stairs themselves, rather than having to be heaved up one step at a time with brute back strength. Roto-Rooter didn't sneer at this somewhat fanciful project. Indeed, when Alan's boss learned of it, he told Alan that if the contraption works, the company will reimburse Alan for his development costs and provide the machine to all its workers.

Once you're alert what to look for, examples of Alan's constant improvement program are everywhere.

He's got huge street maps of New York City mounted on window shade rods over the windshield on the driver's side in his truck. At stop lights, he can pull a map down, consult it, and when the light turns green, one tug and the map disappears.

Alan works mostly at night—it's cooler then, and there's plenty of business—and to safeguard his van in New York's dark streets, he's rigged up a simple burglar alarm. He opens the microphone of a two-way radio in the truck, then takes a portable radio into the house where he's working. It's basically a powerful version of the ever-popular baby monitor. "If anyone even knocks on the truck, I can hear it," he says.

Using an old telescope, he's created a lighted periscope device so he can peer into pipes, like an orthopedic surgeon using an arthroscope on a crippled knee.

SUGGESTION BOXES SHOULD OPEN BOTH WAYS

Alan Wilk is a great source of ideas for his company, and the company is smart enough to occasionally adopt some of his innovations as policy. Roto-Rooter realizes that equipment and procedures can always be improved, and that it is the people working in the field—outside the office—who are most likely to stumble onto those innovations.

Those ideas of Alan's that are not adopted as policy are often disseminated to other drivers informally. Not all ideas have to become policy; they can become suggestions. Morale would suffer if Roto-Rooter mandated that all drivers mount maps on window rods. But Roto-Rooter is doing its drivers a disservice if it doesn't make them aware of the idea. Management should see part of its role as being a clearinghouse of ideas and successful techniques that come in from the field from someone and get disseminated back out to everyone.

All of this makes it sound as if Alan Wilk is merely an inspired tinkerer. But he is also a student of human behavior, which he has occasion to observe routinely at what is often a time of surprise, frustration, and disgust: the moments after the toilet overflows.

Alan, for instance, never goes to the bathroom in his customers' homes. He perceives something most other workers—plumbers, painters, exterminators—either ignore or overlook: customers don't want him to.

"Some people feel really funny about that," he says. "Most people, if they don't like it, they wouldn't say no. But I don't want to impose on anybody. It's not a policy of the company's, it's just sensitivity. Rather than put somebody on the spot . . ." And, in fact, most people *are* slightly put off at the prospect of strangers using their bathrooms.

It's not a problem for Alan: he's rigged up a urinal in the back corner of his truck. It's next to the hand-washing station. And the shower.

Paying Attention to More than the Drains

It's a simple thing: Alan doesn't use the bathrooms in his customers' homes—bathrooms he is often responsible for returning to good working order. It's exactly the kind of insight that demonstrates one of the five critical elements of outstanding service: empathy.

Alan knows that many customers are uncomfortable with service people using their bathrooms; he also knows that a request to use the bathroom is almost never refused. How could it be?

So Alan simply never asks.

It's a small matter, but it shows how Alan Wilk approaches his customers. He's constantly trying to see the world from their point of view, and to accommodate them, rather than forcing them to accommodate him. Such sensitivity to customers is difficult to train, but not impossible. The best way to inculcate it is to have your most thoughtful and percep-

tive employees train your new employees. Then such cus-
tomer-centered thinking begins to be part of the culture of
your company.

SING THE JINGLE FOR THE FOLKS, ALAN

Alan Wilk is, quite simply, a great guy.

He is a cheerful man by nature, and determined, and he usually figures that time is on his side. A challenging problem makes
him more determined, and frequently more cheerful. As the
hours—and the snakes—unspool without success, most people
would get progressively more pessimistic and discouraged. Alan
simply senses victory getting closer and closer.

"I come in and you're in a tizzy," he says. "I will not leave
you till everything's working properly and back in order. Relax.
It's like Allstate: you're in good hands."

Alan is short and fairly handsome. He looks like Jack Lem-
mon's slightly pudgy, happy-go-lucky brother. After a while, you
realize that much of what is appealing about his appearance is
how he carries himself—straight, proud, eager without being aggressive. He seems *ready*.

Alan doesn't hurry—unless he senses that you want him to
finish and get out. Although Alan and all his fellow Roto-Rooter
service people work strictly on commission—between 30 and 40
percent of each job—you would never guess it from his manner.

"The first thing I do in a house is smile," he says. "That's
hokey, I know. But I'm a hokey guy. And a sincere smile seems to
relax people."

He gives no sense of being antsy to get one job over with so
he can race to the next one—although theoretically, the faster he
works, the more jobs he does, the more money he makes. Alan
often takes the time to do a little more than he's actually asked,
and he always cleans up after himself—trying to make no mess
at all, and often leaving the basement or bathroom where he's
working far less wet and smelly than he finds it.

What is truly amazing, given his unhurried approach, is that
most years, Alan Wilk is one of the most productive, and there-

fore one of the highest paid, Roto-Rooter men in New York City. Many years he earns seventy thousand dollars or more, and says of his customers: "I enjoy seeing the look on people's face when they realize they're not being taken advantage of."

His customers are equally pleased: in 1989, 1990, 1991, and 1992, his customer satisfaction rate was a flat 100 percent—something Roto-Rooter knows because it calls all its customers to see if they are satisfied after the service person reports in by radio that a job is complete.

There are several reasons why Alan is so productive—one being that customers are so happy with him that they routinely call and ask for Alan by name. Roto-Rooter dispatches calls just like a taxi company: the next call goes to the next available service person. In slow times, when there are few calls and plenty of service people, the Roto-Rooter men cruise around in their trucks, waiting their turns. But if a customer calls and asks for a particular service person, he gets to jump out of line and go on the call. In slow times, Alan Wilk still does plenty of business.

FASTER ISN'T ALWAYS BETTER

Much of management's focus in the nineties has been on speed. How can we make things happen faster? How can we react to market changes faster? How can we build it faster or fix it faster? Much of this emphasis on speed has made companies more competitive and more sensitive to the customers' needs.

But not all customers want speed—and it's important to recognize that speed is not always the answer. Anyone analyzing the commission structure of Roto-Rooter could quickly conclude that the person who handles the most calls will make the most money. Wrong! Alan Wilk makes sure that his customers realize that he has been thorough. He also goes about his work in a way that lets the customer feel that he doesn't have anything better to do than stay with their problem until it's completely fixed. You can be sure that they don't hear comments about how many more calls he has to make before he goes home. They feel like they're the only call he's going to have. That's how Alan builds repeat business—for himself and Roto-Rooter.

Before making speed a priority, make sure that speed is really the way to maximize productivity. It isn't always.

Another major reason for Alan's success is that he is as patient with the pipes as he is with the customers, taking the time to solve problems other service people give up on, giving up on their commissions in the process. Often, he comes in and clears the clog after a less-experienced or less-able Roto-Rooter man has called it quits.

SERVICING THE SERVICE CALL

Plenty of companies would do well to take a page from Roto-Rooter's program for ensuring outstanding customer service. The company is available 24 hours a day, 365 days a year, and the charge is the same whether service is rendered on any Wednesday afternoon at 2:30 or on Christmas Day at 10:00 at night.

The customer orientation is reflected in the company's phone contact with its customers—each service call involves at least three phone contacts with a customer: the initial call from the customer; a call from the dispatching room back to the customer just before the service person arrives, to make sure the time is convenient for the customer; and a follow-up, postservice call to make sure the customer is satisfied with the service just completed.

The phone strategy does several things. A complaint consumers routinely have about service people is that they don't come when they say, and you never know when they're going to show up. Roto-Rooter's phone call just before the service person arrives is a simple, thoughtful courtesy that sets the tone for the kind of service the customer should expect.

The follow-up phone call gives customers a chance to complain immediately about poorly done work so that Roto-Rooter can correct the problems. (The original service person gets the first shot at correcting inadequate work.) It also allows the company to set standards and maintain them, giving the company a chance to monitor the performance and attitude of its workers with the people who really count: the customers.

At fifty years old, Alan Wilk has in fact achieved a complete state of grace as a Roto-Rooter man. He loves the work, he loves the people, and he still marvels at his luck in stumbling into exactly the right job.

"I've been doing this sixteen years, it fits me to a tee," he says. "I see a problem, I diagnose the problem, I solve the problem. People are happy to see you."

Fridays make him glum, because it means the weekend's coming. "When I have to go off, I get depressed," he says. "I look forward to Mondays—then I can go back to work."

Alan knows that his family—wife Patricia and daughter Karen—have made sacrifices because of his job, despite the swimming pool, the vacations, the theater tickets his income helps the family afford.

"It can be a curse, finding a job you like," Alan says. "It has more of a cost on my family than it does on me. My wife is accommodating—she sees how much I like it."

Patricia's accommodation does know some limits. One of the tools Alan almost never leaves home without is his vise grip. "My wife says to me, 'We're just going out to dinner. You don't need the vise grip.'"

Alan has a gentle, appealing sense of humor and is not the least bit self-conscious. He mentions in passing the well-known Roto-Rooter jingle. How's that go again? He bursts into song: "Call Roto-Rooter, that's the name, and away goes trouble, down the drain!"

In a different universe, Alan might have had the opportunity to go to college and become a scientist or an engineer or a surgeon. But he has no regrets.

"If I'd gone to college," he says, "I might not have found this."

INTO THE SEWERS OF NEW YORK CITY, PART I

Alan Wilk jumps out of his truck, opens up the back door, and winches out his junior Roto-Rooter machine, the one on baby-carriage wheels. It is just after four in the afternoon—his regular shift is four to midnight—and he is double-parked in front of the house of Nellie Dwiczkowski, who has a preventive-maintenance contract with Roto-Rooter. She has her sewer connection scrubbed out twice a year by Alan Wilk, who proposed the contract after she had a problem a couple of years back.

Nellie has a little white house, and she turns out to be a little white-haired lady, eighty-three years old and delighted to see Alan, whom she trails into the basement.

The whole process takes less than ten minutes.

When Alan's done, Nellie says, "The faucet on this utility sink drips." It's the cold water faucet. Alan is a soft touch. He pulls a folding screwdriver from his utility belt and sets about dismantling the cold water faucet. "Maybe it's just a washer," he says. The washer he pulls from the faucet is tattered. "Do you have any washers around the house?" he asks Nellie. Alan doesn't carry plumbing supplies—he considers plumbing a completely different line of work.

From upstairs Nellie fetches a mason jar filled with years of cast-off screws, nails, bolts, and washers. Alan spills the contents out on the dryer, picks a likely replacement, and reassembles the faucet. He turns the water on, then off. No dripping. "It works!" he cries. Nellie beams.

Alan begins to clean up, then looks at the screws and washers spread across the dryer. "You know what we didn't do, Nellie?" he says. "We didn't put a piece of newspaper down so we could fold it up and slide all that stuff back in the jar, like a funnel, like my father taught me." Alan shakes his head, then uses his workman's hands to sweep the stuff back into the jar.

For Nellie with the twice-a-year service contract that takes ten minutes to fulfill, replacing a washer seems a minor courtesy. As he heads out to the truck, she tucks a tip in his hand.

He's tickled by her generosity, but he says, "I lost money doing that. I probably lost my place in line. But anything I do that

I don't have to do makes me feel good and makes them feel good."

Alan has no trouble identifying the sources of his work ethic and his life philosophy.

Alan's father was a real estate manager. From the time Alan was little, he says, he remembers his dad telling him to always give more than expected. "He would say, 'If you're sweeping a floor, sweep it better than anyone else ever swept it. If you can do it a little better than the last guy, do so.'"

Alan's dad did all the repairs and maintenance on the buildings he managed. "He was very handy, very inventive," Alan says. "I never knew him to call anybody to do anything. He told me, 'Never be afraid to take anything apart.' That's how I learned how to replace the rear brakes on my car—I took one side apart, and kept moving back and forth between the two sides to see what I was doing."

Alan's parents could quickly see their lessons taken to heart. When he was a boy, Alan says, "I would be lying in bed, it would get hot, and I would hate to get out of bed to open the door. So I rigged up a pulley—pull one rope, the door opened, pull another to close."

INNOVATION AND NONCOMPLIANCE OFTEN GO HAND IN HAND

People who innovate often do so because they feel that they've got a way that works better for them. Alan isn't happy with anything as it comes—a piece of equipment or a procedure. He's always trying to make his life easier, simpler, better. One of his large Roto-Rooter machines, for instance, has an old car tire around the spinning cage where the snake is stored. The tire—which took hours to get into place—prevents the spinning snake from spraying dirty water all over a customer's house as it rewinds back into the cage. Roto-Rooter provides a cover, but it is made of metal, and if you have to roll the heavy cage across a tile floor, it leaves scratches and marks.

This desire to improve upon everything carries over to the

company rules. Alan doesn't seem particularly bound to them—he puts more stock in providing maximum customer service than in following all the rules. So, for instance, he does a little extra work for Nellie Dwiczkowski that he doesn't charge for, because it costs him almost nothing and makes her happy. He carries extra equipment that helps him quickly and efficiently serve customers but that isn't strictly Roto-Rooter issue.

The company is smart enough to overlook such minor rule infractions. Roto-Rooter understands that when you get an Alan Wilk, you get *all* of Alan Wilk.

INTO THE SEWERS OF NEW YORK CITY, PART II

Back in the truck after taking care of Nellie, Alan sets off in no particular direction as he radios in what he's done for her.

As Alan roams the streets and highways of Long Island, the truck sways and rattles as if it were a huge wagon belonging to an old-fashioned tinker. When he goes over a bump, there is a tremendous cacophony. "That sometimes rearranges the furniture back there," he says.

As it happens, Alan hasn't lost his place in line. "We have a request for you in Glendale," the dispatcher tells him. It is none other than Charlie Mihulka, who meets Alan on the street. "We just bought a house on Eighty-sixth Street," he says. "We'd like you to take a look and clean out the drains and the main sewer."

The new house is a mess. The basement is filled with junk, so much so that Alan can't find the sewer trap. There is an ancient porcelain utility sink in the basement, filled to the edge with filthy water. It is this that makes Mihulka suspect the main sewer connection is clogged—a sink so close to the connection would surely drain unless the sewer itself were stopped.

Upstairs, Alan does a quick survey of sinks, turning on faucets, watching them drain. Of the downstairs bathroom and the main kitchen sink, he tells Mihulka, "I can't improve on that. They don't warrant spending money on."

He snakes out two upstairs bathroom sinks, bringing along

an old rubber shower mat to drape on the sink edge so he doesn't scratch anything with his equipment.

Next up is an island sink in the kitchen, which, like the basement sink, is filled to the brim. Alan looks beneath it. "This all has to be replaced," he says, pointing at the piping. "It's rotted out." He gives a couple of modest tugs and the pipes pull away in his hands.

The basement sink looks to be the real challenge. "This here I don't like," he says quietly. He doesn't mean the sink. He's been with Mihulka almost an hour. "All these sinks in one house. Others may need me. I'd rather do a lot of little jobs, help a lot of people rather than just one."

But he betrays no impatience back in the basement. It takes him another fifteen or twenty minutes to clear the basement sink of a rust clog that has built up over years in the sink's iron piping. When he's done, the water burbles cheerfully down the drain of a sink that probably hasn't flowed cleanly in decades—and Alan hasn't had to snake out the main sewer.

"Now I feel good," says Mihulka, as Alan stows his gear and washes his hands at his hand-washing setup on the back door of the truck. "I've learned more about the plumbing in this house in the last hour than I ever would have on my own."

THE VIRTUE OF THE HOLISTIC ROTO-ROOTER MAN

In general, the only people who do a good job with the intangibles—with empathy and assurance—are those who have the tangibles down pat. What makes Alan Wilk so effective is not just his competence, but his friendliness, his holistic approach.

On balance, Charlie Mihulka would rather have his drains cleared out. But listen closely to what he says about Alan. Having Alan hasn't just solved the problem, it's taught him about his plumbing and his house. He is left with several of the mysteries of his new home solved. He feels better about his purchase.

And that is precisely the multiplier effect that comes from

adding the intangibles to the tangibles. It's clear why Charlie Mihulka wants Alan Wilk to service his plumbing: Alan also services Mihulka's psyche, his self-esteem, his sense of himself.

It's chilly out, and Mihulka joins Alan in the truck for the writing of the bill. Customers are required to pay the service person. "Cash? Check? Raisinets?" Alan asks. The bill is $266.37 for two and a half hours of work—Alan has charged full price for the first sink and half-price for the other three. "I'm not required to discount like that," he says, "but I was doing multiples, and he asked for me. That's a nice compliment."

Mihulka couldn't be happier. "I've dealt with a lot of people," he says. "He's the best. He was the only one who could unclog my old house. I have to sell that house before he retires."

"Well . . ." says Alan, eyes twinkling, "if you sell it, you could just mention my name . . ."

ALL SALES JOBS AREN'T THE SAME

Alan Wilk didn't become a Roto-Rooter man until he was thirty-four years old. Before that he was in the Army, worked for a ship's chandler, and was a manufacturer's representative for a line of women's clothes—a salesman. He was responsible for four states, was never home, and didn't like the work at all.

"It didn't have any redeeming value. It was just selling a line of clothing," he says. "It didn't have any satisfaction for me. If there was something I didn't think was a great item, I didn't push it. My conscience didn't let me, and the manufacturer didn't like that."

With Roto-Rooter, though, Alan is a great salesman: he routinely wins sales-promotion contests for selling service contracts and drain-cleaning products. The difference is that today Alan Wilk is selling himself, a product he can have absolute faith in. It's important to keep in mind that selling a service is very different from selling a product, and selling an intangible is different from selling a tangible. Don't auto-matically assume that success with one *type* of selling trans-lates to another—and don't assume that failure at one trans-lates into failure at another.

WILK'S HANDBOOK FOR LIFE: THE 1911 ARMY OFFICER'S MANUAL

Sometimes Alan Wilk seems to be simply a one-man rescue squad. In his personnel file at Roto-Rooter, for instance, is an August 1985 letter from a Long Island man who broke down with his wife on the Van Wyck Expressway, bound for Kennedy Airport.

Appeals to the police were fruitless—indeed, three police cars drove right past the couple, ignoring them. Six hours passed. The man even had to chase away what he wrote were "three hoods who were about to start stripping my car."

Who should pull up but Alan Wilk, in his Roto-Rooter truck. He tried to start the car, without luck, and then he simply took a chain from inside the truck, hooked up the couple's car, and towed them off to a service station. Alan refused any sort of money, the man wrote, "saying he was only too happy to help."

Indeed, on an information form he completed, under the cat-egory "Non-work activities you enjoy," Alan included "Highway rescue (nonmedical)."

"I'm forever stopping to help people. I don't take money," he says smiling, as if this is part of some grand joke he's concocted. "It takes the fun out of it. People expect to pay you. It feels good to say, 'No, you've had enough trouble.'"

Alan's attitude about his work is woven into his person-ality. Alan can recall the moment, some thirty years ago, when he discovered that he was not the only person to think like he does. It was 1963 and he was a twenty-one-year-old enlisted man in the Army, doing KP in the officers' mess at Fort Dix, New Jersey.

"I came across something I wasn't supposed to come across," he says. "It was an officer's manual from 1911. It said things like, 'Always do your work better than anybody else'; 'Do one

more step than everybody else'; 'Don't report to your commanding officer about every little detail—just do it.'

"I felt like I wrote it. I copied all that down by hand."

Later, Alan's wife Patricia would type it up for him on a single page: six rules from chapter 1 of the 1911 *Manual of the U.S.
Army*—"How to Succeed in the Army."

And it does sound like it was written by Alan, or someone
who had spent a month watching him work. "The one who
through zeal, energy, enthusiasm, patience and persistence
stamps everything he does with his personality, making it individual and distinct, is the one in the Army, like in every other
field of human endeavor, who will succeed," it says. And, "Do
not confine yourself to thinking, to dreaming. It is not enough to
have ideas . . . They must be put into effect."

Matthew Gullo, who is Alan's current supervisor at Roto-
Rooter, says the real secret to Alan's productivity—besides his
persistence and his willingness to work beyond his normal shift
hours—is that "because of the way Alan is, he has a lot of customers who call up and ask specifically for Alan. These customers are Alan's future."

Alan does pose some management challenges, but Gullo says
in the end they all come out to his advantage. "I call Alan a good
nudge. Alan calls, stops by, he's constantly suggesting things. If I
had fifty good nudges like him, it would make my job a lot easier."

One thing Gullo has not had any luck doing is persuading
Alan to leave the road. "I've tried to get him to come inside and
become a field supervisor. But Alan likes to be well-liked. He
does not want to be perceived as someone who hands down decisions. Managers are not always well-liked, and he doesn't want to
be a manager." Gullo also admits Alan would probably make less
money if he came off the road.

"They wanted me to go internal years ago," Wilk says. "Then
I wouldn't have the fun I have. I don't think Matthew has the fun
I have. He has to put up with sixty guys and all their nonsense.

"I'm a great volunteer, but if it becomes part of the job, I
don't like that. I need that 'thank you.' "

What Alan likes in particular about Roto-Rooter is that it allows him the best of both worlds—part independent entrepre-

neur, part employee. He works on his own, at his own pace, with his own style. But Roto-Rooter takes care of the infrastructure— the advertising, the dispatch system, the record keeping, the money.

"It's an easy company to work for. They have rules and regulations, but they're not rigid," Alan says. "They're open to suggestions, of which I've made many.

"There is no sick time, and you buy all your own equipment—but if you just say that, you're looking at the glass half-empty."

ENTREPRENEURS DON'T ALWAYS WORK FOR THEMSELVES

Alan likes the way Roto-Rooter is run for several reasons: it has rules, but realizes the value of flexibility; it gives technicians independence; the company is open to new ideas, to change, and frequently adopts changes that Alan suggests— showing that those suggestions are valued by the company.

In short, Roto-Rooter is organized to combine the best incentives from both the entrepreneurial and corporate worlds. It sets performance standards and lays the bureaucratic groundwork—the advertising, the dispatch system— then allows its technicians what is akin to a sole-proprietor role in handling individual customers.

Although the relationship between Roto-Rooter and its technicians is not a classic employee-employer one, the lesson here is still applicable in more classic business structures. Entrepreneurial environments attract people who view themselves as self-employed. And the self-employed tend to have a higher level of interest in the outcome of the business. Less structure in your business and more freedom for the people who do the frontline work will allow you to attract the kind of people who will care as much about the final results as you do.

There is one thing that makes Alan uncomfortable about his job: giving people the bill.

"People are happy about everything except the bill," he says. "This is expensive. It's $140 for standard service.

"If I won the lottery, I would keep working for a year, and at the end of the call, I'd say, 'This one's on me.' "

■

What follows is the text that Alan Wilk found so compelling, directly from the 1911 edition of the *Manual of the U.S. Army*, chapter 1: "How to Succeed in the Army."

The advice—which perfectly embodies Alan's approach to his work—is a reminder that the wisdom of the modern business gurus notwithstanding, most of their "ideas" are rediscoveries of very old ideas. Except for the outdated sexism, this advice—more than ninety years old—is as fresh as the twenty-first century, and bracingly unbureaucratic. The only thing the least bit odd about it is that it doesn't sound much like the performance one expects of the modern American Army.

1. Make yourself useful. Whatever you do, it matters not how unimportant, do thoroughly with all your might, with all your whole heart and soul, as if your very life depended on it, and then look for something else to do.

   Almost any officer can do a thing fairly well, many can do a thing very well. A few can do a thing superbly well. But the one who through zeal, energy, enthusiasm, patience and persistence stamps everything he does with his personality, making it individual and distinct, is the one in the Army, like in every other field of human endeavor, who will succeed.

   Such a man cannot help but succeed. You might as well try to stop the waters of Niagara as to stop him from succeeding.

2. Do not confine yourself to doing what you are told to do. Do more than you are told to do. There are always other things to be done. Hunt for them. You will be able to find them and do them.

3. Do not procrastinate. Whenever you have something to do, do it and do it at once. Don't put it off. Make it an invariable rule at the beginning of your career, never to put off until tomorrow what you can do to-day.

4. Always endeavor to anticipate the wishes of your supervisors, putting yourself in their place and doing what you would have your subordinates do for you.

5. When directed to do a thing, if you can't do it at first, do not then report you can't do it. Try some other way and keep on trying some other way until you have either succeeded or have exhausted every possible means you can think of.

It is really astonishing how comparatively few things in this world cannot be done if one only tries hard enough to do them. When given a task by the commanding officer or any other superior, do not pester him by continually reporting what you are doing, the difficulties that are being encountered, getting his opinion about this and that.

Remember, it is the result that your superior wants. The result that is up to you to accomplish. He doesn't want his time taken up and his patience tried in the manner stated by sharing your troubles, etc. Probably he has some of his own.

6. Do not confine yourself to thinking, to dreaming. It is not enough to have ideas. Ideas alone mean nothing. They must be put into effect. One idea that is carried out, that is given body and form, one idea that assumes definite, tangible form and bears concrete results is worth a million ideas that are born but to die.

Remember, the man who succeeds in this world is the man who attracts attention, and the man who attracts attention is the man who does things, not the man who talks about doing things.

WHAT'S ALAN WILK WORTH?

Alan Wilk provides a great example of word-of-mouth advertising. Putting aside that he has a substantially higher amount of billable time than his colleagues because he is so frequently requested by past customers, he also gets a lot of requests from people who have heard of him from friends—word-of-mouth advertising. You can bet that a lot of that word-of-mouth advertising goes not to Alan, but to Roto-Rooter generically.

What do you suppose that's worth? If Roto-Rooter receives one call every other day as a result of Alan's customers' positive referrals (this is reasonable if you consider the number of people Alan comes into contact with and individuals' propensity for making referrals on household services), and if Roto-Rooter earns 45 percent of the approximately $130 average service-call fee (which is entirely incremental revenue and goes directly to the bottom line), then over the course of a year Alan has generated:

$130 per service call

× 45 percent margin (Roto-Rooter's profit per service call)

× 365 days per year (drains have been known to clog on weekends)

× .5 (every other day)

= $23,725

Note that this $23,725 is additional profit from word-of-mouth referrals alone. It doesn't take into consideration the amount of business Wilk generates for himself and Roto-Rooter because of his performance.

HOW DO YOU FIND ALAN WILK?

1. Alan Wilk is a repair person—like Keith Spring—but Alan's line of work doesn't necessarily require prior experience (in part because Roto-Rooter has an extensive training program).

    To find Alan Wilk, you need to be alert to the signals that he is a natural problem solver. Indeed, from the way he's configured his truck and from his approach to drain cleaning, you can tell that he is an obsessive problem solver. He can't resist. That trait did not develop recently; it goes back to the boy who rigged up pulleys in his bedroom to open and close the door so he wouldn't have to get out of bed.

    When you're hiring for a job that requires persistence and problem solving, ask how the candidate approaches such problems. With Alan, the answers would be clear and persuasive, despite his lack of specific plumbing experience. He would talk about his father's mechanical skills, his father's performance standards, and how Alan himself has absorbed both into his own life—including teaching himself how to service his own cars.

    That's the kind of person you want tackling your customers' drains.

2. Alan's other skill is his personability—his thoughtfulness, his ability to connect with people, his soothing effect on them in the midst of a crisis. All you need to do to discover this trait is interview him in person.

CHAPTER 8

SERVICE

ACCOUNTABILITY

photo by Jim Spelios

DANNY WILLIAMS

WHEN ONE CAN DO THE WORK OF THREE

A colleague of ours tells an entertaining and illuminating story from his childhood. He was out picking potatoes in a neighboring farmer's field. His friend Andy came up, and the boy asked if Andy could join him in picking potatoes. The farmer agreed.

Then a third boy, Joe, came along, and the boy asked if his friend Joe could join him as well.

This time the farmer balked. "Absolutely not," he said. The boy was baffled.

"One boy picking potatoes is great," said the farmer. "Two boys picking potatoes is not quite two boys, but still okay.

"But three boys picking potatoes is less than no boys at all."

There are all kinds of benefits to team-style management, but only when it's used in the right situations. The farmer was smart enough to realize that one boy working alone picks more potatoes than three boys working together.

The farmer instinctively understood what we regard as the central principle of solo service: taking responsibility.

There are service situations—like in the potato field—where one person does more work than three. And where one person does *better* work than three.

The key is that there is only one person with responsibility for taking care of the customer—and that person is totally accountable. There is no division of responsibility.

Let's show what we mean. We have another colleague who recently moved and bought a house. He went to a national retail chain to buy a refrigerator, washer, and dryer for his new home. He picked out the refrigerator, then asked the salesperson to walk across the aisle and help him pick the washer and dryer. The salesperson couldn't cross the aisle: refrigerators only. The man had to use another salesperson for the washer and dryer. What's worse, coordinating the simultaneous delivery of all three appliances ended up being a lot more work for the customer than for anyone at the store.

There was no one who was responsible for taking care of the customer in this case. All the salespeople could do was shrug and look regretful. No one could be held accountable.

Here was a team system—of selling, in this case—that made a lot more sense for the store (and the organizational charts) than for the customers. This is a persistent problem in retail. In many stores, the salesperson who sells you the suit can't help you with the tie. But for the customer, buying the tie is an integral part of buying the suit; buying the washer is no different from buying the refrigerator.

The team or group approach to many tasks ends up being a lot less efficient and responsive than an individual approach. It's not only an absence of any sense of responsibility, the employees have no sense of ownership of the customer, no sense of proprietorship.

Many non–retail sales organizations understand this problem, which is one reason sales areas are usually divided into exclusive territories. There's no question who is responsible for calling on and servicing a particular account, there's no dodging the tough sells or hogging credit for the easy ones.

The key is to think like a customer—to watch for times when the customer is best served by one person instead of a group of people, or a series of people. When one can do the job, the multiplier effect for increasing the quality of service, and *reducing* staff, can be truly astonishing, as we discovered.

Danny Williams is a telephone service technician in South Florida for United Telephone, a local phone company that is a division of Sprint. For years, Danny serviced a Florida county along with two other technicians. No one took responsibility for making sure the terminal boxes in the area were in good order— any one of the three who did keep them neat and tidy might end up having his painstaking work undone by the other two being sloppy. No one took responsibility for doing preventive maintenance—because any advance work done might benefit not the person who was doing it, but one of the other two technicians.

In short, having three equal technicians service the same area was not producing particularly good service, for either the telephone customers or United Telephone.

Danny realized this and asked to take care of the area all by himself. And voilà! By the company's own measures of service, the quality soared. One was not only doing the work of three— one was doing better work than three. (Just like the farmer suspected would be the case in the potato field.)

Danny's success has in fact been clearly linked to his working his territory alone. It is his and his alone. As a result, he takes pride in everything in it. Because it is really too big for one person to handle in a forty-hour week, Danny earns considerable overtime, so that his total pay is in the range of seventy thousand dollars per year—as a lineman for the phone company!

And United Telephone is delighted to pay that much. First, it's much cheaper than adding a second technician (not to mention a third). Second, in part because of his pay, Danny isn't going anywhere. Where else in rural Florida can he get a frontline job with that kind of pay? He will probably be in his position for some time (perhaps with occasional added training or coaching responsibilities). This keeps him close to his customers, and encourages him to increase his already considerable local knowledge base.

The danger of this approach, of course, is that if you hire a disaster, if Danny Williams were incompetent, your service quality falls through the floor. But you can spot such disasters a lot more easily when other members of the "team" aren't covering for them, and cut your losses quickly.

And when single-member service works, as you'll see, it seems almost too good to be true: the quality is unbeatable, employee morale is high, pay is high, and costs stay low.

THE TECHNOLOGY IS DIGITAL, THE SERVICE IS HAND-CRANKED

Danny Williams has pulled his truck to the side of a narrow road, left the keys in the ignition, as is his frequent habit, and is standing alongside a pair of narrow trenches, each nine feet deep. Between the trenches stands a sixty-foot-tall power pole. It looks innocent enough.

The trenches and the firmly planted pole mark the scene of two things: tremendous carelessness, followed by twelve hours of work, which began at about five-thirty one Sunday evening and ended at about five-thirty the next morning. Around the trenches and the pole is littered evidence of the carnage that the night of work required—pieces of mangled telephone cable as thick as a man's forearm.

The carelessness was the work of a contractor who is planting power poles along the side of nine miles of State Road 78, which runs along the west shore of Lake Okeechobee, the vast, shallow inland body of water in South Florida that is the fourth largest natural lake within the nation. The contractor was doing a little work on Sunday, planting power poles, trying to keep his job on schedule. During the week, the pole-erection operation is accompanied by someone from United Telephone, a person whose sole job is to make sure that as they are pounded into the ground, the bottoms of the power poles stay clear of the buried telephone lines that link tiny Lakeport, a town at the western compass point of Lake Okeechobee, to the rest of the world.

On this Sunday, though, the contractor was working without a cable locator. And late in the afternoon, he poked a pole dead-on through a thick, black phone cable that was buried nine feet deep in a vain effort to protect it. The cable was what phone companies call two-hundred-pair cable—it contained two hundred pairs of old-fashioned copper wires, each a single phone line, for a total of 400 wires. Puncturing the cable left Lakeport without any phone service. One Lakeport man had a heart attack during the hours the phones were out.

Danny Williams and two colleagues worked all night to bring back the dial tones. Lakeport falls into the area where Williams normally works, which also happens to be the area where he grew up. The first thing he needed that Sunday afternoon was a big piece of earth-moving equipment to dig down nine feet to the cable. The quickest, most convenient place to find that piece of equipment happened to be right down the road, at the ranch of a man Danny Williams has known for many years. Williams knew the rancher had a backhoe, and at six on Sunday evening, the rancher came out and did the Williams boy a favor: he dug the two trenches Williams needed, finally snagging the severed cable and hauling it up out of the holes on either side of the pole, so the men could get to work. Just getting to the cable took until nearly nine o'clock.

TRANSFERRING EMPLOYEES IS COSTLY

Danny Williams is a local, and the benefits to United Telephone and its parent company Sprint are evident in his work every single day, in routine matters and in crises. It would have taken hours for the company to hire a backhoe and operator after the cable was cut late Sunday afternoon; Williams knew where one could be found and was able to borrow it at no cost.

Perhaps more significantly, people in the area Williams services identify him with the company. They know whom to call when they have a problem, and although they are plugged into what has become a huge conglomerate, they feel like they're being taken care of by "the phone man" they know so well. As one older woman—irritated with explanations of why deregulation made it impossible for United Telephone, her local phone company, to fix her long-distance bill—declared defiantly, "I'll just call the phone-company guy, Danny. He'll help me. I've known him since he was in diapers." Transferring Danny to another territory would certainly be disruptive to him and his family. But the price United Telephone would pay would be much greater. More companies need to think about the repercussions of transferring employees from one city to another. If they did think, they'd probably transfer people much less often.

In the dark that Sunday night, the men set to work splicing in a new piece of cable, a temporary splice, and checking and rechecking to make sure they were hooking up everything correctly.

Williams shakes his head. The bill for the repairs to the cable will go to power-pole contractor. "It wasn't worth it for him, working on Sunday," he says. Then he nods toward a point just a little farther off the road and grins. "He's just lucky he didn't cut the fiber-optic cable that runs along here."

Danny Williams tells the story in a few flat sentences. He's a fairly quiet fellow, and he doesn't have any inclination to turn up the gain on any of his stories. By the time the work was done that night—work for which Williams and his colleagues were paid overtime—Danny had just about enough time to go home, get cleaned up, catch a quick nap, and report for his regular shift at about eight-thirty in the morning.

DANNY IS THE PHONE COMPANY

As telephone service moves into twenty-first-century technology almost a decade early—offering everything from call forwarding and caller I.D. to the promise of a universe of video and computer services—Glades County, Florida, can sometimes seem as if it has barely left the nineteenth century.

This is sugar country—vast fields of sugarcane, the stalks far taller than a man, roll up to the sides of the highways and roads. The town of Clewiston is just over the border from Glades County—it is the place where United Telephone has its district office, and also the place where Danny Williams was born. Clewiston calls itself "the sweetest town in America." The area is dominated by sugar companies.

Moore Haven, about sixteen miles up the lakeshore from Clewiston, is the town where Danny Williams grew up and went to high school. Many of the county's six thousand or so permanent residents live in mobile homes, as do many of the flood of snowbirds who winter in the county.

In Moore Haven and Lakeport and all the rest of rural Glades County, Danny Williams is not only the phone man, he's the phone company. He handles everything from the major cable breaks to the routine reconnections of snowbird couples returning for their twentieth season. He understands the culture and the rhythms of the place, and he isn't particularly surprised when snakes, spiders, and ant colonies take up residence in his telephone terminal boxes.

Although Williams, who is thirty-four years old, has never left the area and has been with the phone company almost fifteen years, he only returned to Moore Haven proper to work in the middle of 1986. When Williams first took his white company-issued Ford van across the bridge over the Caloosahatchee River to Moore Haven, the area was officially the worst maintained of ninety exchanges statewide in United Telephone's Florida territory.

On the 100-point index United Telephone uses, Moore Haven rated 60.5 in 1986. For a while, Williams rotated in with two other telephone service technicians assigned to the area.

"When I took over, I had three people over there," says

Richard Holey, a forty-year phone company veteran and Williams's boss. "We had people spending their time in the coffee shops, doing a half-assed job." Ninety percent of the time Danny's calls were following up on these people having not done something right. Eventually, he said, couldn't he just have the area by himself? "I figured it couldn't be any worse."

By 1988, Williams, working alone, had raised Moore Haven's rating to 95.9—from dead last in the state to first. The index was at 99.3 in 1990, another first-place. Williams's 99.9 rating in 1991 was good for only second place—someone else scored 100.0. That was fine with Williams: through Thanksgiving of 1992, he was scoring a perfect 100.0 for the year. In 1991, Sprint, the parent company of United Telephone, chose Williams out of forty thousand employees to receive its first annual companywide employee-recognition award.

How was Williams able to do the work of three people, and do a better job alone than they had done together? "I don't know what they did," says Williams, with characteristic reserve. "They didn't do the job, that's basically it."

SEEING TROUBLE BEFORE IT COMES: THE CRYSTAL BALL METHOD OF PHONE SERVICE

Danny Williams tops a rise, following a road over one of the dikes that keeps Lake Okeechobee from flooding the surrounding farmland—and waves and nods through his front windshield at a man in an oncoming car. He waves at almost everyone. Of this particular man, he says, "That's my dad's nephew." He thinks a minute. "I guess that'd be my first cousin."

Williams has spent the morning over in Moore Haven, doing a routine hookup for a snowbird couple in a little trailer park where in some cases the modern phone equipment looks to be in better shape than the mobile homes. The installation didn't take long, at least in part because the trailer park was already ringed with a set of new desert-green terminal boxes and each lot was set up with an individual gray interface box, bringing a line to the trailer from the terminal box.

"I prewired all these lots," says Williams. "I do that when there's nothing else to do." Rather than waiting for an installation call at the park, then running a line with outdated equipment, or spending the whole day wiring the entire facility to install a single line, Williams takes an aggressive posture about caring for his territory. He uses slow times to anticipate where demand will grow—Lakeport, for instance, didn't exist when Williams was a boy—and to prepare for that growth. And he is constantly on the watch for old equipment, even old equipment that hasn't yet started to fail, that he can upgrade.

THE ADVANTAGES OF A ONE-MAN SHOW, PART I

Danny Williams knows that ultimately he's going to have to wire the trailer park, or replace the outdated equipment at a particular house. Since he knows no one else will ever do it, he does it himself during his slow times (time for which he's already being paid). If there were more than one person in the area, there might be a subtle (or not so subtle) competition to do the least amount of work possible, with each person confident that the others would pick up the slack. Why should any particular employee hustle to do extra work during the slow periods when that person might just be doing the work for some lazy colleague?

The way United Telephone has the territory set up, it is in Williams's interest to use his time as efficiently as possible—to take advantage of the slow times to do the kinds of chores that make his future work life much easier. And, when customers call for hookups, it will be possible for Williams to make those connections much more quickly than if he had to wire everything from scratch.

Rather than having several layers of people within a territory, United Telephone has figured out that it pays to give frontline employees like Danny Williams as much responsibility as they are willing to take.

Phone lines come to homes and businesses through a series of steps, stopping first at a fairly large box, called a cross box, the phone company's version of a substation, a place where large trunk lines come in and smaller bundles of lines go out. The next step down is the familiar, postlike terminal box, which takes in a group of wires for a small area from the cross box and sends the wires on to individual homes and businesses.

To be easily usable, both the cross boxes and the terminals need to be neat and well-maintained, the tapestry of colored wires inside hooked up in a precise, predetermined manner. Williams can slide the top off a well-kept terminal, or swing open the doors of a cross box, and read the wiring arrangement inside with the ease with which everyone else reads the phone book.

Williams is in and out of cross boxes and terminal boxes all day long. When he first came to the Moore Haven exchange, the cross boxes and terminals were a confusing tangle, making the phone service unreliable, and making repairs time-consuming and difficult.

Williams is neat and orderly by nature, and his terminals and cross boxes are trim and shipshape. "If I keep stuff neat, I don't have trouble," says Williams. "If you've rehabbed things, you don't have trouble." Indeed, the diagrams for wiring the boxes could hardly be more orderly than the boxes themselves.

"You take pride in what you do," Williams says. "If you don't maintain the area, it does take three people to do it. It's like defensive driving. They didn't look for potential trouble. If you take the extra step, you find it."

Holey, his supervisor, is so impressed with the advantages of the one-person, one-area method that he's thinking of expanding it to more densely populated Clewiston. "Danny's the only one going back [to that equipment]," Holey says. "He doesn't leave a mess. He knows if he doesn't do it right, he'll have to come back and do it again."

THE ADVANTAGES OF A ONE-MAN SHOW, PART II

Another advantage of single-person territories is that they force service workers to own their own territory. They have to live with all the choices they make about how they handle their duties and maintain their infrastructure. Most people will try to minimize their own work loads—and the way to do that when you are responsible for your own territory is to keep things organized and in good condition so they are easy to work with.

Ownership is a great motivator. Even a large public utility can find a way to give the feeling of ownership to its employees. The payback includes emotional and financial dividends to the employee and financial dividends to the company.

Because he is the only technician assigned to his area, Williams logs a fair amount of overtime, at least ten hours per week, sometimes more. Williams makes sixteen dollars per hour for regular work hours, twenty-four dollars per hour for overtime. But even with the overtime, Williams working alone in the area is still cheaper for United Telephone than having three people working the area. And through Thanksgiving of 1992, the company's follow-up phone surveys with customers found only one installation customer dissatisfied with Williams's service, and only one service customer dissatisfied—in eleven months of work. Williams frequently goes on fifty calls per week, two hundred calls per month. The technician in Williams's district with the next fewest complaints had five in each category.

OVERTIME CAN BE CHEAPER THAN STRAIGHT TIME

Many managers cringe at even the mention of overtime. The first thought that comes to mind is of lazy employees who couldn't get the work done during normal hours because they'd rather gouge the company by getting paid more money for doing the work after-hours. If that's the overtime scenario you face, you definitely have a problem.

But there is another overtime scenario that's a win-win for both the employee and the company. That's the Danny Williams scenario. By having a little more work than one person can do in a normal day, day in and day out, the company has opted to pay Danny overtime instead of incurring the extra cost of an additional full-time person. The company makes more money and Danny makes more money. In fact, the company has turned an average paying job into a really good paying job for Danny—and the service is better than ever.

As companies continue to look for ways to downsize and streamline, overtime becomes a much more desirable option for the future. It may not only keep your costs down, it may be the vehicle to allow you to attract more people like Danny Williams, and keep them happy.

HONING THE COMPETITIVE EDGE

As Williams wraps up a call and prepares to head back along the lake from Lakeport to Moore Haven, a Klaxon begins to sound. The noise is nearby, coming from where locks go through the dikes around the lake.

"Hear that?" Williams asks. "That's a phone ringing. I wired that up on top of the locks for the lockmaster, so he could hear his phone ringing outside."

Williams gives the people in his territory the kind of service they might expect if the phone company were a Glades County business, rather than part of Sprint, an international communications conglomerate with ten million customers.

Williams didn't figure on going to work for the phone company. He was a good high school baseball player, and there was the hint of a baseball scholarship to Western Kentucky University. But during his junior year in high school, one of the big sugar mills shut down—Williams drives by its sprawling, abandoned skeleton twice a day, going to and from Moore Haven—and Williams's father thought the sugar business looked too uncertain for his son. He also didn't think college provided a solid foundation for earning a living.

"My dad talked me into going with the phone company," he says. "After the mill closed, my dad said, 'Get in with the phone company. It's a good, five-day-a-week job.'" Williams joined up when he was eighteen years old. Now he's thinking about starting to earn a college degree a few classes at a time, so he stands a better chance of promotion into management eventually.

"It's an interesting job. What's neat about it is that it's different every day. You feel like you're doing something," he says. "But I don't want to be a lineman at fifty."

What gives him his edge, he says, his desire to keep his area's rating high, is something he learned all those years playing sports. "I've got an attitude of making things a challenge. Make it competitive," he says.

COMPETITIVENESS IS A NECESSITY FOR WINNERS

Danny views his job as competitive. Not everyone doing it would share that view, but it is what the individual service performer thinks that counts. Danny has turned his job into a game—a game he is determined to win.

Not everyone loves competition. Some children thrive in a competitive school environment while others languish. But if you're looking for someone with a competitive spirit, there are some easy indicators.

Danny Williams was active in sports as a youngster. He loved it and did well. That's a pretty good indication that Danny enjoys a competitive environment and won't easily shy away from a challenge. An involvement in sports is an obvious place to look for competitiveness, but it's certainly not the only place. Chess is very competitive; and, if you've ever seen couples yell at each other across a bridge table, you know that game is very competitive.

"THE PHONE COMPANY'S CHANGED"

Deregulation has brought competition to even the local phone business—especially to installation and service—and Williams has tried to help United Telephone adapt. "The telephone company's changed," he says. "You gotta move."

Sometimes for Williams this means not always following the rules precisely.

One afternoon he went on an installation call at a relatively new RV park, where he met up with an old man in blue coveralls named Johnson, who had a lot for his gold Plymouth Voyager and a pop-up RV. Technically, the rules of deregulation say Williams is only supposed to take the new phone line to the interface box. The rest of the job is considered internal wiring—although at an RV park, this means twenty feet of cable snaking from the phone box to the camper.

Johnson—who says his son works for the phone company in Alaska—is prepared for this with a spool of phone wire from Radio Shack.

"You want this buried?" Williams asks.

"Yes, I would," Johnson says, looking a little mournful.

"I'll tell you what," says Williams, working with his usual crispness. "I'll help you dig the trench, if you'll put the line in it and cover it over. I'm not supposed to, but . . ."

It takes the strapping Williams less than five minutes to dig a trench. Johnson lays the cable in the trench, and working from one end, starts pushing dirt in over it. Working from the other end, Williams buries ten feet of cable before Johnson can bury two. Johnson is cheerful, but doesn't seem to think Williams is doing him much of a favor.

Williams says later, "He doesn't understand the new way. If I didn't help him, he'd just say, 'He's just using that as an excuse not to dig the trench. He's lazy.' And that doesn't do anything for me or the company.

"It doesn't take much to help him a little."

WHAT'S DANNY WILLIAMS WORTH?

Danny Williams's situation is difficult to assess because he works for a monopoly. The opportunities for incremental revenue due to service are few, but they do exist, and there are savings from other sources.

Incremental revenue might result from Danny's upgrading equipment in the field, permitting more residents to use new, sophisticated telephone services at an additional charge. It might also occur due to less downtime when lines are out of service (as they were more frequently before Danny took the job). Both of these are difficult to measure.

It is not difficult to measure the cost savings associated with Danny's sole proprietorship of the district, however. Danny earns about $16 per hour, straight time, including vacation and holiday pay. We know that in the past, there were three people doing Danny's job. They were not earning any significant overtime. The bill for the three, assuming that the hourly wage rates were the same, was $99,840 (40 hours per week × 52 weeks per year × 3 men × $16.00 per hour).

Clearly, even if Danny ends up with about 15 hours of overtime per week (say, 750 hours per year), he is a bargain, saving upwards of $20,000 per year in wages alone, not to mention that United Telephone has to pay for benefits for only one technician instead of three. What's more, Danny provides dramatically improved quality and incremental revenue opportunities. It would seem that there is not necessarily a relationship between cost and quality.

HOW DO YOU FIND DANNY WILLIAMS?

Because United Telephone listened to its own employees, it discovered a service superstar right in its midst. When

Danny Williams suggested taking on sole responsibility for his area, United Telephone gave him a chance to do it. Listen to your employees, especially when they volunteer to take on more responsibility.

CHAPTER 9

BOUNDARYLESS

SERVICE

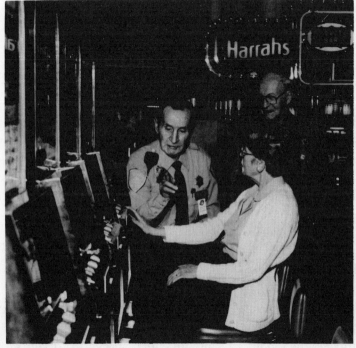

photo by John Ries

JOSEPH SABELLI

LOOKING OUT FOR THE CUSTOMER

IS HIS ONLY JOB

Already in this book we've seen modest instances of
people and organizations that are doing away with
the traditional boundaries that define—and confine—
most jobs. At Paula Doricchi's Ruby Tuesday, when a
customer's food is ready, the first available server delivers it, even if that server is not assigned to that

table. In Keith Spring's garage, all the mechanics do every job: there isn't one service bay for transmission work, another for electrical, a third for tires—and a lot of waiting as the car moves from one bay to the next.

Smart organizations have begun to see that dividing up the work too finely, and preventing employees from crossing the boundaries, often hurts the customers, reduces the quality of service, and damages the company.

There is a tremendous loss of efficiency across those boundaries when a customer has to be handed off to another service provider, or has to wait for the only person who can do the job (while the food gets cold, or the check-in time lengthens).

And, as we've already seen with Danny Williams, such division of responsibilities means that no one in particular takes responsibility for the customer, because every employee owns only a particular part of the customer's needs. When no one takes responsibility for the whole customer, it is only pure luck if the customer actually ends up satisfied (and think how many times you are multiplying the chances for service failure if the customer must speak to two or three employees to get all needs filled).

Finally, if people are only trained to do one particular job, a company's flexibility and responsiveness are dramatically reduced. Your employees can't fill in for each other—because they don't know each other's jobs.

These are the kind of situations when an employee ends up shrugging at a customer (the worst sort of customer-service signal) and saying, "Hey, it's not my job, sorry." And the kind of situations when a customer fumes.

When companies truly understand the frustration this kind of organization causes, they provide a different kind of service for their high-end customers.

Department stores have personal shopping services for the customers who spend the most money. A customer comes into a lovely reception and dressing room area, tells the personal shopper his or her needs, and waits while the shopper races from department to department, assembling the requested merchandise. For most of us, assembling the same kind of ensemble would mean doing the racing around ourselves (with multiple chances for inadequate service). Many banks provide a personal banker for their biggest depositors. No need to see the teller for a deposit, the customer-service desk for traveler's checks, the loan officer to preapply for a car loan, the assistant manager for an error on the statement. One smiling, gracious person handles it all.

We call this *boundaryless service,* and there is no question that it should be the standard—for fast-food restaurants and luxury hotels alike. Some organizations, even low-price organizations, are beginning to see the value of boundaryless service for all their customers. When was the last time you had a clerk at Home Depot tell you he or she didn't know where the picture-hanging hardware was?

In America, the epitome of the carefully divided business organization is the casino. There is perhaps no business with as many organizational boundaries, and those boundaries are important to maintaining security within a casino, for both the company and the customers. When new chips are delivered to a blackjack table, two people watch them counted at the cashier's counter, there is a receipt, and at least three people (dealer, pit boss, and the security guard who makes the delivery) verify the count as the chips are moved from carrying trays to the green-felt gaming surface.

So we were delighted to find a most striking example of a boundaryless server in a casino.

Joe Sabelli is a security guard at Harrah's casino in Reno. His formal job is to escort money and chips as they move around the casino, among the tables, the cashiers, and the counting rooms; to keep track of customers on the gaming floor; and to handle patrons who are intoxicated or otherwise behaving inappropriately.

But Joe has taken on a whole set of responsibilities that go well beyond his job—that in fact overlap the jobs of others in the casino. Joe spends much of his time making change for customers—taking their twenty-dollar bills and turning them into rolls of quarters or dollars. He does this even though there is a whole staff at the casino devoted to nothing but making change, including a set of roaming change makers who are frequently not as quick on the draw as Joe.

Joe also fixes jammed slot machines—although, again, there is a whole technical staff set up to service the machines. The repair technicians are often backed up, and Joe doesn't see any reason why the customers should have to wait for some mysterious technician to arrive to fix their machines if Joe can unjam them. (What's more, why should the casino have to wait for a particular staff person to appear in order for the collection of coins to continue when there is an able member of the staff standing right there?) For the time being, in fact, Joe is the only security guard trusted with keys to the slot machines—a remnant of the careful division of security and access in casinos.

Sabelli is in many ways a combination of host and concierge. He gives advice, directions, encouragement—he'll even fetch drinks. He is the only security guard at Harrah's to behave in such a fashion.

Joe Sabelli understands the need for the casino to have boundaries and areas of responsibility for security reasons. And he honors those boundaries—except when it comes to taking care of the customers. He views the customers as his responsibility, and he never says, "That's not my job."

The kind of service Joe delivers, if it were to be put in place across the casino, would require a different mind-set on the part of managers. It would mean training new employees completely differently—just as in the case of a car mechanic who can do any repair job, it would mean training security guards and waitresses and change makers in all aspects of the casino's operation. It would require giving new employees not just a brief tour of the whole facility during orientation, but actually giving everyone enough knowledge of the whole business so they could do anything a customer might need done.

We aren't suggesting eliminating job division entirely; there is tremendous value in specialization. But we are suggesting doing away with an attitude that assumes an employee can only take care of one part of a customer's needs. It means changing the organization and the corporate culture so that all employees understand that any customer, and any customer's needs, are that employee's responsibility. Changing that attitude will bring tremendous efficiency to the company. It will mean not wasting time and energy (and money) when a customer needs something.

Joe Sabelli is remarkable in many ways, as you are about to discover. But one of his most amazing traits is his perception that boundaryless service is the service of the next century. The American companies that grab and keep a global competitive edge will be the ones with employees like Joe Sabelli, who believe that *nothing* is more important than taking care of customers.

GENTLEMAN JOE

Joseph Sabelli works in one of the vast, gleaming, frantic palaces of pure American capitalism, Harrah's casino in Reno, Nevada— a place where the gloss is about fun and entertainment, but the glint in every eye is about greed. It is the American dream, artificially sweetened: success without toil. There is money and the sound of money everywhere in the casino, and the whispered promise that all that money—perhaps a whole lifetime's worth— is just the drop of a quarter away.

Joe Sabelli is a security guard at Harrah's, and most of his time and responsibility involves watching all that money—the large sums that belong to Harrah's. But Joe also takes personal responsibility for the smaller sums tucked away in the purses and pockets of the guests. He's done the job for nine years—he now makes seventy-one dollars per day, about nine dollars per hour, double what he got when he started—and it's fair to say that in a setting where both the casino and the customers concentrate on getting, Sabelli concentrates on giving.

There was the day, for instance, when Sabelli happened upon a slot-machine customer in an argument with a casino employee. The customer insisted she had given the man a twenty-dollar bill to change into coins. The man, whose job in the casino is to make change, claimed the customer had given him a ten-dollar bill, and a quick balancing of his money didn't show an extra ten dollars. This didn't calm the customer. Sabelli, though, brought her unhappiness to a brisk conclusion. He reached into his wallet and gave the woman ten dollars. A few minutes later she hit a fifty-dollar jackpot, tracked Sabelli down, and returned his ten dollars.

More routinely, Sabelli escorts intoxicated patrons from the casino and reaches into his own pocket to give them cab fare. It makes even Sabelli's supervisors shake their heads in wonder.

"I try to pay him back for the taxis," says Mike Hagan, director of internal security at Harrah's, "but most of the time we never even hear about it."

To Joe, it's no big deal, it's just money. "My methods are a lot different than everybody else's," Sabelli says. "You gotta give. If you don't give, you're no good. Whatever I give a person, it comes back to me."

Before he started at Harrah's, Sabelli had never been a security guard, and he doesn't see himself the way most of the security guards see themselves. In fact, he's all but turned his job inside out. He sees himself as anything but a silent, steely-eyed protector. He has left his job description far behind.

"My main function, well—no one takes the time to know people," he says. "I do that."

Job Descriptions Can Be Limiting

Joe Sabelli hasn't let the traditional definition of a security guard interfere with his own sense of what his job is really about. Joe sees security as an extension of hospitality. In his mind, the reason the hotel has given him a uniform is so guests can readily identify him.

Limited job definitions simply put restrictions on employees' ability to take a global view of their roles. Redefining a job, or better yet retitling it, can make a huge difference in the approach people take to their roles. How does a security officer view his job if his employer thinks of him as the vice president of hospitality?

Enlightened managers today want staff members to think of their job functions from a wider perspective. The best way to get them to start is to take the blinders off their job descriptions.

Joe Sabelli has turned what could be an anonymous job into a hospitality franchise. He makes change for casino customers— literally running with their bills to get the rolls of coins and running back with the coins—even though there is a whole staff in the casino that does nothing but make change. This occasionally irritates the change makers, but Sabelli is unconcerned. He sees his role as keeping the customers happy, not his colleagues. He sees his role as making it as effortless as possible for customers to spend money.

When Sabelli is checking floors in the hotel, he often sees guests who are checking out struggling with their luggage. "A lot of people can't carry their luggage, and they can't afford to tip the bellman," he says. "If I see that, I take it to the elevator for them."

Anyone who works in a casino quickly becomes a student of the superstitions of the steady players. Many customers like to play one machine continuously, rather than hopping from slot to slot. No one wants to leave a machine, only to turn around five minutes later and see someone else drop in the dollar that brings a jackpot.

"A lot of people don't like to leave the machines. If someone is handicapped, or whatever, and they want a hamburger, I'll go down and get it," says Sabelli. "If a lady wants to leave to go to the powder room, I will stay right by the machine for her"—preventing anyone else from playing it until she can return. "These are the little things you do to make them happy."

FOLLOW THE ROUTINES OF YOUR CUSTOMERS

Joe Sabelli has paid enough attention to the casino's customers that he knows what they like, and he makes an effort to accommodate them. No, Harrah's probably doesn't have a policy that urges security guards to "guard" a player's machine while she goes to the rest room (if anything, we suspect, there is a policy that says just the opposite: an unplayed machine is open for anyone). But Joe has adapted the casino to the quirks of its players, and in the process has made the casino a much more hospitable place.

This is a strategy anyone with customers can use. Watch their habits. Where their habits conflict with those of your business, see if you can adapt. Restaurant customers, for instance, much prefer to pay their checks at their tables rather than stand in line at the cash register themselves. Regular rental-car customers like to come from the airport gate directly to their cars, without a lot of standing in line and producing of various forms of identification. The smart rental-car companies have easily adapted to this preference, making their businesses much more efficient in the process.

Sabelli doesn't neglect his routine security-guard duties—filling orders for chips for the gaming tables, escorting shipments of money in and out of the counting rooms—but those duties consume so little of his workday that he fills the rest of it greeting and taking care of customers. While most of his blue-uniformed colleagues are standing around solemnly, Joe is racing from one end of his area to the other, doing favors for people.

Sabelli knows hundreds of regulars by name or face, and many more know him. His warmth and personality are so powerful that the part of the casino where he normally works, the Virginia Street casino, which is about one third of the hotel's gaming area, is known by staff and customers as "Little Joe's." Harrah's is well aware there are customers who will game only in Sabelli's area.

"We get a lot of security officers who are Rambo," says Mike Hagan, the security director. "They come in with the supercop mentality. That's not why we're here. We point to Joe's picture and say, 'This is what we want you to be like.' "

And they're pointing to a picture of an eighty-five-year-old man who came to America from Palermo, Sicily, seventy years ago and doesn't have a high school education.

JOE SABELLI IN ACTION

Money is more common in a casino than popcorn in a movie theater—it is everywhere, loose in the payoff trays of the slots, piled atop video poker machines, rattling in oversized plastic cups people are carrying, stored inside gray utility cabinets for the staff, collected in stacks in the form of richly colored chips on the green felt of the gaming tables. Money is so common, it is possible to lose sight of the fact that it really is money.

But the casino never loses sight of that fact. Money that is going any distance in the building is escorted, usually by more than one person. This is clearly for security reasons, but it's also often physically necessary—so much of the money is in the form of coins that moving it around in casino-sized quantities is taxing work.

It may be that all the loose money tends to make the folks who work in casinos sober, exacting, often humorless people. Even the dealers are reserved. In this setting, Joe Sabelli seems particularly impish. Sabelli is like nothing so much as a cheerful Sicilian leprechaun.

ATTITUDE IS MORE IMPORTANT THAN EXPERIENCE

Joe Sabelli had never been a security guard in his life before he applied at Harrah's. In fact, he had never had a job that was even remotely similar to a security guard. But Harrah's hired him anyway.

What Harrah's was looking for was an attitude. The company knows that the ideal security guard is someone who likes people and likes helping them, even though the typical profile that comes to mind is a hulk of a man who doesn't smile.

The next time you get ready to hire someone, don't start with the job description and a profile of ideal prior experience. Instead, focus on the kind of personality that best fits the position. Some people smile every chance they get and others can go all day and never come close. Is that an important issue in the job you're trying to fill?

Dashing along a row of slots on a bright Friday morning, Sabelli beams at an older Asian woman, points at her pile of coins, and says, "You don't have enough for a steak dinner yet! I need a steak dinner! You gotta keep pushing it!" She giggles like a schoolgirl, never pausing in the rhythm of her gambling.

Joe greets an older man, who turns from his slot machine to shake hands. "Where the hell have you been?" Joe asks the man, a local who has been ill. "No wonder I didn't get a raise. It's good to see you back."

As he scurries through the Virginia Street casino—row after row of slot machines broken up with gaming areas—Sabelli snatches up empty, peeled coin rolls from the carpeted floor and from between the slot machines. His eyes—he doesn't wear glasses—can pick them out at twenty paces. He also picks up discarded drink glasses and beer bottles—even at eleven in the morning, these are plentiful—and returns them to the bar.

It is not Sabelli's job to collect the cast-off coin rolls and the glasses, but he likes helping the housekeeping staff. "With cleanliness," he says quietly, "you always win, you can't lose"—as if repeating something he might have been told eighty years earlier.

The only challenge in watching Joe Sabelli work is in trying to keep up with him. Sabelli moves through Harrah's at an amazing pace—one literally has to run to keep up with him, and given his agility at dodging around the guests and the gaming tables, it is often simply a case of trying to keep his small, retreating form in view.

One of Sabelli's jobs is to check the guest floors he's assigned in the hotel four times per day. He can sweep through four floors—checking the service elevators, the rooms with the soda and ice machines, looking for anything out of place, or for people who don't look like they belong—in less than ten minutes, which includes time to greet each member of the housekeeping staff.

On the elevator headed back downstairs, Sabelli instantly becomes the elevator man. "What floor, Sir?" he asks a guest getting on. "The lobby?" He punches it. When Sabelli reaches the floor where he is getting off, he stays on the elevator until everyone getting on at that floor has had the chance to board, and he has punched each of their floors.

Back in the casino, a pit boss flags Joe and gives him a request slip to fill an order of chips for a blackjack dealer who is about to open her table. Sabelli races for the cashier to fill the order. He is often moving so fast that people who see him coming can't figure out which way to dodge to get out of his way, and he bumps into them gently, smiling, and slides them off to one side in a friendly way.

Sabelli's whole approach has something of the air of cheerful charity work, as if he were a candy striper in a hospital, constantly looking for minor tasks to do. That impression is only reinforced by many of his colleagues who treat him almost like a beloved grandparent rather than a security guard.

Having delivered the chips, Sabelli cycles through another pit area to make sure no one needs anything, and Sharen and Nina, two young women who are pit bosses, commence teasing him.

"Joe always says nice things about us," says Sharen.

"He's blushing," says Nina.

"We love to make Joe blush," says Sharen.

Joe is indeed blushing, furiously. "These girls make us look good," he says.

"It's your own reflection," says Sharen.

Sabelli spots an older woman at the twenty-five-cent progressive slots who has stopped playing and is rummaging in her purse. He is at her side in a flash. "Can I help you?" She produces a twenty-dollar bill.

"Twenty dollars in quarters?" Joe asks, even as he's edging off. "I always repeat the amount, to confirm the bill," he says. "And I hustle so she doesn't think I ran off with it."

There is a circulating change staff—men and women in purple and green outfits, pushing around small carts loaded with coin rolls. Sabelli often moves faster than they do, and the ability to get fresh coins to the customers as quickly as possible, so as not to slow the gambling, is a priority for both the customers and the casino. At Harrah's in Reno, the casino marketing slogan is: "Better slot service? We guarantee it!"

Sabelli takes the lady's twenty-dollar bill to one of the change people, saying with a smile, "I need some lucky silver," and returning the rolls of quarters to the woman. "You're gonna make it, believe me!" he says.

Sabelli can sometimes seem almost naively upbeat, but in fact his style is a mix of calculated teamwork and wizened independence. In general, for example, he refuses to take tips. But if he *must* take a tip to avoid offending a patron, he breaks it up into quarters and distributes it among the cocktail waitresses, coming up behind each in turn, stooping down as if finding a quarter on the floor, then tapping each woman on the shoulder and saying with a grin, "Hey, did you drop this?" and dropping the quarter on her tray.

"A little bit goes a long way," he says. "If I ever need their help, they do not refuse me, because I help them more than they help me."

He worked for more than two years to earn the right to have the key to open and service the slot machines in his area. The fact that he is the only guard with a key, and the only person outside the slot department with a key, makes him a target of resentment by both his fellow guards and the people in the slot department.

"I know they don't like it," he says, "but I couldn't care less. I'm trying to prepare them for what's coming. Eventually they're gonna have to do it. Because they're going to have less employees, everyone's going to have to do more. And the security people just walk around like a bunch of dummies." He shakes his head. It's no different than his making change while the other guards stand around. "They are lazy. I hate to say the word. My next project—I'm going to have the key [to the slots] on all floors."

REDEFINE JOBS FOR THE FUTURE

Although Joe Sabelli has only modest formal education, he certainly understands the future economic facts of life for service businesses. Manufacturers in the United States have already learned the painful consequences of not being low-cost producers. Service businesses are facing similar challenges in the area of personnel recruitment and deployment. Managers need to look for ways to flatten their organizations by challenging old divisions of responsibility that simply add layers of cost. Joe Sabelli seems to grasp this instinctively.

And while we redefine the work that people need to do, we need to look for more people who have the energy and interest to continually expand their own areas of responsibility.

As Sabelli passes a blackjack table where four guests are waiting impatiently to begin playing, he says brightly, "Everybody ready for a good day?"

Joe Sabelli, though, doesn't know how to play blackjack, or craps, or roulette, and although he knows something about the slot machines, so he can unjam them, he has never in his life put a quarter in one.

"I'm no gambler," he says, "I don't know how to play any of 'em. If you gamble, you never have nothing."

He is not speaking with malice or disrespect, just from his own experience. "Money is a funny thing. Money is god here, but to me, it's just an exchange."

The man who routinely reaches into his own pocket to give a drunk patron cab fare home points to the nearest slot machine. "That's like throwing it away."

He has no trouble cheerfully wishing the guests luck, he says, "because these people are gonna do it anyway. With them, it's a habit. When it's real busy, we have a ball here. They're losing their money, but we have a ball."

He shrugs, "In the old country, we call people like this suckers."

RATE CUSTOMERS, DON'T JUDGE THEM

In the old country they may be called suckers, but at Harrah's they're called customers. And nobody knows that better than Joe Sabelli. Casinos constantly rate customers as they play; it helps them determine how much action the customer is giving them and influences decisions on what freebies to offer the customer to induce him or her to return. They also rate customers' credit worthiness, just like every successful business does.

Evaluating customers is important. Judging them can be fatal. Customers come in all shapes, sizes, and colors. The ones with lots of money often don't look it, while the ones that look it often don't have it. Neither you nor your employees should make value judgments about customer tastes or habits. It is not important for the people who deliver the product or service to want the product or service for themselves. What is important is to recognize every customer's right to set his or her own standards, have his or her own tastes, and be content in the quality of what he or she receives.

THE CONNECTION BETWEEN CUTTING HAIR AND CASINOS

Joe Sabelli has an old, tattered picture of himself and his little brother Nick as boys, standing side-by-side, both barefoot, both wearing goatskin skirts and very somber expressions. The picture was taken at Ellis Island, after they got off the boat from Sicily. Joe was fourteen. His face brims with determination, his hands balled into fists at his sides. By the time he reached Ellis Island, his determination had already served him well.

"When I was ten years old," says Sabelli, "I was behind the plow. For corn. We had to eat. My dad came over here several years before we did. So from the time I was ten until I was fourteen, I was the dad. Taking care of the goats, milking the goats, selling the milk. We would milk right into people's cups.

"Maybe once every three or four months we would get a letter from Dad. At first, he was working in the coal mines of Pennsylvania."

When Sabelli's father had saved enough money, he sent the fare for Joe, Nick, and their mother. "We came over on a ship—third deck below the water," says Sabelli. "It was terrible—they wouldn't let us up on deck. And Mom was smaller than I was."

The family moved to Boston. "In those days, it was hard to feed a family, hard to support a family of four," he says without elaborating. His mother, he says, "was the kindest lady I ever met. She would always take the smallest portion when she would cook for us."

His father "was very strict, but fair. What did my pop used to say? 'Giuseppi—what you sow is what you're going to reap.' At that time, I didn't know what that meant."

Sabelli had gone to school in Sicily. "All I remember is Sister Bernadine," he says. "In those days, the only thing the sisters were interested in was good manners, catechism, Bible, and a little reading." He never went to high school in America.

Indeed, as soon as they could, both he and his brother joined the Navy. "We got paid seventy cents a day each. My pay went home, and we lived on Nick's."

Joe was in the Navy for twenty years, rising from seaman to chief petty officer. Nick was killed aboard the *Arizona* at Pearl Harbor.

By the time Sabelli left the service in 1946, he was already married to his wife, Rose. A Navy admiral who took a shine to Sabelli hooked him up with a job at Westinghouse in Cleveland, and he and Rose settled there.

He ended up in a department that made transformers, winding coils of wire before the transformers were assembled.

"I figured this is not good enough," says Sabelli. He expressed his desire to move up to two colleagues, engineers at the plant who had befriended him. The problem was that Sabelli not only didn't read and write English too well, he also couldn't read plans and engineering drawings.

"After work, I'd go up to the fifth floor and they would teach me to read the drawings," he says. "I didn't have much education. I got my education by watching other people. If I saw someone smarter, I learned from him. There is always someone smarter than I'll ever be."

EDUCATION SHOULDN'T BE A LITMUS TEST

We would never minimize the value of a formal education, but managers must stop viewing it as a prerequisite for outstanding performance. Although it's obvious that it doesn't take a college education to be a security guard, it should be equally obvious that it doesn't take a college degree to be a successful computer salesperson, a sales manager for a large manufacturing company, or even a CEO of a large company. A formal education is merely one criterion by which to evaluate an applicant—and as Joe's life shows, it isn't even necessarily a good measure of an applicant's desire to learn.

Sabelli's after-hours learning got him a position as a group leader in the transformer division. "It took me two years to get to group leader," Sabelli says, "and then I was twenty-eight years as a group leader."

All the years he was at Westinghouse, Sabelli worked five days per week from three-thirty in the afternoon until eleven-thirty at night.

From eight in the morning until two-thirty in the afternoon every day during those same years, and on Saturdays, Sabelli also ran a barbershop, which he opened the year he left the service. It is as a barber, Sabelli says, that he learned what he eventually brought to Harrah's: "If you don't give service, no one comes."

Sabelli's shop—Little Joe's, on Detroit Avenue, near the Cleveland lakeshore—had a front room, where the haircutting got done, and a back room where the waiting got done. In the back were two pool tables, two card tables, and a couple of bottles of liquor.

"Instead of them sitting there waiting, this would keep the guys occupied," he says. "I had a whiskey bottle back there—they were on their honor to pay. I always came out ahead. You know, they always say, if you let them pour it themselves, they pour a little less, and leave a little more."

Eventually, his business expanded to the point that he took on two other barbers. "I gave them 90 percent of what they made," he says. "That way, they won't steal from me. If I give them, say, 65 percent, how do I know they aren't cutting the hair and just putting all the money in their pockets?"

THE SCHOOL OF HARD KNOCKS OFTEN GRADUATES WINNERS

When looking over the employment history of job applicants, pay close attention to the obstacles they overcame to get where they are. Joe's entire history, not just his employment history, shows more than a thirst for knowledge and growth. There is ample evidence that Joe is a self-starter—

that he is entrepreneurial, even when he's working for a company.

Most employment applications don't include the kind of questions that would have revealed Joe's story. And most resumes you receive highlight where applicants are and where they've been. Once you know where an applicant is, it's your job—the tough part—to find out how he or she got there.

The barbering gave Rose and Joe and their two daughters a secure life. Just from cutting hair, Sabelli says, "I never made under fifteen thousand dollars a year"—at least in the later years. "It was all gravy. I turned it all into bonds. That's the way I built my nest egg."

He retired from both Westinghouse and barbering in 1974. He works now not for the money but to stay busy. He and Rose have tried retiring more formally twice—once in California before he started at Harrah's, once again briefly in Florida after he'd been at Harrah's four years. They didn't like it either time.

REHIRE THE RETIRED

Our population is aging. And our older people are in better health—both physically and mentally—than ever before. They can bring incredible experience and maturity to a variety of jobs. More important, most of them have limited career-advancement goals. They've already climbed their ladders and they're now more content than their younger colleagues to stay with the jobs they are hired to do. Age discrimination is not only against the law; it goes against smart business principles.

The Sabellis now live in Carson City, south of Reno, and their routine is unvarying, a mix of habit and regimen.

"Mom is up at four," Sabelli says. "I get up at ten to five. I take a shower." Joe still shaves every day with a straight razor—he has a different one for each day of the week. By the time he's done in the bathroom, breakfast is ready.

Breakfast for Joe Sabelli is unvarying. Each morning, Rose

makes him a bowl of oatmeal, two eggs, bacon, and home fries—
"fresh, not frozen ones," Joe says of the home fries. Sabelli tops
that off with five slices of bread, spread with jelly. Looking at
him, it's hard to imagine him consuming even half that amount
of food at one sitting. "It gives you energy," he says with a little
glint in his eye. "I have coffee with that. One cup."

WALK SOFTLY AND DON'T BOTHER WITH THE STICK

In contrast to the first instinct that having an eighty-five-year-
old as a security guard would be silly or ineffective or at best an
indulgence that only a large corporation could afford, Harrah's
and Sabelli have both discovered that his age and manner are often an asset in going about his guard duties. Harrah's routinely
makes citizen's arrests of patrons who are running scams or causing trouble, and the casino can produce as much muscle as it
needs while waiting for police.

But in the elegant, relaxed, carefree world Harrah's is trying to create, the preferred method for dealing with trouble is
as subtly as possible. Little Joe can get away with things that
even he himself wouldn't have been able to pull off forty years
ago.

The first thing he often does to get drunk or belligerent patrons to leave the casino is put an arm around them, which seems
natural coming from a guy who looks like a leprechaun, and also
has an almost instantaneously calming effect.

"I get these people to go out without any problem," he says.
"I don't have no troubles." Sabelli has never once used his hand-
cuffs. "I never *have* to use them. But if someone has to be thrown
out and these guys come"—the younger security guards—"I walk
away. Because they don't have manners. Right away, they start to
push. Because they've got a uniform and a badge."

Harrah's is occasionally reminded that its customers look at
the casino in a different, far more human way because of Sabelli.
"There was a rumor he was going to retire," says Hagan, the security director. "I don't know where it came from or how people
found out about it—it wasn't true—but we had guests calling in

who wanted to be here for the party, wanted to make reservations to make sure they get in in time."

HANDLING DIFFICULT CUSTOMERS CAN BE EASY

Like several other people featured in this book who occasionally find themselves in uncomfortable positions with customers, Joe always treats people with dignity. It is possible to deal with belligerent customers without making them more defensive and hostile. Sabelli is invariably calmer than those he is trying to eject, and he makes no effort to muscle them. In some ways, he deals with them as one does an unruly child—by getting them to realize that the time has come to calm down and take a time-out. His approach isn't always enough—but it is enough far more often than most people might realize. It takes two people to have a confrontation— and most of the time, there's no need for it.

Char Pferschg is a pit boss who started at Harrah's nineteen years ago making change, and she says that simply by watching Sabelli, "he taught me how to handle people. He has a knack— he can go to the most obnoxious person, put his arm up and around his shoulder, walk him to the door, and the guy will shake his hand on the way out. He doesn't put people on the defensive.

"The most important thing he told me was: 'I never take away someone's dignity.' "

Sabelli, says Pferschg, "taught me more than anyone else in my life.

"If he could write, he would write this book."

WHAT'S JOE SABELLI WORTH?

What is Joe Sabelli worth to the casino because he fills the time he could be standing around being bored by instead helping patrons have fun? Let's see.

The question is really, what is an incremental customer worth to a casino? The answer is, a lot. Casinos are largely fixed-cost businesses. Most of that staff and all of that space, machinery, and air-conditioning have to be there whether or not there are customers pumping quarters into slot machines. Let's guess that the average customer loses $50 per day at a casino (we'll focus on the slot machines, where Joe really does his stuff). Needless to say, a lot of the money goes to the casino. We'll say 10 percent for an incremental customer. Given that a customer can play anywhere, a friendly face like Joe's can really make a difference. Of the thousands of people who go to a casino every day, how many might be influenced to come back by an eighty-five-year-old man with an impish grin? For the sake of argument, let's say 15. So there's not much gambling involved with a guy like Joe Sabelli:

15 people per day

× $50 per person

× 10 percent (margin)

× 365 days per year

= $27,375

HOW DO YOU FIND JOE SABELLI?

1. The quick and dirty answer to how you find Joe Sabelli is, you don't. He finds you. You just have to be smart enough not to reject him out of hand when he comes along. Joe might not have fit anyone's ideal profile for this job—on paper. You would never be able to grasp Joe's personality, his charm, his energy, in any way except by meeting him in person. Then you wouldn't be able to miss it. What's more, Joe is exactly the kind of person who wouldn't do too well with a resume and a phone interview. Joe

doesn't write particularly well and he's impatient with the phone. Neither of which, as it turns out, is a particular handicap for his job.

In an interview, you need to ask the right questions. If you ask about Joe's work history, about why he was in the Navy, about his tenure at Westinghouse, about how he got promoted there, about his barbershop, you would have no doubt about his customer orientation. What's more, you'd quickly see that Joe Sabelli is not a man bound by convention. Despite his age, he thinks globally, outside the box—he's always looking for ways to make people happy. Even if you were to decide he was too frail to be a security guard (which would obviously have been a mistake), any hospitality business could easily find a niche for Joe.

2. Sabelli himself makes an important point about the value of hiring older people. Too many organizations think senior citizens are difficult employees, past their prime and prone to absenteeism or low energy levels. In fact, as Sabelli so vividly illustrates, people who are retired are much more likely to be content with jobs a little below their abilities because they have finished their careers. They have nothing in particular to prove, they are just looking for a way to feel valuable and earn a little money. Employ them, and you'll find they have wonderful attitudes, often better than your younger employees. What's more, all the studies show that senior citizens are no more likely to be absent or out ill than workers from any other age group.

CHAPTER 10

PREPARING

FOR PERFECT

SERVICE

photo by Bobbie Stone

WALLY BOJORQUEZ

CARING FOR CUSTOMERS BEFORE THEY ARRIVE

Although we have only spent a little time talking about it up to now, a good deal of customer service happens before the customer shows up. Consider:

The guy who washes the silverware and the linens

at a restaurant is as important in terms of customer service as the server and the cook.

The woman who cleans the floor of an auto-parts store each night is as important to the customer's satisfaction as the stock clerk or the person who actually helps the customer pick the right oil filter.

The guy who cleans the hotel room in preparation for the arrival of a new set of guests is as important as the bellman or the front desk clerk in terms of welcoming the customer.

If this idea—that much of customer service is in getting ready—gives you pause for even a moment, consider the consequences when this part of service fails:

What's your reaction as a customer when the silverware at your dinner table features a little baked-on fettuccine Alfredo from the previous person to use your fork?

How do you feel about the reliability of car repair advice you get at a store where the floor looks like it hasn't been swept (let alone waxed) in a week or more?

How do you feel about your hotel room when you find a little congealed toothpaste on the bathroom counter? when the shower is sprinkled with dried-on hair from the last person to use it?

Those people—the dishwasher, the janitor, the hotel housekeeper—are typically thought of as support personnel. But in fact they are as much frontline service workers as the waiter, the clerk, the bellman. They just operate a little less publicly, and they generally get a little less attention, and a lot less credit. But they are critical to making sure your business is ready to do business—that it is ready to provide the best possible customer service.

We've touched on the idea of getting ready for the customer in several previous chapters, discussing Paula Doricchi, David Greene, Rich Ciotti. We've done so largely in the context of product knowledge—that preparation is half the battle when dealing with customers, particularly in a retail setting.

In this chapter, we extend that idea to include a much broader notion of getting ready for the customer. It has to do with the whole way your business presents itself to the world. It has to do with being ready for the customers before they arrive— because there are all kinds of instances when if you're not ready, there is almost no possibility of service recovery. A clean fork, presented after discovery of the dirty one, hardly erases the unpleasant impression the dirty one has created.

Don Burr, the founder of the defunct People Express airline, used to make a similar point. We're paraphrasing him, but his idea was this: a coffee stain on the flight attendant's serving tray makes the passengers nervous about the maintenance of the plane.

What we're really talking about in part is first impressions—although at a different level than the first impression Phil Adelman is responsible for.

It is a question of merchandising.

One of the companies that brings great artistry to the idea of getting ready for the customer is the home-furnishings chain Crate & Barrel. A Crate & Barrel store doesn't simply look ready for business, it is positively seductive. The merchandise is displayed simply but dramatically, and the displays are also the stock: what you see is there to be purchased. Since many of the items sold by Crate & Barrel are impulse purchases, or gifts, such inspired display is a great merchandising tool. It is also a customer service—because the goods are presented in such a way that customers can see their aesthetic appeal, and can pick them up and test their utility.

This issue of how a company presents itself cuts across all lines of business. ServiceMaster is a nationwide company that performs janitorial services for hospitals. When ServiceMaster gets a new client, the first thing the ServiceMaster employees do is work on the lobby of the hospital, stripping and shining the floor to a mirror finish. A hospital whose lobby floor is so clean that patients can see themselves is a hospital that is not only clean, it is one with high standards across the board. That cleanliness sets a standard, and it sends a message.

Wally Bojorquez is someone who combines the merchandising skill of Crate & Barrel and the service standards of ServiceMaster. Bojorquez is the produce manager of a Vons supermarket in San Diego, and he sees his job as much more than making sure the department gets stocked.

He wants the produce to be appealing in just the way the housewares are appealing at a Crate & Barrel—displayed in such a way that they inspire the impulse purchase. And also displayed in such a way that someone who might not know how to pick a cantaloupe is encouraged to buy one. (What's more, he performs the first impression function for his store, because his is the department you enter when you walk in the door.)

Bojorquez wants the produce managed so that fresh stock is always available, and arranged so the produce moves out logically, with the slightly older merchandise selling first. Nothing should have a chance to spoil.

Although Wally Bojorquez works throughout the day while customers roam his department, most of his job is focused on getting ready for those customers: stocking, sorting, arranging, ordering. If you have any doubt that such tasks are really customer service, Wally will eliminate that doubt.

Part of Wally's appeal for us was that when we found him, he had just recently changed stores. His insight into customers is as powerful as his insight into fruits and vegetables. He knows that the produce department at his new store has to be handled differently than the one at his old store. The lettuce and the apples are the same; the customers, though, are different.

A Portrait of the Artist as a Greengrocer

They are lined up, pile after pile for twenty-five feet, perfectly stacked head-high, creating a series of flat-topped pyramids— one right next to another. The colors are fantastic—blushing orange, pistachio green, stop-sign red, fluorescent yellow—like nothing out of nature, and all the more outrageous because they *are* natural. Between the colors and the shine, the pyramids throw off a glare—as if someone had put in some serious time polishing.

If you are a little dazed when you wander into the Vons Supermarket on Midway Drive, not far from the beach in San Diego, the apple table will wake you right up. If you're fully awake, the apple table will make your mouth water, it will make you instantly hungry for the crunch and spray of a crisp, cool red Delicious. And, as Wally Bojorquez knows, not everyone will resist that impulse, which is okay with him.

"I say, go ahead and taste it. I ask them how they like it. I smile and say, 'If you try it, maybe you'll come in next time and buy a couple pounds worth.' They won't, but you joke along."

But the real reason Bojorquez doesn't mind the occasional grazing off the apple table—or the banana table or the vegetable table—is that it's a compliment to him. It means his artistry is working. Bojorquez, who manages this produce department, wants his fruits and vegetables to be irresistible—he spends eight or ten hours per day, six days per week, polishing, arranging, rotating, in a constant battle against two forces far more powerful than he is: chaos and decay.

To visit his department in Vons #53 in San Diego is to believe that Bojorquez has both his enemies in retreat. Along the right wall of the department is the wet rack—lettuce, carrots, celery, radishes, fresh herbs. The heads of long-leaf lettuces are stacked like well-cut logs on a wood pile—butt ends to the right, leaf ends to the left. The butt ends have been trimmed to leave a clean base and the ragged leaves have been stripped away leaving heads of red leaf, green leaf, and romaine that look ready for the salad bowl. The bunches of celery are cleaned, each bundled neatly with a twist tie, and they too are stacked in parade formation—butt ends to the right, tips to the left.

In midmorning, Bojorquez will sometimes stride past the wet rack, perhaps headed for the cold room for a fresh box of melons, when he'll notice that people have been buying lettuce, and the stacks have become uneven. Not disorderly, exactly—the department's very crispness inspires a certain neatness even in the customers—it's just that the left side of the romaine pile has gotten much shorter than the right side, or the red leaf has been outselling the green leaf.

In a flash he's in front of the wet rack, hands flying across the stacks of lettuce with the speed of a Las Vegas blackjack dealer, rearranging and reordering the bundles.

"You have to do it so everything is even," he says. "You don't want the roller-coaster effect. It's not pleasing to the human eye."

SHOWING YOU CARE

There are a lot of ways to deliver a quality message. Often, the way something looks says as much about quality as anything else. The way Wally stocks the produce department tells customers that someone is paying attention to the department, that the company cares, that it respects its merchandise, and its customers. Wally's produce department sends a strong message about quality.

It's also important to note that the quality message doesn't come through because of any grand show. It's the little details like the perfect stacks of apples and the celery all pointing in the same direction that makes the point. In an increasingly self-service retail economy, what you stock and how you stock it can be as important to customers as whether someone is in the department to smile at them.

Bojorquez, who is thirty-seven years old, has been thinking about produce since well before he went through puberty, and he has become an odd blend of artist and merchant, a repository of vast stores of information about fruits and vegetables, a psychologist of people and produce.

He's only been at store #53 for eight months, but he came to a department that was off track. There were problems with rotation, problems with freshness, problems with presentation.

Bojorquez, for instance, likes his mounds of whole melons—cantaloupes, honeydews, watermelons—to be sprinkled with cut melons.

"One thing they were not doing when I came—they weren't on a cut-melon program." He says this with solemnity. "That's one thing I stress. Cutting melons open brightens it up, it makes customers want to reach for it." As he talks, he is using a machete-sized stainless steel knife to slice cantaloupes in half, wrapping each half in clear wrap, placing each one carefully on the pile. The orange half melons sparkle in the pile of rough-skinned winter cantaloupes. "A lot of people don't want a whole melon," Bojorquez says, "they live alone, or they can't pick a melon.

"And it adds to the department—you see cut melons, it puts you in a good mood. It makes you proud of your grocery store.

"And it's more profit for us." Two half melons cost a dime more per pound than a single whole melon.

GOOD MERCHANDISING IS GOOD SERVICE

Wally Bojorquez makes a critical point here: good merchandising isn't merely a way of marketing your products, it can be a customer service. Sure, cutting the melons in half makes the whole display more attractive. But it also tells customers that those melons are ripe and ready to eat. For people who aren't certain how to test a melon for ripeness without cutting it open and tasting it (and we confess that includes both of us), the cut-melon program is a wonderful service.

A display can make a product less intimidating, and a display can show customers how to use the product. Take advantage of both opportunities. It's not just good for your business, it's good for your customers.

Vons #53 is the third Vons store where Bojorquez has been produce manager. His previous store is Vons #44, fifteen miles east across San Diego in El Cajon. Bojorquez opened Vons #44, and it is where he earned his reputation.

Linda Wdowiak, store manager of #44, has worked for Vons for twenty years and says Bojorquez "is the best produce manager I've worked with." The transfer from #44 to #53 was part of a routine rotation of managers that Vons does, but it also put Bojorquez in a store that does 30 percent more business than his old store. For Bojorquez, it was a promotion in terms of stature and challenge, if not in the hourly wage that, with overtime, brings him about fifty thousand dollars per year. As Bojorquez puts it, "In the grocery industry, the store where you are is how you're regarded." Tom O'Neill, store manager of #53 and Bojorquez's current boss, says with a grin that when the transfer was announced, "Linda called me up and told me she hated me. That's how I knew I was getting somebody good.

"To me," says O'Neill, "in the perishable departments, the most important thing in the world is the product. That's where the customer relations start. Wally is focused on the product. He puts quality out for people. From the business perspective, he merchandises for gross [sales]. You can display it so they buy what you want to sell."

At #53, Bojorquez sells between seventy and eighty thousand dollars worth of fruits and vegetables per week. That puts his gross sales second among Vons' sixty-odd greater San Diego stores and, O'Neill says, in the top ten among the chain's 350 stores.

During Thanksgiving 1992, Bojorquez's first holiday at #53, his department's sales were up over the previous Thanksgiving weekend, although the store's sales were down. Day to day, week to week, Bojorquez's produce department routinely grosses more than the meat department—particularly remarkable when you compare the cost of a bunch of bananas to the cost of a pound of ground beef.

"He had so much pride in his department," says Wdowiak, "you would think his was the only department that was important."

Indeed, if you dig deep with Wally Bojorquez, you eventually discover a not too subtle bias against the whole rest of the store.

"A can's a can," he says. "What can you do with a can?"

THE MAYOR OF #44, THE TECHNOCRAT OF #53

As intent as Wally Bojorquez is on his produce—its arrangement, its quality, its variety—what he was really known for at the El Cajon store was his service. Over three years, he says he had come to know four or five hundred customers by name. The last Christmas he was at #44, he gave Christmas cards to 150 of his closest customers.

"It was like a second family," he says. "I really missed that store when I left it. The hardest part of leaving was that of all those people I knew, 80 to 90 percent of them I'll just never see again."

Linda Wdowiak says Bojorquez was like the mayor of #44.

"He interacts with the customers so well," she says. "He could be working on the lettuce, he'd get a customer who said, 'I need some bell peppers.' He'd say, 'I've got a fresh box in the back,' and he'd stop what he was doing and go get it. No matter how busy he is, he always smiles, and he always helps the customer.

"Sometimes we get so tied up in the work, in getting the can on the shelf, that we forget about Mrs. Smith who has to buy it from you for you to have a job. He's so up—he showed me that it's so easy to be nice. I think I was better at customer service when he was here than I am now.

"That attitude just breeds in a store, it's very infectious. The reason I miss him so much is because of that."

Another reason Wdowiak misses him—aside from the fact that her department doesn't have what she calls "the polish" it used to—is that since Bojorquez was transferred, her produce sales are off two thousand dollars per week.

As 1992 wound to a close, Bojorquez was still settling in at #53. He says he knows only about twenty-five customers by name. Part of the reason is that #53 needed some work on the basics: getting produce displayed neatly and dramatically, getting the produce properly rotated, making sure older lettuce was out front, where it could sell before it rotted, and the fresher lettuce was in the back, since it would keep. And part of the reason Bojorquez has focused more on stocking and stacking and less on socializing is that the dynamics and the demographics of the two stores are different.

"In the El Cajon store, we had a lot of older people who came in every morning. They liked to chitchat," Bojorquez says. "I think they looked forward to that, coming in and seeing me.

"I think the customer here is not as friendly as at El Cajon. You've got a lot of young people, they're into fitness, they're in and out quick." Indeed, more than half the women customers are wearing either spandex or sweatpants and sweatshirts. In general, the customers at #53 have much more of a self-service attitude—they view the grocery store as a place to stock up, the more convenient the better. Vons #53 carries several different varieties of prewashed, precut, premixed salad greens, sealed in plastic bags and stacked right alongside the fresh stuff on the wet rack. Bojorquez says that with his time-pressed yuppie clientele, the bagged stuff flies out of the store. "The best way to service them is to keep it well-stocked—variety and freshness. They like variety here, and they like freshness.

"To me, customer contact always meant more than stock levels. But I'm just now getting to where I can start that here."

But O'Neill thinks Bojorquez's focus has been just right. "To me, the customer-relations performance out there is pretty simple. Anybody but an idiot is going to do okay with that. It's not the verbal contact so much—it's the product that's important."

DIFFERENT STROKES
FOR DIFFERENT FOLKS

The easiest mistake to make in operating a retail chain of any kind is to forget that different stores require different approaches. Bojorquez had the same job in El Cajon as he does now at Midway. But the customers are different, the problems are different, and so Bojorquez's approach has to be different.

The personality of a store has to be in accord with the personalities of the customers. Since customer demographics and psychographics vary greatly from market to market and from neighborhood to neighborhood, you can be sure that if all your outlets have the same personality, some of them are wrong.

In both the El Cajon and Midway Drive stores, customers come in through a door that routes them first into the produce department. And there is more to Wally Bojorquez's air of self-importance on behalf of his department than just proprietary pride.

"Customers pick stores by the produce departments and the meat departments," says Bojorquez, "but first and foremost it's the produce."

Wdowiak says all the studies agree. "Women look at produce departments, and that's how they pick their grocery stores," she says. "When you do a survey, the two things customers notice most are the produce and the floors. You need good-looking produce and a nice clean floor—and they think you've got a great store."

It is one of the reasons that good produce managers are so highly prized. A good produce department has the power to woo customers and instill loyalty in them—not just to a particular store, but to a whole chain. Especially as the nation becomes more health-conscious, fruits and vegetables are the stuff of longevity not only in diets but in grocery merchandising as well.

The previous produce manager at the Midway store was transferred, to Vons' store in Rancho Bernardo, which does among the highest produce volume in the chain. It was a job Vons offered Bojorquez—but the commute would have been more than forty miles in each direction, and Bojorquez declined.

Tom O'Neill, for one, was not sorry to see Bojorquez's predecessor leave. "I didn't think he was any good," O'Neill says. "He didn't rotate and cull. He always put the new stuff on top of the old. He was a dump-and-run man—he dumped the produce out and ran on to the next task. And your help works up or down to that standard."

With Bojorquez, says O'Neill, "It's cleaner, it's neater, he hand-stocks. It's gotta look like it was hand-stocked.

"And we've got better goods—when I stick my hand into the middle of the bunched goods or the lettuce, it's fresh and crisp, not slimy."

O'Neill says it's tough yet to tell what impact Bojorquez is having on sales, although he says he notices the department is "throwing a lot less produce away," which improves profitability. The public relations impact of Bojorquez's style, however, has been immediate. "We're getting much more favorable comments on our produce," says O'Neill. He knows just why Wdowiak was frustrated to see Bojorquez leave.

"He's the greatest thing since canned beer."

SOMEBODY ALWAYS LOSES AT MUSICAL CHAIRS

When Vons made the decision to move Wally, they put the sales of at least three stores at risk. As of the end of 1992, the store Wally left has already seen its produce sales drop. Sales at the store Wally moved to, though, are up. And the jury's still out on the Rancho Bernardo store, which now has the produce manager Wally's boss was only too happy to see go. And let's not forget all those customers that Wally misses and who undoubtedly miss him. That's a lot of turmoil caused by one move.

The policy of rotating people from store to store is certainly not one that's exclusive to Vons. In fact, for the past several years it has been more common than not. But changing personnel is anything but routine. People are put under a great deal of stress when they have to deal with new faces, systems, and relationships. When Vons made this series of moves, the company introduced change into Wally's life, the lives of the employees and managers of at least three stores, and the company certainly changed the buying experience of Wally's old customers. In such a scenario, it's highly unlikely there aren't some losers. As a manager, you need to make sure when you shift personnel that there are more winners than losers, that you end up with a net gain given all the turmoil reassignment involves.

There is no way to know for certain how such a set of transfers will work, but there is a way to do some simple analysis to minimize the risk. Just make a list of the likely positive and negative consequences for each of the transfers—and attach dollar values to those consequences. Sales will likely drop in Wally's old store, but they will increase in his new store. What will happen to sales at the busiest store? Add up the positives and the negatives, and if the net is not positive, re-think the transfers. Or look for ways to solve the problems without moving people around. Transfers only rarely solve fundamental problems, because people have a tendency to take their problems with them to their new positions.

JUST THREE WORDS FROM WALLY: ROTATION, ROTATION, ROTATION

It is just past seven-thirty on a fall Sunday morning (the store is open every day from six in the morning until two in the morn-

ing), traffic in Vons #53 is still light, and Wally Bojorquez is using mushrooms to illustrate the basic principles of produce.

"One of the big things," he says, "is rotation—taking off the
old and putting in the new." As he talks, he is sweeping out three
clear plastic bins of the remnants of the loose button mushrooms left over from Saturday's raiders. There are just a couple
of handfuls of small mushrooms left, and to Bojorquez's eye,
none of them pass muster: they are bruised and brown and starting to slime. He dumps them all in his trash box, on a cart at his
elbow.

The larger mushrooms are another story. What's left wouldn't
be mistaken for freshly stocked, but neither are they in particularly poor condition. Bojorquez moves all these to the bottom of
the three large-mushroom bins, culling through them briskly
with practiced hands, the occasional rejected large mushroom
landing with a soft plunk in the trash box.

Rotation is the produce department's version of stocking, and
it is how Wally Bojorquez spends most of his time. Rotation
means moving the produce that has been on display the longest
down and forward, toward the customer, into the positions where
it is most easily reached and will sell most quickly. In a well-run
grocery store, the instinct of the picky customer to reach far into
the back of a display is correct: that's where the freshest produce
should be.

"When I came here," says Bojorquez, "they had a big problem with rotation. They weren't rotating the stock, they were
leaving a lot of bad product out there. The manager showed me
some letters the customers were writing. That's what I was up
against."

Rotation is as important to the customers as it is to the stores.
A produce display that is well-rotated stays far fresher than one
where new stock is simply dumped on top of old. There is far less
waste, which keeps prices down, and in a department where the
produce is consistently rotated, it is likely that it is also carefully
culled, so fruits and vegetables that really are past their prime
are discarded.

Even Stuff that Doesn't Spoil Does Go Stale

Inventory management is a critical issue of Wally Bojorquez's work life because his inventory starts spoiling the day it is picked in the fields or orchards.

But everyone who works in retail needs to worry about whether the inventory is going stale. When that happens with produce, it's hard to miss. But it happens in all kinds of stores, just a little more subtly. Packages get dusty or faded or punctured; clothes get rumpled or dirty or overhandled.

If your inventory looks tired, it won't sell. And as a poor produce department casts suspicion on the whole of the grocery store, so stale inventory casts a cloud over the whole of any store in the customer's mind.

Bojorquez looks the part of a produce manager—he's a little taller than medium height, with close-cropped black hair, wide shoulders, robust arms, and a quick smile. He looks authoritative in his apron. He keeps his produce knife, blade down, in the apron's upper pocket, just below his chin. And Bojorquez claims to eat just about everything he sells.

Although he is the department manager—responsible for ordering the produce that is in his store, responsible for scheduling and managing a staff of four full-timers and a dozen part-timers—Bojorquez is as much a frontline worker as any of his colleagues. His "office" consists of a tall white cabinet next to a battered white chest of drawers, the top of which Bojorquez uses as a desk. In the cabinet is a miniature picture album with snapshots of some of Bojorquez's favorite displays from his El Cajon store—like the one he did for kiwifruit featuring a giant kiwifruit on a surfboard.

Everyone Belongs on the Front Lines

Wally's "office," such as it is, couldn't be closer to his customers unless it were actually out on the selling floor, adjacent to the banana table. This puts him where he needs to be—near the produce, near the customers, near the people who stock the produce.

Too often, managers end up physically isolated from the place where the work of their employees is done—and everyone misses out as a result. A plant manager might do better if his desk is in the plant. A store or department manager could see a lot more of what's going on if his office or desk is right on the floor of the store.

Don't worry about how it might look to the customers. They might just get the message that management wants to have a hands-on approach to the business.

Bojorquez is a big delegator. He likes the specialists in his department to do their own ordering. Jim, the wet-rack man, comes in every day at two in the morning, when the store is closed, to begin getting the lettuce butted, cleaned, and stacked, and he does his own ordering every day. Craig, the second man, does the scheduling.

A point of pride with Bojorquez is that his cold room is every bit as orderly as his display racks: boxes are arranged by category of produce and stacked neatly to the ceiling.

"I'm very organized," he says. "It all starts in the back room. Every box has its place here—you don't lose productivity with people looking around for boxes of things they need."

Bojorquez could rise in Vons, and the logical track would be to jump next to being an assistant store manager, and then on to having a store of his own. He shakes his head.

"I'm not interested in being a store manager," he says. "I'm a greengrocer. I want to stay in the produce field. That's what I like. That's what I know.

"I'm not interested in cans."

WHAT'S WALLY BOJORQUEZ WORTH?

For Wally Bojorquez, we won't consider the value of a shopper for a year, we'll think about the value of a shopper over his or her life as a customer, assuming that the store is able to retain the customer—and if that store has Wally, there is a high likelihood it will.

The average supermarket probably has a net margin of around 4 percent. But we want to consider the incremental customer—just one more shopper who happens to come into the market and is impressed with the service (thanks in part to Wally) and becomes a loyal shopper.

This incremental shopper is quite profitable, relatively speaking—providing perhaps a 12 percent profit margin.

So, consider that the average incremental customer might spend $100 a week on groceries. If we assume that the customer is 35 years old, and if we are conservative in our assumptions, the individual may have another 30 years of eating to do.

The equation is then:

$100 per customer per week

× 12 percent (margin)

× 52 weeks

× 30 years

= $18,720

So Wally delivers a customer who is worth almost $19,000. Pretty good. But the good news doesn't stop there. Wally doesn't just deliver one customer, he probably delivers hundreds over the years that he is at a particular store. You decide how many customers will shop at a particular market for a quality produce section (don't forget the research saying that produce and meat are the areas leading to decisions as to whether or not to use a particular market).

INCREMENTAL CUSTOMERS ATTRACTED BY WALLY	LIFETIME VALUE TO VONS
100	$1,872,000
200	$3,744,000
500	$9,360,000
1,000	$18,720,000

If all those numbers seem a long way to go to figure out Wally's value, well there is a much easier, though slightly less precise, way to figure his value. We know for a fact that since Wally Bojorquez left the El Cajon store, his former manager says produce sales are off about $2,000 a week. In that store, at least, having Wally means at least $104,000 per year in additional sales—just in produce.

That falloff in sales may represent customers who are just buying less produce, or buying their produce elsewhere. But what if it represents customers who have actually switched grocery stores—to a store with a more consistent produce section? Those customers are completely lost, and since produce is only about 6 to 8 percent of total grocery store sales, the lost produce sales could represent overall lost sales of $1.5 million per year to the store.

Suddenly, evenly stacked heads of crisp lettuce seem much more important.

HOW DO YOU FIND WALLY BOJORQUEZ?

1. Wally Bojorquez is just as happy dealing with things as he is dealing with people—he may in fact be happier with things. He sees his displays as modest works of art (he keeps pictures of his favorite efforts). He loves the process of arranging the produce, of touching it, sorting it, stacking it. Equally important, he has a talent for arranging. When he's done, he likes to be able to stand back and view his

work—it gives him great satisfaction on its own, before the customers even arrive and begin to appreciate it.

So you need someone who is self-motivated, who sets his own standards, and who is happy performing without an audience—at least without an immediate audience.

2. Wally Bojorquez is inherently concerned about neatness, he is fastidious, and if you're looking for someone to do an advance service job like this—and we include in that everyone from hotel housekeepers to window-display designers—you need someone who is neat, and who insists on neatness.

Wally could be thoroughly knowledgeable about produce—when it's ripe, how to cook it, what to order when—but if he were unconcerned with neatness, he would make a poor produce manager. His department would be a mess. The lettuce would not be neatly stacked; the mushrooms would be slippery and brown.

Where organization and careful stocking matter, you don't just need someone with an artistic touch, or someone with product knowledge, you need someone who doesn't want an apple out of place.

It is easy to get at both these traits—pleasure in dealing with things and neatness—not only with interview questions, but by taking a prospective employee out on the selling floor. (Or, in the case of a hotel housekeeper, into the hotel rooms.) Ask for a critique of the way things are done now; your candidate's standards will quickly become apparent.

CHAPTER 11

GUARANTEEING GOOD SERVICE

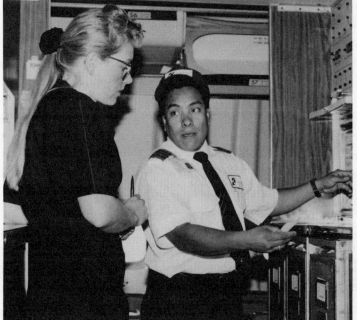

photo by Gerald Blackman

JORGE ALVAREZ

WHEN YOU ONLY GET ONE CHANCE TO DO IT RIGHT

During most service performances, there are several chances for a skilled service provider to recover from any problems the customer has midstream. Indeed, what distinguishes many of the people in this book is not simply that they know how to make things work right, but they know how to handle themselves when things go wrong.

Many companies build in opportunities to check their service as they are delivering it—a retail clerk at the cash register will ask, "Did you find everything you needed?" A restaurant manager will visit each table and ask, "How is everything tonight?"

But there is a small but crucial category of company where the service delivery is absolutely final, where there is no chance for recovery, or where recovery would be so costly as to not be economically feasible.

We call this last-chance service.

Last-chance service pops up in all kinds of places. Someone receiving a meal at a drive-through, for instance, may be four miles down the road before discovering that he was given one diet Coke and two Sprites instead of two diet Cokes and one Sprite. A minor service problem, unless you're the one stuck drinking Sprite instead of diet Coke. Most of the time, it's just not feasible to turn the car around and head back to the drive-through; the crew filling those orders needs to be particularly careful, because there is no chance to recover.

At the other end of the spectrum of significance, the mechanic who services rental cars needs to be insistent on perfection. When a component seems on the verge of wearing out, it's time to replace it. Because nothing is more aggravating than a rental car that breaks down—stranding its driver in an unfamiliar city, without the time, inclination, or resources to deal with car repairs. An emergency 800 number, even brisk delivery of a fresh car, hardly compensates for the inconvenience of a car that fails. A rental car needs to run; indeed, a broken-down rental car is far worse than none at all. At least if a company has no car, you can go to another company. (The problems of last-chance service are a major reason the rental car companies replace their cars after only a few months and a few thousand miles of use. The companies try to avoid giving the cars time to break down.)

The best place to see the idea of last-chance service is in the airline industry, because once a plane leaves the ground, there is no chance for the companies that serviced it to fix mistakes they may have made.

There is in fact a television commercial that perfectly illustrates this problem. When the pilot of the plane discovers he has taken off without Colombian coffee, he wheels the plane around and heads back to the airport. What makes the commercial funny is how divorced it is from reality.

When a plane runs out of orange juice on a breakfast flight, or runs out of pillows on a red-eye, the passengers simply go without. This makes the passengers cranky, and it also makes the flight attendants cranky.

What we discovered is that to be good at delivering last-chance service—to be effective at being the last quality-control check—a service performer needs a detective's ability to see what's not quite right, a fortune teller's ability to imagine what might happen once the customer is out of reach, and a jazz musician's cool ability to improvise.

We found all three in Jorge Alvarez, who works for Caterair, one of the world's largest catering companies. Jorge's job is to board airliners that are minutes away from take-off and make sure all the catering supplies are in order.

Most of the time, he finds something wrong—from missing special-order meals to an insufficient balance of regular and diet soda. The problems are not the kind of thing that would endanger a flight, or even seriously impair the comfort of the passengers. But they are problems that can't be solved once the door is closed, which magnifies Jorge's responsibility.

Jorge has earned a reputation among the people who rely on him—the flight attendants who fly out of Phoenix's Sky Harbor International Airport—as someone who can be relied on to absolutely guarantee that they will not be stuck six miles up without what they need. He not only prevents the flight attendants from being unhappy—which is what someone performing last-chance service should do—he often goes the extra step to do things that make them happy.

Indeed, one of the things that captured our attention about Jorge is the number of compliments he's inspired from flight attendants. His file is filled with glowing letters about his attentiveness.

The other thing that initially captured our attention was a story about how Jorge once had to cater an airliner from the bed of a pickup truck, tossing supplies up into the plane in an effort to make sure it got off on time and fully supplied.

Jorge Alvarez lives every day with the pressure of knowing

he's the last backstop for his company. The service he delivers reflects that.

Just because your business doesn't send airliners aloft hundreds of times an hour doesn't mean that the quality of the service it delivers isn't just as final.

THE MISSING POTHOLDER AND OTHER MYSTERIES OF AIRLINE CATERING

The great missing potholder mystery begins with the first flight of the day, USAir #358 from Phoenix to Philadelphia.

Jorge Alvarez is standing in the forward, first-class galley of the USAir 737, going through the flight's meals and supplies with Sherry, the flight attendant for first class.

Alvarez shows Sherry where he's put the vegetarian meal for one passenger. He opens the menus for first class and shows her that they match the food in the compartments. Alvarez shows her where various supplies are stowed: the linens, the rolls, the peanuts, the carafes for a flower on each meal tray.

This is Alvarez's job—cross-checking that the plane is properly catered and equipped, and giving flight attendants tours of their own galleys.

"In here," he says, popping open a compartment, "all the plates, the mints, the ramekins, the oven lifter . . ."

"A potholder?" Sherry asks.

"No," Alvarez admits, searching through compartments. "I think they left the old one." But the old one is nowhere to be found.

"*That* I definitely need," Sherry says in a tone the pilot might use about fuel.

"Okay, no problem," Alvarez says, "I'll get you one." He whips out his walkie-talkie, which he holds upside down, with the antenna pointed at his feet.

"This is Jorge to base. I need some potholders for USAir 358." The passengers headed for Philadelphia are already walking onto the plane. "I'll need them right away," Alvarez says into the walkie-talkie.

Jorge—his colleagues most often pronounce his name as if it

were spelled *George*—wiggles his way to the back galley of the 737 around the passengers stowing their carryons. A team of caterers is still loading supplies. Alvarez grabs a bag of used headphones and tosses them out the rear door of the plane, into the raised bed of the catering truck. He checks a few things in the rear galley, then ducks out the door into the truck and begins going through the stripped-off gear and dirty dishes from the in-bound flight, looking for a potholder. On two more USAir flights that day, he will have the same problem—no potholders in the catering setup. In those cases he will do what he does here: find one in the stripped-off equipment.

He gives it to a flight attendant in the rear galley, who is calmly applying her makeup in the galley mirror as the caterers try to load meals, trays, and drinks around her. "This is for her up front," Alvarez says. "I called for one, but I'm not sure we're going to make it."

Alvarez helps the caterers finish their work, cross-checking as he stows ice and ice cream. When the plane is loaded, Alvarez and the caterers step back into the truck and seal the plane's rear door. As soon as the truck bed is lowered, Alvarez jumps out the rear and dashes to the front of the plane and up the Jetway stairs. "I gave the potholder to the flight attendant in the back," he tells Sherry. "Anything else you might need?"

She looks up, a little surprised. "Can I let you know in-flight?" she asks.

The flight attendant is only being half-flippant. The great missing potholder mystery is the very reason Jorge Alvarez's job exists. Caterair supplies food to more airlines in more airports than any other in-flight catering company, and he has a job that some consultant looking at the organizational charts might think is a waste of time and money, an admission of management failure.

Alvarez is what Caterair calls a coordinator. He visits airplanes just as the catering is being completed, to make sure the catering is done right and is complete, and to show the flight attendants that they have everything they need—potholders, carafes, an extra six-pack of Pepsi on a flight that routinely runs out—and to show them where it has all been stowed.

Of course, if the cooks and prep people have done their jobs right, if the caterers have done their jobs right, if the flight attendants could remember from one week to the next where the orange juice gets put, Alvarez's job wouldn't be necessary.

But about forty thousand meals per week come out of the kitchen where Alvarez works, and the world of airline meals is far from flawless. Although Alvarez has nothing to do with the quality of the food that gets served, he often has plenty to do with the attitude with which it gets served. Nothing irritates flight attendants like running out of orange juice or finding themselves without a potholder.

Give the People What They Want

Alvarez thinks of the flight attendants as his customers, and no matter how upset they get—and regardless of whether their irritation is justified or not—Alvarez doesn't lose his temper. He does everything he can within reason to accommodate them—finding a potholder when there isn't one, replacing food that's not right, pointing out the special meals, even when he's got something much more urgent to do. He proves that it is possible to deal with sometimes irrational customers and yet not surrender one's humor, competence, or dignity—or lose the customers.

But he doesn't do it by himself. Alvarez gets lots of understanding and support from his supervisor. And that's the important lesson here for managers. If unpleasant customers have to be dealt with by the people that report to you, you can help the situation tremendously by letting the people who service them know that you understand what they're going through. And make sure that they know that even though some customers may not appreciate everything they do, you as a manager do.

Alvarez's job is a combination of quality control, mini-crisis management, and pure public relations. It is a role that is transparent: when Alvarez does his job right, no one knows, because everything goes as it should.

Alvarez has an uncanny talent for seeing what's missing,

what's not right—and he is incapable of overlooking it. What's more, he manages to find a way to fix what's wrong. Alvarez is a master of improvisation. He also manages to be a pillar of calm in a business that operates on constant deadlines, in the closest of quarters, with people who aren't always in the most charming moods.

Alvarez has earned something of a reputation for doing whatever it takes to make flight attendants happy—so much so that his file at Caterair is filled with letters from grateful flight attendants, most often written on the stationery of hotels where they are laying over between flights.

Most of what Alvarez does involves minutiae. It also involves soothing and coddling skittish and snappish flight attendants who convey a distinct sense that on more flights than not, they are left holding hot dishes without a potholder.

"I sympathize with them," says Leon Salzman, who runs the Caterair kitchen where Alvarez works at Phoenix's Sky Harbor International Airport, "because when a flight attendant is up at thirty-seven thousand feet, there's nothing she can do. Except curse."

SERVICE RECOVERY ISN'T
ALWAYS POSSIBLE

While it's always important to recover from a service error as quickly as possible, in some cases there is simply no chance to recover—quickly or otherwise. The whole point of Jorge's job is to make sure every airplane goes off as near to flawlessly catered as possible.

Although you may feel that quality is everyone's job, it is important to understand that sometimes you have to make it somebody's responsibility to get it absolutely right the first time.

From Kitchen to Tray-Table, from Dish Room to Airplane

Airline food is the food Americans love to hate. It's a lot like school cafeteria food for adults.

So one approaches a kitchen that produces two million airline meals per year a little gingerly. The kitchen that is Jorge Alvarez's base of operations is only four years old and sits just outside the gates of the Phoenix airport, one of two Caterair kitchens in Phoenix.

Airplane food embodies two seemingly contradictory qualities. Regardless of the menu or the airline, it all seems to have been prepared from the same cookbook. But regular fliers insist that some airline food is better than other airline food. Both things turn out to be true.

Caterair, out of this one kitchen, prepares meals for Continental, USAir, American, Northwest, and Alaska airlines. But the quality of food does vary. It is exactly as good as the airlines want it to be. Alaska Airlines, renowned for its meals, insists on fresh ingredients and fresh preparation and spends seven dollars per passenger. At the opposite end of the scale, there are airlines for which Caterair takes frozen, prepared meals—basically airline TV dinners—and simply heats them before loading them on planes.

Almost all of Jorge Alvarez's duties now are done not in the kitchen, but in the airplanes. Being a coordinator is an hourly wage job—paying just under twenty thousand dollars per year—but out at the concourses, the coordinators have responsibility for making sure planes get off on time and with everything they need. The stakes are not trivial—there is at least one other major airline-catering company competing for business at most airports, many of the airlines do at least some of their own catering, and the airlines are ever in search of a better deal. What's more, Caterair offers its customers a service guarantee: if the catering crew delays a flight's rollback from the gate for even sixty seconds, the airline pays nothing for the service on that flight.

Alvarez, who is twenty-seven years old, started in the kitchen and on the catering trucks, and his experience there is critical to being an effective coordinator—he knows how things are supposed to be, how problems happen, how to solve them.

Alvarez conveys much of the determination and ambition often associated with immigrants. His mother brought him from Guatemala when he was fourteen, along with his six brothers and sisters. His father, a construction worker, remains in Guatemala.

Alvarez graduated from high school in Mesa, just outside Phoenix, and has become an American citizen. His English is expressive if choppy.

Alvarez started at Caterair in 1986 after being laid off by Big Surf, a Phoenix water park, which closed for the winter. "A friend of mine used to work over here. He was a supervisor in the dish room. He said there's an opening here. I said, 'Of course, like a miracle, I just got laid off and you offer a job.' Not a great job, but I needed a job."

The dish room is unpleasant. "We worked with hot water, it's greasy, it's a mess," Alvarez says. He was only there a few weeks, "which was enough for me." A boss came back to talk to him. "He saw I am a good worker, he asked if I am interested in the transportation department.

"I said, sure, if it's more bucks, I'll do it."

Caterair was impressed with Alvarez's energy and performance from the start. Al Cerato, now Alvarez's direct supervisor, remembers him from his early days. "He was a go-getter, a hustler. He's always been a guy you could rely on."

Alvarez has risen quickly through the ranks at Caterair—promoted three times in his first four years, and has spent more than a third of his time as a coordinator, Caterair's highest nonmanagement job.

Alvarez was already working on the catering trucks when Leon Salzman came to Phoenix. "He was always, always moving," says Salzman, "just a whirling dervish, like the Tasmanian devil."

HIGH ENERGY CAN BE A NECESSITY

If what you're selling is speed—and that's certainly a big part of what Caterair is selling—your people better be fast.

Constant speed requires high energy. And if you're going to offer speedy service, the people who deliver that service will have to be high-energy folks.

The problem is that high energy isn't something you can teach. Some people have it and thrive on it; others don't and become anxious even thinking about it. You need to be sure that your high-energy jobs are filled with people who have it.

DENVER DOESN'T DO ROOT BEER

Aside from a red pickup truck he uses to get from the kitchen to the concourses, all Alvarez needs to do his job is a clipboard with the flight schedule, his walkie-talkie, his wits, and his patience. Alvarez, a left-hander, is short and powerfully built. Coordinators wear black pants, a white shirt with military-style shoulder boards, and a necktie. In early June, with summer just gathering force in Phoenix, the official temperature at the airport is 102 degrees. On the tarmac—amid the jet exhaust, the trucks, and the glare off the white concrete aprons—and inside the idle airplanes, it is often ten degrees warmer. But Alvarez's tie never gets loosened, and he never looks less than composed.

"I try to be very clean for the flight attendants," Alvarez says. "We are in the food business. If they look at you and you are all dirty, they are probably expecting the same service—dirty."

HOW SERVICE LOOKS CAN BE AS IMPORTANT AS HOW IT FEELS

Alvarez and his colleagues work in difficult physical conditions—in and out of airplanes, trucks, the terminal, racing around in the heat of the tarmac. But Alvarez is acutely aware that even if he does his job perfectly, he may be perceived as a slob if he looks like one. He also realizes that the food business is a delicate one—built as much on the perception of neatness as on the reality.

Even if your employees deliver outstanding customer service, it is important that they also look the part in terms of uniform and grooming. Workers who look sharp frequently work a little sharper, and good grooming has another, hidden advantage. It gives the impression of a well-run organization, so customers may forgive lapses in service that would be aggravating from a sloppy company.

Alvarez is responsible for launching nine flights per day, always the same flights, and he is so intently focused that although he knows the airline, flight number, gate, type of plane, kind of meals to be loaded, and galley setup in each case, he has never bothered to learn where the planes actually go. It has absolutely no bearing on his task.

The second flight of his day is Continental Airlines #780, a 727 to Denver, which leaves at twelve forty-five. First-class passengers get lunch, coach passengers are presumed to have eaten before boarding and get only a snack. Alvarez arrives at the plane before the catering crew does.

The galleys in this 727 are not only different from those in the 737s, they are also different from those in other 727s. The variety of equipment—even within an airline—is part of what makes catering an unforgiving business. Show up at an airplane with the wrong kind of equipment and a delay is almost guaranteed.

The caterers arrive, nestling their truck against the forward galley door, and immediately set to work. A Continental flight attendant sits in the first row of seats, eating a Pizza Hut pizza from inside the terminal. She doesn't acknowledge either Alvarez or the caterers, who have to step around her to do their work.

The caterers start to fill the trays in the galley that hold cans of soda. The preferences of passengers vary from route to route, but on individual routes they are quite predictable. This is the kind of insight Alvarez has absorbed, and he puts it to regular use. While he's never needed to know that Continental #780 goes to Denver, Alvarez knows the flight another way. He advises the caterers to stock plenty of Pepsi and diet Pepsi. "They tend to run out on this flight," he says. "But they don't use much root beer, I know that."

In six years of working around flight attendants, Alvarez has become a connoisseur of their moods and behavior. They often treat the caterers and coordinators with disdain and outright disrespect, an attitude Alvarez says springs in part from their experience with caterers elsewhere, from their own working conditions, and from simple prejudice.

"A lot of it depends on what airline they work for," Alvarez says. "All of those who work for Alaska Airlines are very friendly. Others . . . yes, some of them come with a bad attitude."

One of the most important roles Alvarez plays is as an ambassador, from his company to the flight attendants, and he seems to be constantly looking for ways to make their jobs a little easier.

He always shows flight attendants where their special passenger meals—kosher, vegetarian, low-cholesterol—have been stowed, and where the crew meals are. For a three-person cockpit crew, there are two different kinds of meals, so the pilot and the copilot eat different food. The goal is to make sure a minimum number of people are felled if there should be an outbreak of food poisoning.

Most USAir planes do not have ovens in coach class. Hot meals are boarded already heated, in insulated plastic trays. Because storage space is so limited, the stacks of hot entrées often end up stowed right next to the ice cream sandwiches. If that happens, Alvarez wraps either the meals or the ice cream in a big red USAir blanket.

Alvarez doesn't let even the smallest problem slide. In early afternoon, servicing a Northwest 727 headed to Memphis, Alvarez is checking the serving tools in the first-class galley to make sure everything is in place. He spots a serving spoon with food baked on it by the dishwasher. Although he doesn't have a replacement, he peels back the shrink-wrap and removes the spoon, so a flight attendant doesn't inadvertently use it.

SOMETIMES DETAILS ARE MORE THAN IMPORTANT

What Jorge Alvarez does is all details—it's not a question of the details being important, the details are the job, so the details have to be perfect. There is no catering truck at thirty-seven thousand feet.

Alvarez has a passion for details. He's obsessed with them. Here, as in finding people with high energy, it is certainly possible to identify those people who do well with details as opposed to those whose strengths may be in other areas. For a job that requires a detailed mind, make sure you fill it with the right type of person. One way to evaluate the extent of someone's detail-orientation is to ask a simple question during a job interview: "What did the details of your previous job consist of?"

The word *details* will not tip off those who aren't really detail oriented, and the truly detail-minded will use an invitation like that to train you for the job they've just left.

All too often people are doomed to fail right from the beginning because the job requirements aren't consistent with their strengths. Matching up strengths is a lot more important than finding people with prior experience.

Even when the pressure mounts, Alvarez is the kind of person who can improvise, and who can work fast without seeming harried or peremptory.

On this particular afternoon, Alvarez learns that a Continental flight of his, which normally arrives at 3:24 and departs again at 4:04, isn't scheduled to arrive until 4:05. So around 3:30, Alvarez heads off to service Northwest #108, an MD-80 bound for Minneapolis. As he's standing in the aft galley of the Northwest plane, watching the caterers work, he spies his Continental flight pulling up to its gate—at 3:45. The Continental flight will be racing to leave as close to its original 4:04 departure time as possible.

On the Northwest plane, Alvarez swings into action, helping the caterers so he can get to the Continental plane as soon as possible. He pulls out trays of discarded drink cans and shoves them out to the truck, loads trays of fresh soda and bags of fresh ice.

He briskly walks the coach-class flight attendant through the galley—"You're supposed to have thirty-five [regular] meals, plus seven specials. That's forty-two, plus I'm giving you all ten banks." Banks are extra meals in case there are standby passengers. Normally, Alvarez holds the bank meals in the Jetway, and finds out the final passenger count from the gate agent just before the plane leaves. If extra meals are needed, he hands them to a flight attendant just before the door is sealed. One of Alvarez's own innovations is to board all the banks when things get crazy—so neither he nor the flight attendants have to worry about whether a plane will have enough meals.

"Forty-two plus ten banks," Alvarez says, "that's fifty-two meals." He shows her where they are.

Boarding the bank meals when time gets pinched isn't standard Caterair procedure. It means, inevitably, that meals get wasted. And Alvarez doesn't charge the airlines for all the meals if he boards the banks—he goes back after things calm down and finds out how many bank meals the plane would have needed and only charges the airline for those.

"Sometimes," says Alvarez, "I break the rules. It's better to lose those meals than delay a plane. I take my own decisions over there. So far, I haven't taken any decisions I've been sorry for."

DON'T ALWAYS PLAY BY THE RULES

He who mindlessly plays by the rules often loses. And one of the risks of hiring detail-minded people is that they can sometimes confuse the details of their jobs with the whole job.

Jorge Alvarez doesn't have that problem. He sees both the trees and the forest.

Alvarez's technique of boarding the banks is a minor breach of normal company policy that enables him to meet the real goals of the company—getting the food onto the planes without delay. The sacrifice of a few meals is nothing compared to the goodwill and peace of mind Alvarez's tactic creates.

Empowerment means more than just giving people the right to make decisions. It means that they also have to have the freedom to break the rules when the rules are getting in the way of delivering on the goal. Allowing people to exercise their judgment when dealing with the rules means that most often the customer and the company will win.

THE FEW, THE PROUD, THE CATERERS

Jorge Alvarez wanted to be a Marine. When he talks about it now, even though he is only twenty-seven, he has the air of a man looking back on his childish dreams.

"They look so tough, so respectable," he says. "People get respect for them. You see the uniform, people say, 'Oh, a Marine, I don't mess around with that.' But I failed some of the tests, and I lost interest."

Jorge Alvarez probably would have made a great Marine, and Caterair as a company was sharp enough to see something the Marines ignored, to look beyond Alvarez's test scores to his energy, his sense of responsibility, his eagerness to learn.

When Alvarez was a helper on the catering trucks, servicing planes for the first time, he was teamed with an experienced driver. "He taught me a lot," says Alvarez. "I learned to assume responsibility, to do things right. I learned not the hard way, but the easy way to do it right. He always said to me, if you find a better way, do it that way."

That's why Alvarez holds his walkie-talkie upside down. He says the reception is much better with the antenna pointed at his feet.

Alvarez is under no illusions about the significance of airline catering in the cosmos—he hopes eventually to go to college and become a psychologist—but one thing he likes about Caterair is that the company appreciates and rewards his performance, and that he can always see the next level available to him in the company. Caterair allows him to imagine himself growing and gaining responsibility.

"You know you're not going to be stuck," he says. "If you're satisfied, you can be there. If you have dreams, you can move."

Everyone Can Have a Career Path

Most frontline service jobs have no opportunity for career growth. Caterair has consciously built in a career path—not only within the frontline service jobs, but also from the dish room and the kitchen to the frontline, customer-contact jobs, and even on into management.

Such career migration is vital. It provides employees with a sense that they can move up in a company. It also means that many frontline employees will have worked in the back room, as Alvarez has, and will understand how the whole company works, how problems happen and how they can be corrected. Leon Salzman, now the general manager of the kitchen where Alvarez works, started out, like Alvarez, in the dish room.

The result of Alvarez's experiences—both in coming to America and in the examples and culture he found at Caterair—is that when he heads out in his red company pickup, he feels like what happens at the airplanes is a direct reflection on his integrity.

"When I'm over there, I'm really like—how do you say?—I'm responsible. They give me these flights, and I feel like I'm in charge of them. I see things, they aren't satisfactory for me, I say, do it this way."

It is precisely that kind of independence on behalf of both customers and Caterair that Alvarez's managers appreciate.

"They have to use their own judgment," says Al Cerato, operations manager of the kitchen. "And if they make a mistake, you can't beat 'em over the head, because then they won't make decisions. They'll quit making decisions, and you lose the empowerment."

Know When to Keep Your Mouth Shut

If you give people the latitude to make decisions, you can't berate them when they make mistakes—and they will! Everyone, even a manager, makes mistakes, and when you give frontline workers the power to use their judgment, mistakes are inevitable. Plan on them and consider them part of the training process.

When mistakes are followed by harsh criticism, people will simply stop making decisions. And—as in the case of boarding the bank meals—no decision can be far worse than a mistaken one.

Many companies and organizations would have stopped promoting Alvarez quickly—perhaps even in the dish room—because of his rough English. Caterair, in contrast, quickly concluded that Alvarez had intangible skills that were more important, and that when the time came, the company could help him polish up his English.

EFFECTIVE COMMUNICATION DOESN'T REQUIRE PERFECT DICTION

We've seen that good service transcends race, sex, ethnicity, and age. Now we see that it even transcends language skills. Most companies wouldn't realize that somebody who doesn't speak perfect English has the skills to be a high-level customer-contact person whose job requires effective communication.

But it didn't take Alvarez's supervisors more than a couple of weeks to realize he was diligent, energetic, and perceptive—and he has turned out to be an enormously valuable employee.

Despite Alvarez's language difficulty, Salzman says one of the things that makes Alvarez so valuable is his ability to communicate.

"He anticipates problems," says Salzman. "Airlines are very poor about communicating to us about time changes, for instance. Alvarez does one hell of a job communicating to us from the field.

"When he sees things out of place, things that are irregular, he notices, and I wish everybody did. We give him the technical skills, but he applies those things. He's taken it one step further."

And Alvarez maintains a remarkable cheerfulness given that his principal customers—the flight attendants—are so often sour, fussy, and unappreciative. "It is very easy to become demoralized," Salzman says. But Alvarez doesn't ever let a sullen flight attendant undermine his dignity, and he knows how to use his sense of humor to keep things in perspective.

One day, Alvarez happened to have extra ice cream sandwiches in the cooler on his pickup truck, and he gave them to the flight attendant on his next flight. "I said to her, 'Here, there's some ice cream for you.' She said, 'Oh! Thank you.'

"Right the next minute, she finds something wrong, she starts throwing everything to the ground."

The flight attendant pulled the food and equipment from the galley compartments and dumped it on the floor.

"I ordered new food the way she wanted it, then it came and we put it on. I said, 'Okay, well, have a nice day.' And I grabbed the ice cream. I said, 'No ice cream for you.' And I left.

"Some people think they are better than the caterers."

WHAT'S JORGE ALVAREZ WORTH?

It is a little harder to put numbers to what Jorge Alvarez does, but let's give it a try.

Jorge's industry has a small number of large customers (and the number changes daily). American, United, Northwest, Delta, USAir, Continental, TWA—these are the big names right now. There are also a few international carriers with one-way catering requirements.

What does this size market mean in terms of *losing* a customer for Caterair? Two things. First, a big chunk of your revenue is likely to go with that customer, and second, there aren't that many other customers to get from your competition, particularly if they (and there are only two big players in the airline-catering industry) are doing well enough to capture your customers. So what is the cost of losing a customer as a result of poor service? Or what is the cost of losing a customer as a result of being underbid by a competitor and not having developed a relationship based on anything other than price?

Let's see. Seven major domestic airlines, plus some internationals—maybe ten shares, of which each of the big U.S. carriers represents (on average) one share, or 10 percent. What usually happens to a company that loses 10 percent of its business? Its profit declines by at least 10 percent (if it is a pure variable-cost business), probably by substantially more. What does that mean for Caterair? Hundreds of thousands of dollars. Not bad if you can prevent that loss by diving into the trash in search of potholders—and you can, as Jorge does.

Let's not forget the guarantee that Caterair offers its customers—if Caterair is responsible for delaying a flight, there is no charge for the catering on that flight. An employee of Jorge's skill and determination is worth even more every time he keeps Caterair from having to make good on that guarantee.

Finally, consider the value to Caterair of getting a reputation for good service—a reputation that can result in an even greater increase in profit as a result of increased incremental revenue as you acquire your competitors' customers.

HOW DO YOU FIND JORGE ALVAREZ?

1. The first thing to remember about Jorge Alvarez is that the company found him at Caterair—right in the dish room. He has been steadily promoted based on his performance.

   Caterair is organized specifically to encourage such internal promotion, a personnel strategy that seems to be less common in this era of downsizing. But it is a potent strategy. It breeds loyalty in employees, it provides an incentive for those in entry-level jobs to perform at the top of their abilities, and it creates a mid- and top-level staff that is completely familiar with how the organization gets its work done, and what its goals are. Promoting is also quicker and less expensive than conducting a search for mid- and top-level employees, and when they are put in place, there is far less of an adjustment period than if you bring in an outsider.

So the most important lesson of Jorge Alvarez's hiring is that when you're looking to fill jobs, make sure the best candidate isn't right under your nose—already working in your organization.

2. Jorge Alvarez brings a critical attitude to his post: he believes the customer is always right, even when the customer is clearly wrong. He is single-minded in his determination to do what the flight attendants want, even while realizing that what they want is occasionally irrational.

Not every service job should have someone who views customers this way, but last-chance service positions always should. These are jobs where simply arguing with a customer can screw up the service interaction beyond recovery.

3. Caterair looked carefully at Jorge Alvarez and made a vital distinction between the valuable, deep skills he possesses (empathy, ability to improvise, critical thinking, sense of responsibility) and the superficial skills he lacks (perfect command of English).

When you are thinking about *not* hiring someone, make sure the reason for not hiring them is solid. Especially in issues of cultural differences, make sure you as a manager are not magnifying some gap or handicap out of proportion to its real significance.

Jorge's language skills are more than adequate for his job; and his other skills are truly extraordinary.

CHAPTER 12

INTERNAL SERVICE

photo by Lou Chase

JACOB SMITH

WHEN COWORKERS ARE CUSTOMERS

Here is something we are absolutely sure of: it is impossible to create a service organization that takes good care of customers if the people who work in that organization can't take good care of each other.

It's an old service-business axiom, but one that wears well: if you aren't servicing the customer, you are servicing someone who is.

And it is critical to the quality of service you deliver that your employees see each other as customers, and treat each other as customers.

Internal service quality is no different from external service quality—indeed, the rules, suggestions, and insights of the previous eleven chapters all apply inside organizations as well as they do to external customers.

In internal service, something is either done well or it isn't. Value is delivered or resources are wasted. Internal customers are just as fussy as external customers, perhaps fussier. The one problem is that they tend to be quieter in most institutions for fear of retribution, which could jeopardize a promotion opportunity, or a job.

So why should you pay attention to any of this?

Because frontline service workers simply cannot do a good job for your customers unless they receive quality service from within their organization.

Think back to the beginning of the book and consider Paula, the waitress at Ruby Tuesday. She and she alone creates fantastic service for her customers—remembering their names, knowing the menu as if she did the cooking, timing the arrival of their food perfectly, doing anything to make them happy.

But if Paula didn't receive good internal service, her own skills wouldn't satisfy a single customer. If Paula didn't have a kitchen that consistently turned out good meals, she couldn't satisfy her customers. If the air-conditioning were to break in her restaurant in August, very few of her customers would wait for a table, let alone stay through coffee. Without air-conditioning even Paula's charm would be insufficient.

What about Wally Bojorquez at Vons? No amount of rotating and arranging and stacking and culling can make produce that arrives in poor condition attractive. If Vons' distribution system (or those of its suppliers, who are chosen by Vons' purchasing agents) weren't capable of delivering produce in good condition, Wally would likely either go crazy or quit.

We have found a perfectly pure example of internal service— a man who is never seen by most customers, but who not only determines their fate, but also determines the speed and satisfaction they get from their interactions with actual frontline service workers.

Jacob Smith works for the Bank of America in Los Angeles, evaluating loans, responsible for approving them or rejecting them. His customers are the loan officers in Bank of America branches scattered across California (a job Jacob himself once had). Their performance is largely dependent on his; loan customers only get approval or rejection from their loan officers when Jacob passes that decision along.

If Jacob does a lousy job evaluating a loan, turning down a credit-worthy customer, that customer receives unreliable service from the bank. If Jacob dawdles, taking a long time evaluating a loan request, the customer receives poor, aggravating service from the bank. In both cases, the customer receives poor service, but not due to anything in the control of the frontline service worker, the person the customer deals with—the loan officer at the local branch. The poor service is a direct result of the failure of an internal service worker.

But the customer does not know or care who is responsible, and will probably take his or her frustrations out on the local branch officer. This is a good example of how poor internal service is really a double whammy—it hurts not only relations with your customers, but also corrodes the morale of the frontline service workers. That poor morale will in turn further diminish the quality of service at the front line.

How many times have you been forced to fly a poor airline, rent a car from a poorly run car-rental company, eat at a poorly run restaurant? You will often encounter valiant frontline service workers in such instances, and you can often tell by their own frustrations that the reason they aren't able to take good care of you has nothing to do with their competence or attitude. They simply aren't getting the kind of support they need from their company—they are victims of poor internal service, as are you.

By the same token, outstanding internal service pays a double bonus: it makes it easier for frontline workers to do their jobs, and so reduces their frustration level and increases the satisfaction and control they feel in their jobs. Good internal service is good not just for a company's external customers, it's good for the morale of the whole company.

One thing that attracted us to Jacob Smith is the clarity with which he sees his role, and the role of internal service—more clearly even than most senior managers of organizations the size of Bank of America. Although he has been promoted out of the bank branches and has considerable authority, he sees himself as a service worker, as someone constantly stretching to take good care of his customers.

Jacob Smith also understands the value of communicating—giving both his colleagues and the ultimate customers as much information as he can about the bank, the loan process, and the specific applications under consideration. Smith knows that information is power, and he wants to give the branch loan officers and the bank's customers as much power as he can in the loan-making process.

The final thing that so impressed us was that Jacob's boss found a way to spread Jacob Smith's attitudes and values across the organization. Jacob's boss created the Jacob Smith Challenge—and showed his own organization how important internal service is, and how to use the high standards of one employee to raise the standards of the others.

MEETING THE JACOB SMITH CHALLENGE

Jacob Smith grew up on a farm in the forties and fifties in the wide, empty spaces of the Texas plain north of Houston. His mother and father had fifty-six acres—Edgar Smith was born in 1897 and still lives on that farm—and most of what they grew and raised went to feed the family. Edgar Smith earned his living as a carpenter—he built the family house, and when it burned down, he built it again. Jacob had a comfortable spot in the family—second youngest. James was younger, and Edna, Jessie, Laura, Leslie, Willie, Betty, Thomas, Lillian, Edgar, Jr., Helen, Herbert, and Guide Belle were all older. The Smiths were a proper clan—fourteen kids, whose ages spanned two complete generations.

Jacob says his childhood on the farm was "wonderful, in a word. We had the greatest parents you could have. They taught us right, they gave us great examples." Jacob spent his time mostly outside, riding bikes, playing basketball, rolling tires, and doing farm chores. There was no television, although there were plenty of books. The nearest store was three miles away. School was fifteen miles away and the student body was all black. In fact, Jacob Smith grew up with only occasional interaction with white people.

The only hint of what was to come was that Jacob says he was "always somewhat business-minded. I was always with paper and pencil, figuring. If I was picking cotton, if I picked this much, then I'd have enough money to buy this pair of pants. I was always kind of figure-oriented."

Jacob Smith grew into a serene, watchful forty-eight-year-old—and if he commuted each day to a job on a space station, his world now could not be more alien than the world of his childhood.

Smith lives in Los Angeles, a city where there are now more people than there were in all of the state of Texas when he was a boy. He works in a nondescript, two-story office building in Brea, on the far eastern side of the city, about ten miles north of Disneyland. Smith's desk is on the second floor, amid hundreds of identical desks, row after row nearly to the horizon, each desk anchored by a telephone and a Compaq computer with a color monitor.

In baldest terms, Smith has become a faceless bureaucrat for the Bank of America, a sprawling California institution, with 830 branch offices in Southern California alone. Although Smith is a loan officer, he doesn't work at a bank, and the appearance of an actual Bank of America customer at the building where he works could only be a sign of trouble. Indeed, the only external suggestion that the place has any connection to banking is an ATM out front.

Smith never meets the people whose loans he helps approve or reject. Only rarely does he talk to them on the phone—and then usually to explain, with a gentle reasonableness, why they've been rejected. Smith knows the bank's customers through the information that comes to him on their credit applications, through the credit reports that appear on his color computer screen, through their tax returns. Sometimes the only hint of personality in the process, the only suggestion of character, is the handwriting of the applicant.

This is the way Bank of America handles loans now. What happens in the bank branches is the *sale* of loans. The loan applications for all of Southern California flow into two loan service centers (there is another like the one where Smith works). The first service the centers perform is deciding for the branches whether a loan—a consumer loan, a boat loan, a car loan, a mortgage loan—should be made or not. The centralization has completely separated the decision about the loan from the branch officer who initiates it, and indeed from the customer who is seeking it. There is not much talk of the "upstanding character" of an applicant in such a system: the lines on an applicant's TRW credit report carry far more weight than the calluses on his or her hands. In terms of loans, Bank of America's branches have been turned into sales offices, little different from a car dealership's selling floor or a branch office of a real estate sales company.

The system Bank of America uses for loan processing is designed for efficiency. Using an internal mail system, routine applications can move from a branch to Smith's building to computer to approval and back out to the branch in a week. Rejections take even less time.

But back in 1988, Bank of America officials began to worry that the system was so impersonal that it was even beginning to wear on the bank's own employees—that there was tension and misunderstanding and resentment between the branches, which sold the loans, and the service centers, which approved or rejected the petitions with the regal inscrutability of a potentate.

EFFICIENCY ISN'T ALL THAT'S IMPORTANT

Bank of America had developed a loan processing system that was very efficient, but dehumanizing—particularly to the people who administered it. To the company's credit, it realized that the efficiency of the system wasn't enough. So managers took a step back to see if there was a way of making the system more appealing while still retaining its efficiency.

The pressure is on all businesses to streamline their

processes wherever possible, often replacing people with technology. The challenge, however, is to accomplish this without taking the humanity out of the business.

Bank of America undertook an effort to improve relations between the service centers and the branches—first to measure how well the branches thought the service centers were doing (there were four smaller centers then), then to gradually improve their performance.

The idea was to do something that Jacob Smith already did—have the service centers treat the branches like customers instead of supplicants.

CREATING INTERNAL CUSTOMERS

The key flaw in the new loan-approval system was that it set the people in the branches and the people in the loan service centers against each other. Their interests were very different: bank branches wanted to make loans, because branch employees were paid on commission; loan officers wanted to act more cautiously to avoid making loans that would go bad. Because the people in the two groups saw their missions so differently, there was little incentive for them to work together. Indeed, the loan service centers appeared to have been given most of the power that had previously resided with the branch officers, causing plenty of resentment. Bank of America's solution was to get the loan officers to see the branches as customers who were "buying" their approval services.

In any business, there are staffers who deal directly with customers, and staffers who work behind the scenes. Those employees who aren't serving the customers are serving someone who is. As a manager, you can't look at the parts of your company in isolation. In this case, Bank of America couldn't afford to consider the needs of its customers, separate from the needs of its internal customers, separate from the needs of the bank. It had to view making loans as an internal process—and work to create a culture where departments viewed each other as customers rather than competitors.

What Bank of America learned was something that would only make Edgar Smith—farmer, carpenter, father of fourteen—smile. Bank of America discovered that Jacob Smith, the farm boy, was the most gracious, most highly respected—most beloved, if such a word is possible in such a bureaucracy—loan officer in California. He consistently averaged greater than 90 percent "excellent" ratings from branch employees, who evaluated loan officers not overall, but loan by loan. Right from the start, Jacob Smith was number one in the state, month after month, year after year.

As Bank of America's chairman and CEO Richard Rosenberg said, "Jacob literally is the standard for other consumer loan employees." And to make sure no one would miss the point, his service center actually created a contest called "The Jacob Smith Challenge": beat Jacob Smith's service ratings and win one hundred dollars.

LEARNING TO FIND REASONS TO MAKE LOANS, NOT REJECT THEM

Jacob Smith's desk is remarkable for the spare, uncluttered condition in which he maintains it. There is not a single personal memento in his space—no pictures, although he is married, no sports paraphernalia, although he is a modest athlete and a serious fan.

Even the inside of his desk is neat—he has a little box to prevent the pens and pencils in the pencil tray of his top drawer from straying from the very center of the tray.

"You're right," Smith says, as if noticing the austere character of his desk for the first time, "I don't have that many things that don't help me do my job."

Smith does have a copy of Bank of America's regulations for making loans—*products*, the bank calls them. The manual of rules for the kinds of consumer loans Smith is involved with is more than three inches thick, and sits at Smith's left elbow.

On his desk are neat stacks of manila folders, each containing the paperwork for a loan application. One thing that is surprising in the era of computers is how much actual paper each loan application generates, and how much of that paper is handwritten.

Smith is a low-key fellow, the kind of guy who gets calmer as things get more chaotic. He has exactly the kind of personality you'd want in a loan officer if you could still meet one face-to-face: thoughtful, open-minded, willing to listen, but always conveying the sense that you won't be able to head-fake his analytical skills. There is nothing like having strangers paw through your financial data—your application, your credit reports, your pay stubs, your tax returns—to make you feel like you're standing naked before a jury. Smith seems to be able to do what he has to do and allow the customers to keep their clothes on.

MANAGE THE CUSTOMER AS WELL AS THE TASK

Jacob Smith doesn't blow your socks off the minute he meets you. In fact, he's modest to a fault, almost unassuming. But his calm demeanor is perfect for the role he plays. When branch employees or loan applicants get aggravated at a bank decision, Smith cools them off rather than aggravating them further.

The stereotypical loan officer is the kind of person people love to hate. In fact, it's hard to imagine a customer-initiated phone call in this business that isn't unpleasant by nature.

Jacob Smith is anything but unpleasant. He understands his customers' predicaments. He knows that the branch loan offices are dealing with real people who don't want a bureaucratic answer. He realizes he has to take care of the customers—the people—as well as the paperwork.

First up on Smith's agenda this morning is a woman and her husband who want a second mortgage. The application has already been rejected by Bank of America's computerized ranking system based on the initial financial data supplied, and based on a quick scan by the computer of the couple's credit reports.

"Still, we can look at it further," says Smith, "and we can override. That's where I come into play."

The woman is a bank employee, which makes her application a little special. Smith works for a team in his loan service center that handles more difficult loan applications—boat loans, mobile-home loans, unsecured lines of credit, and loan applications from employees.

Employee loans are the most notorious among loan officers. "Nobody wanted to work with the employees," says Smith. "That's where I got my niche.

"Employees can be hard to deal with. They think they are entitled to more because they think we can throw the credit requirements out of the window in the case of a twenty-year employee.

"They say, 'I've got bad credit? So what?' Or, 'My debt ratio is too high? So what?'"

In fact, there is no special weighting for bank employees. "Sure, they've been at the bank twenty years, but they might be unemployed tomorrow," says Smith. "There are no special underwriting requirements for employees." They do, however, get a discounted interest rate if they are approved.

The problem with employees is that they think they deserve a loan from their own bank—and telling them no can be a delicate task.

"I thought, how different can it be?" says Smith. "You have to be straightforward. I found it wasn't any more difficult, if you explain it to them thoroughly. You give them the rationale why it's that way, rather than just saying, 'It's that way.'

"You give those kind of explanations—the rationale for some of the rules, rather than just saying, 'That's the rules.' Rules don't do a lot for people."

THE CUSTOMER IS ENTITLED TO UNDERSTAND *WHY* AS WELL AS *WHAT*

Jacob Smith has to play by the rules. In fact, his three-inch-thick rule book sits right out on his desk where he can easily consult it. But Smith uses rules exactly the opposite way most people do. He uses the rules as a jumping-off point, not as a weapon. Smith is never afraid to explain his decisions—on the contrary, he's eager to make sure people understand what's happening. And because he knows he's going to have to explain his choices, he thinks them through carefully before making them. He doesn't simply use "the rules" as an excuse for behaving imperiously. And he's discovered that when people understand why something has been done, even if they don't agree with the decision, they are more inclined to accept it and consider it fair.

Smith summons the credit reports for the woman and her husband, available instantly on his computer because they've applied for a loan and their application is pending. He is reviewing the file to see if he should recommend that the rejection be overruled. Smith is no longer a line loan officer—in early 1992, he was promoted to being the assistant leader of his team. He now wrestles with more complicated cases, reviewing rejections when the branch office disagrees with that decision, or reviewing applications for sums that exceed the lending authority of routine officers.

In the couple's file are letters they and their branch officer have submitted, explaining how some of the problems appearing on their credit report—problems that probably caused the rejection—are not really problems.

Credit report problems are called *derogs* (short for *derogatory items*). The letters explain two derogs to Smith's satisfaction. But he keeps looking and quickly finds two other matters.

"Here's a federal tax lien," he says, pointing to a sixteen-hundred-dollar item from 1988. "It's not huge, but it's huge enough, particularly with it not being released. It's not so much the amount as the responsibility to deal with your obligations."

Right below the unsatisfied tax lien is listed a thirty-one-hundred-dollar debt to a company called Pacific Credit. The notation is *SCNL*—skipped, cannot locate.

The only obvious excuse for both items would be if they didn't actually belong to the woman—they are listed with her first name, but with a different last name. All the rest of the information agrees—address, Social Security number—but confusion of credit files of similarly named people is not uncommon.

Smith calls the branch office.

"Peter!" he says, "Jacob Smith at the Bank of America loan service center . . . I wanted to talk to you about the items addressed in your memos."

He assures Peter that the explanations are satisfactory, then moves on, asking if the woman ever went by the other last name.

"She did?" says Smith. "Oh, okay. Well, that's a problem then. There's a federal tax lien of sixteen hundred dollars that has not been released. And there's one more item—Pacific Credit, for thirty-one hundred dollars."

He listens to Peter's explanation. "I'll be," he says meditatively. "I see. I can see that. But back to the tax lien—that's an issue that would prevent us from extending anything to her. Uh-huh. Everything looks good, up to the federal tax lien."

Smith hangs up, and sets the file aside. He looks up. "Divorces are a problem," he says. The two derogs left on the woman's credit report are artifacts from her divorce, disputes that haven't been resolved after four years. Smith sounds regretful, philosophic, almost like a counselor rather than a loan officer. "Divorces are a problem we can't always resolve."

But that brief conversation with the branch officer was a little taste of the trademark Smith style. He didn't simply call Peter and tell him the rejection was affirmed, or even that Peter could call up the couple's credit reports and see just as easily as Smith why they were being rejected.

He walked the branch employee through the problems. He told him what the real hang-up was—the tax lien—even suggesting very obliquely that if that problem were resolved, the couple might be able to get the loan.

"It's a time issue," says Smith. "People are always saying, 'I don't have time to explain this and this and this!' I *do* have the time.

"I take the time to explain to the branches the reasons for things—because they have to explain them to the customers. I also give alternatives—'We'll do it if you take care of this.' Or, 'We'll make that car loan if the car is five thousand dollars cheaper.'

"And down the road, that benefits me. I don't have to explain that anymore, when I tell a loan officer or someone from a branch the same thing. And the word gets out, 'Jacob is fair, he plays by the rules, but he's fair.' "

Much of this attitude comes from Smith's upbringing. But he can actually pinpoint the moment in his fifteen-year career with Bank of America when his attitude about lending money, and about loan applicants, turned around. The transformation was the work of a frustrated intermediary, just like the kind of people Smith deals with daily at the branches.

Smith was working in a precursor to Bank of America's loan centers—an auto-loan center, that handled financing for car dealers and car buyers.

Smith had just rejected a car loan for a car buyer, and the man at the dealership who handled financing was angry. "The man said to me, 'Look for ways to *make* the loan. You're looking for ways to decline loans instead of ways to make loans.'

"That comment always stuck with me."

FIGURE OUT HOW TO SAY YES

This is one of the great secrets of providing outstanding service—whether it be internal or external. Even if you have the power to prevent things from happening, it's really your job to make things happen. It's easy for loan officers to imagine themselves as guardians of the bank's vault—charged with preventing the unworthy from receiving loans.

But it's far more effective, and far more productive, for them to think like Jacob Smith does: the point of being a loan officer is to make loans, not to decline them. Thinking about the job in those terms doesn't turn one into an irresponsible flake, handing out the bank's money left and right. But it does completely transform the attitude a loan officer—or any employee—comes to work with. Jacob Smith thinks he is there to help the bank's customers borrow money. And he's constantly searching for imaginative ways to make loans happen, and giving branch employees and customers enough information so they stand the best chance of getting loans approved.

Make sure that the people in your organization with the power to say no (including yourself), understand that the goal is to figure out a way to say yes.

TURNING A ROLE MODEL INTO A RABBIT

Richard Rushton, who is one of the people who runs the Brea loan service center, came to Brea in late 1988 from the San Diego service center.

"At San Diego, we were number one in the state," says Rushton. "Except that the number-one *guy* in the state was Jacob Smith—who worked somewhere else."

Brea was fourth out of the four centers in the state at that time—and Rushton was moved to Brea to help improve its performance. "It was the worst by far of the centers," says Rushton. "The others were at least at 80 percent [approval ratings]. L.A. was at 60 percent—and it would have been 50 percent without Jacob Smith."

Rushton discovered that the workers at the Brea service center were actually very skilled at frustrating branch employees. "I said at the time, 'Some of you people can actually approve a loan and still piss the branch off to a fare-thee-well.'"

Rushton also discovered that many of the center's employees lacked training. "I said by this time next year, we'll be number one. I spent the first six months doing intensive training. There was no consistency in the operation."

After the training came the Jacob Smith Challenge.

"I sat in this office and told him my proposal," says Rushton. "He was flattered, and he was a little apprehensive about being held up as a role model. He asked for a day to think about it."

What Rushton was proposing was a little dangerous—and it would not have worked with just any outstanding employee. With the wrong person as an example, others might have viewed the contest as favoritism, or they might simply have resented Smith. But despite his outstanding performance, Smith is the farthest thing from smug or arrogant or even faintly immodest about his own performance. And he is nonjudgmental. The way he deals with the branches, he says, "comes easy, because for me it seems like the right thing to do."

Smith never seems to be holding himself above his colleagues, which is one reason Rushton thought management might be able to get away with holding him above his colleagues.

"He's a quiet guy, an easygoing guy," says Rushton. "He came back an hour later and said, 'I'll do my part.'"

The deal was this: anyone who got better ratings than Smith over three months got one hundred dollars.

GETTING THE REST TO LIVE UP TO THE BEST

Richard Rushton had an employee who was doing exactly what he wanted all his employees to do. He didn't hesitate to use that employee to teach others how to work. He was also willing to invest a little of the bank's money to motivate people—to show them they could be as good as the model employee. Rushton handled the project with grace. He asked if Smith was willing to be the example, and he picked an employee he knew would provide the positive incentives of competition without causing any morale problems.

The Jacob Smith Challenge was a tonic. "With the Jacob Smith Challenge," says Rushton, "we went from number four to number one immediately." He ended up paying out a hundred dollars to thirteen or fourteen workers.

"He was a rabbit," says Rushton, "and they chased him."

The whole thing doesn't strike Smith as all that odd in retrospect. "The bank found it needed to do some unusual things," he says. "I didn't have any real problem with being the target—it was more recognition for me."

Smith got a bonus for being the rabbit, and he also got promoted.

"I just maintained my low-key position. I never went around with my head higher than myself."

As for Rushton, he'd encountered plenty of skepticism about

whether the intangible skills that made Smith so effective—courtesy, quickness, respectfulness—could be transmitted to people who didn't have them instinctively. He proved to his satisfaction that, with the right training and the right incentives, they could be.

"It is teachable," Rushton says. "I have the evidence."

GIVE PEOPLE A FAIR CHANCE OF SUCCESS

Rushton showed that getting people to do what you want is often simply a case of setting up the right environment so what you want is the easiest thing for them to do. Many managers might have relied just on the customer-survey ratings to motivate people. But when the survey didn't goad poor performers to better performance, Rushton looked further. He discovered gaps in training, which he filled. He then set up incentives aimed at improving the weak areas. The results were dramatic.

READING BETWEEN THE LINES OF A LOAN APPLICATION

Jacob Smith didn't find banking immediately. He went from high school to the Air Force.

The military suited him okay, he says. "I never had a problem taking orders. I've always been organized, and I've always accepted organization."

When he resigned from the service after his four-year hitch, he went to work for McDonnell Douglas as a cabin assembler for DC-10s and DC-11s. He also went to school part-time, and eventually ended up going to work for Sears, hoping to rise through the sales ranks into management.

"I didn't like sales," he says. "That's not me. I didn't like the uncertainty of the salary. I was good, but not good enough. I never was a persuasive-type person."

He stayed at Sears for five years, long enough to conclude

that the company would not soon take him into its management-training program. By then he was married—his wife Gail was working as a secretary for Bank of America—and he quit Sears and went to school full-time, getting a finance degree from California State University in Los Angeles.

"I had ruled out professional employment—doctor, lawyer—from a practical point of view," he says. "I liked banks. From when I was young, I like the way they looked. There was the aroma of business. You worked with numbers, with figures. It was somewhat analytical. Banks, that was my thought."

Bank of America recruited him out of school, and he's been with the company since, rising to the point now where he has the rank of assistant vice president and earns more than thirty-five thousand dollars per year.

Rushton, for one, has been encouraging Smith toward management, but Smith has been reluctant to leave behind his front-line work with people's loan applications. "He equates management with hassle," says Rushton, smiling.

And Smith clearly enjoys making loans—he is not an exuberant man, but he's almost always smiling when he's typing in the approval code for a loan. He also enjoys the detective work that reviewing a loan application often involves. Different people, reviewing the same paperwork, find different things. His level of approval authority and override authority is a signal of the bank's faith in his judgment.

"Some people can read between the lines of things like tax returns better than others," he says.

He has just been through an application that required reading between the lines. A couple has applied for twenty-five thousand dollars on an unsecured credit line at a modest interest rate of 9 percent. This is one of the products Bank of America is most careful about selling. The application has been reviewed by a loan officer, who recommends its approval at twenty-two thousand dollars. It has come to Smith because the twenty-two thousand dollars of unsecured credit exceeds the officer's lending limit.

Smith starts going over the paperwork and the officer's work sheets. The husband is recently disabled, but shows nine thousand dollars per month in income, including four thousand dollars per month from disability insurance and substantial Social Security benefits.

Everything seems in order. Then Smith notices something odd on the papers from Social Security that explains each family member's benefits.

A number on each sheet is highlighted in yellow, which is identified as the amount of the first check from Social Security for each family member. The first benefit check to the wife, for instance, is to be $3,474. But then the sheet goes on to explain that that amount represents three months' benefits, and that the regular monthly benefit will be one third that amount—$1,158 for the wife.

Smith is puzzled by this. He reads each of the forms from Social Security carefully, word-by-word, to make sure he's not missing anything. He goes back over the application. Apparently, he's the only person to notice this inconsistency. It's unclear whether the couple actually thinks they have the income they say, or whether they are trying to fool the bank.

"It turns out they have only 60 percent of the income they stated," says Smith. "They qualify for no line of credit."

If they really think they have nine thousand dollars per month in income, being rejected for this loan will be the least of their shocks.

"I'll just give this back to the loan officer," says Smith.

An application for a similar line of twenty-five thousand dollars in unsecured credit comes to him because the computer has given it a failing score. The applicant is a professional couple who claim a combined wage income of more than $30,000 per month—$371,904 per year, according to their pay stubs.

Their application is thick with documentation, including two years of complicated tax returns. Smith digs in. "Let's see if they're telling the truth."

Smith notices that the couple are not depositors. Not being a bank customer doesn't hurt—but being one does help.

The couple has annual expenses of $98,000. They also have $66,800 in available revolving credit on credit cards. "That will hurt them," Smith says. One of the critical elements in approving additional unsecured credit is how much an applicant already has—regardless of whether it's used or not.

Indeed, this couple pays off its balances every month. "It may be zero balance now," says Smith, "but it could be $66,000 tomorrow."

Smith can find nothing that would have caused the computer ranking to fail the application. "This one is so clean, I'll send it back for paperwork." He's smiling. "We'll definitely offer these folks something."

It is exactly that kind of attitude that he says his current bosses encourage.

"They have a good outlook on credit and life," says Smith. "If it looks good, do it. If the book says don't do it, well, maybe the book is old. Change the book."

WHAT'S JACOB SMITH WORTH?

The extraordinary way Jacob Smith performs his job benefits Bank of America in two primary ways. First, he protects the bank's traditional assets, its loans. It was his careful reading of an applicant's Social Security documentation that uncovered the fact that the applicants had only one third of the income (from that source) that they thought they had. The loan, for $22,000, was to a couple the bank might have found it very difficult to collect from had the loan gone bad (picture the headline: B-OF-A FORCES DISABLED AMERICAN TO SELL HOUSE—not good). By identifying the problem, Jacob Smith protected the bank's $22,000 and its reputation.

How often does that type of thing happen? More often to Jacob Smith than to most loan officers, because it's his job to review nonstandard or borderline credit applications. For the sake of argument, let's say once per week. Let's also say that while Smith is good, he is really only 25 percent better than his colleagues. So he catches a potential bad loan once every four weeks.

What does that mean in dollars for the bank? Assuming that Smith works 48 weeks (bankers get good vacations), and that between the cost of recovering a bad loan and lost interest, the bad loans are complete losses, then he could be saving the bank 12 bad loans per year (48 weeks per year ÷ one loan every four weeks) at an average (from the example) of $22,000 each, for a total of $264,000 per year.

But that is only half the battle. Smith's real benefit comes not from *what* he handles, but from *how* he handles it. Because he is fast, correct, and communicative, Smith is able to turn down loans without annoying branch officers and without alienating customers (except for those few customers who will be alienated by being turned down no matter what, and research suggests those are very few). Let's consider what this might be worth to Bank of America.

We'll assume that Smith reviews four loan applications every day, or 960 in a 48-week year, and that all 960 are from customers of the bank. Because of the difficult type of loans he sees, let's say he rejects 480 (or half) of those loans. Of those rejected, 240 (or half) are not surprised and not angered. Despite the rejection, they remain customers of the bank. Of the remaining 240 rejected, 20 percent, or 48 people, are likely to be permanently aggravated and close their other banking activities with Bank of America.

Of the remaining 192 rejected people, we can guess that at least half (96 people) would have been lost had they not been handled with care and graciousness; they were treated this way only because their branch officer had a prompt and detailed response from Smith.

The numbers are flying fast and furious here (Jacob would be pleased). Our calculations yield 96 customers per year who cheerfully stay customers because of the great service Jacob Smith delivers in the regular course of his day.

What are those 96 customers worth to the bank per year? Let's guess. Don't forget that Bank of America targets a middle-income or higher customer who may use several services, including other loans, safe-deposit boxes, mortgages, and so on. We'll argue that the life of a customer with Bank of America is 10 years.

PROFITABILITY PER YEAR PER CUSTOMER	TOTAL PROFIT TO BANK FROM SMITH'S 192 CUSTOMERS
$50	$ 48,000
$100	$ 96,000
$150	$144,000
$200	$192,000

Looking at Jacob Smith from the perspective of either retaining assets or retaining customers makes sense. When you put them together, the numbers really start to add up.

HOW DO YOU FIND JACOB SMITH?

The Bank of America found Jacob Smith in its own ranks. Smith was a good frontline loan officer. He was also someone who had an ethic of trying to find a way to make loans.

Those were signals that he might make a good internal service provider—because Jacob understands the importance of customer service, he understands it is no accident.

Not all frontline workers do well behind the scenes, but when you're looking for behind-the-scenes people, when you're looking for service workers to take care of your service workers, it pays to look inside first. People like Jacob Smith not only bring their sense of customer service to the internal service roles, they also understand the problems of the people they are taking care of. They've been there.

CHAPTER 13

SERVICE AS

PERFORMANCE

American Airlines photo by Chet Snedden

JONI STRONG
AND DUDLEY

WORKING THE CROWD AT
FORTY-ONE THOUSAND FEET

How many times have you met a flight attendant on a plane that you'd had on a previous flight? Even very frequent flyers almost never encounter the same flight attendant twice. And no one picks a flight expecting to find a particular flight attendant aboard.

And yet flight attendants are crucial to the overall perception of airline service quality.

They belong to a group of service workers who perform one-time service. One-time, that is, from the perspective of the customer. Such service workers don't really have the opportunity to develop a relationship with the customer, although they have a chance to help their company develop a relationship. They have one shot to leave a good impression, to do what needs to be done.

The average person encounters such one-time service workers most commonly while traveling—the toll taker in the tollbooth, the agent at a rental-car counter, the skycap at the airport, the waiter in a hotel restaurant, the staffer at a tourist attraction.

One company that seems to understand the importance and the art of one-time service is Walt Disney. The whole thrust of the training Disney's employees receive at the company university is that for many families, a visit to Disney World or Disneyland is a once-in-a-lifetime (that is, a once-in-a-bank-account) experience. The employees are responsible for making it extraordinary.

When a guest asks a park staffer the way to the bathroom, Disney points out, it may be the ten-thousandth time the staffer has been asked that question, but it's the first time *that* guest has asked it. And the guest deserves to be treated as if the staffer were just waiting to be asked the question.

Disney recognizes that most of its employees will only interact with a particular customer once. The company has gone to great lengths to make sure its employees know what it wants communicated in each of those one-time encounters: hospitality, friendliness, competence, complete knowledge, helpfulness. Disney realizes that if every encounter embodies those qualities, it will be hard for its guests not to have a good experience.

The most outstanding example of one-time service we found is a woman who really does see herself not as a service *worker* but as a service *performer*.

Joni Strong is a flight attendant for American Airlines. She has a sidekick named Dudley, and together they are determined to make every flight memorable.

Many flight attendants these days seem to see their jobs as little more than passing out watery drinks in plastic cups. They often spend more time socializing with each other than talking to passengers; a special request brings sullen, reluctant compliance.

We blame this as much on the climate in the industry as anything (trimming crew sizes and extracting salary give-backs are hardly morale boosters), although there are exceptions. Southwest Airlines, for instance, actually encourages its flight attendants to bring a sense of fun back to flying, and in fact screens candidates for personality before signing them up for training.

Although Joni has been flying for thirty-five years, it is precisely this sense of freshness and fun that she and Dudley bring to their jobs.

When we say Joni sees herself as a performer, we mean it. Her plane is a stage, her uniform a costume, her passengers an audience. This notion of performance is important to the one-time service encounter. To raise a single encounter above the mundane requires a bit of spirit, a bit of drama. Disney makes this point by calling all its employees "cast members"—they are always on stage for the park guests.

And while a one-time performance is unlikely to bring a customer back in search of the person who delivered it, the performance does leave the customer with a real sense of connection to the company. And that will bring the customer back.

The idea of performance is actually a thread that runs through almost all the people in this book. Surely Paula Doricchi is a performer, and Marie Williams, and Alan Wilk, and Rich Ciotti. This is one way great service workers leave their personal lives at home and get up for their work: they realize that they are performing for their customers, and that a compelling performance is rewarding, if only for the appreciation of the audience.

So let us raise the curtain on Joni Strong, and Dudley.

MONKEYING AROUND AT FORTY-ONE THOUSAND FEET

American Airlines flight #74 pushes back from the gate in San Diego a couple of minutes past its scheduled 8:30 P.M. departure time, and begins the transcontinental leap that will take it into Washington's Dulles International Airport at 5:40 A.M. Most of the interior of the big, double-aisled Boeing 767 is dim and empty.

Before tackling the Rockies and the Appalachians, flight #74 hops up to Los Angeles—130 miles—to pick up more eastbound passengers.

As the 767 idles on a taxiway in San Diego, the pilot comes on the public-address system. "Mmmmm, ladies and gentlemen," he says, sounding like a doctor still pondering a mildly unpleasant test result, "we're in an air-traffic-control hold here, into LAX. We're kind of in the penalty box." The flight from San Diego to Los Angeles is so short that almost as soon as the plane lifts off the runway in San Diego, it's on final approach into Los Angeles. Before it can take off, it needs to be cleared to land. "We won't be taking off for probably fifteen minutes," says the pilot, "and then it's fifteen to twenty minutes over there."

An audible groan rolls through the tourist cabin. The passengers—who on this midweek red-eye are mostly tired-looking business travelers—toss and reposition themselves with restless irritation. Before they can get too rebellious, though, Dudley starts working his way down the plane's port aisle.

Dudley is a child-sized monkey with a furry face and an irresistible manner, a childlike impertinence. He flies crew on American Airlines often enough to have his own employee identification, and he never fails to send a wave of smiles and laughter down the rows of seats. A skeptical older man can't resist grinning when Dudley gazes down onto his bald crown and says to Joni Strong, the flight attendant around whom he has his arms wrapped, "Hey! Look! I can see myself in there!"

One man, nursing his crankiness as if he has earned it, completely ignores the monkey and says sharply to Strong, "Tell me we won't be late getting into Washington."

"No," says Strong, "we'll make that twenty minutes up, no problem."

It takes Dudley about ten minutes to work his way to the back of the plane and up the other aisle. Near the front of the cabin, he comes upon a young man with a full beard. "Hey! That's my daddy!" Dudley cries, looking excitedly from the passenger to Strong and back.

"Now just because a man has a beard doesn't make him your

daddy," says Strong, rolling her eyes at the passenger to show she's been through this drill before. The man is laughing heartily.

Not long after Dudley finishes making his vaudevillian circuit of the plane, the pilot rings the chime to tell the flight attendants to strap into their jump seats, and flight #74 roars off the runway and into Los Angeles International, where some passengers get off. One of the deplaning passengers pulls out snapshots of *her* monkey for Joni Strong to admire.

The only difference is that the passenger's monkey is real, whereas Dudley is a puppet, whose persuasive movements and sassy wisecracks are the work of Joni Strong.

SOMETIMES SERVICE REALLY IS A PERFORMANCE

Some service jobs really do put their performers onstage— one-time service jobs more often than other types. Being a front-desk clerk at a hotel requires graciousness and personality, but it doesn't require much of a performance. The front-desk clerk is not really onstage.

To do Joni's job in any sort of memorable way, though, requires breaking out of the well-practiced routine, and requires breaking through to customers who are often in a travel-lagged trance. It requires, in short, a real performance. And flight attendants are certainly onstage—the center of attention, with a captive audience.

We've seen some other examples of being "onstage" in this book—certainly Phil Adelman and Paula Doricchi are. If you have service workers who are in a position to perform, make sure you look for performers—for people with large, warm, embracing personalities, people who don't mind hamming it up a bit.

Strong, who is fifty-six years old, has been an American Airlines flight attendant since 1957—longer than many of her colleagues have been alive. Only forty of American's twenty thousand flight attendants have more seniority. Strong's tenure is unusual in a job that wears people out, physically and emotionally. She started flying before there were passenger jets—her business card bears a drawing of a vintage World War I biplane.

Strong has logged more than ten million miles, the equivalent of flying around the world once a month every month for thirty-five years—including volunteering for three and a half years of troop-transport charter flights to and from Vietnam. She has seen the planes get larger and larger, the airlines get leaner and leaner, the passengers get more and more demanding.

But what is really amazing is that in a business where the service has in the last decade seemed to be striving to mirror the numb, robotic attitude of the passengers, Joni Strong feels some responsibility to leave the passengers in a better mood when they get off the plane than they were in when they boarded.

"I enjoy people. I see things in a lot of people that others don't. A lot comes out in the puppet—a lot that I would never do myself. I like what you can do for people if they are really grumpy, turning people around. You know, sometimes a flight attendant will say to me, 'Go back to 5B and see if you can make that guy *smile.*"

Strong has an irrepressible, antic sense of humor. Occasionally, in the van taking the flight crew from Dulles to the Holiday Inn at five-thirty in the morning after an exhausting all-night flight, the lead flight attendant will threaten to "stuff a sock in it" just to quiet her down.

BRIEF ENCOUNTERS OF THE BEST KIND

Joni's personality is well-suited for her role. In addition to being able to make friends quickly, she obviously likes people and gets a lot of enjoyment out of making them happy, and she has a comic's ability to get a smile during a very brief encounter.

Today, many organizations don't rely simply on ten-minute interviews to make hiring decisions. Many companies, including some airlines, use personality profile tests to help in the hiring process for jobs like Joni's. Although these tests are certainly not foolproof and can't be relied on as the sole predictor of future success, they can certainly help managers get a clearer picture of a candidate's likelihood to be well-suited for a particular type of job. Interpreting such tests, however, is no job for an amateur. If not used properly, they can negate any potential advantage. Most companies who offer the tests also offer training courses for staff members who will be using the results. You are well-advised to take advantage of such training, so you don't end up misusing the tests.

Strong is sort of like Billy Crystal meets the Munsters. For a while, when she was flying DC-10s, she would climb into a coat that was hanging in the coat closet and hang there—in the coat, on the hanger, inside the closet—and greet boarding passengers. She would reach out of the closet, take their hanging bags, and hang them inside alongside her. "I would just hang there and blow their minds," she says.

Pasted over her picture on her California driver's license is a color picture of E.T. "I got pulled over once," she says, "I gave him my license, and that broke him up, and that was it."

Strong will occasionally make a dribble glass for a fellow member of the flight crew. In the pockets of her navy blue apron, along with a small flashlight and a small screwdriver, Strong also has an old-fashioned squirting nickel, which she doesn't hesitate to use.

"Some other people have tried to do this stuff, and they get in trouble," she says with a devilish twinkle. "I don't. It just depends on who the person is, what I do. And it's in how you do it.

"You can get a smile out of anybody."

Indeed, her personnel file is filled with letters from passengers delighted to find a flight attendant who wasn't wearing a million-mile glaze in her eyes. The letters tell of Strong soothing nervous fliers, entertaining planeloads of delayed passengers, calming squalling children. The operations director of a Dallas-based tour company wrote that Strong was, quite simply, "the single most absolutely wonderful flight attendant I have ever come in contact with."

WHAT DO YOU EXPECT? SHE GOT HER INSPIRATION FROM GROUCHO MARX

One of the duties Joni Strong particularly likes is being "the plucker"—the person who stands at the doorway that leads from the terminal, into the Jetway and the plane, taking tickets and checking boarding passes as passengers get on the plane.

This is not a job flight attendants are trained for. It used to be the job of a gate agent. But as deregulation has inspired cost-cutting, most airlines now have a member of the flight crew from each plane come off the plane to greet the passengers. It is not a task that flight attendants generally fight each other for the privilege of performing. Passengers line up, impatient and loaded with carry-on baggage.

"I like to pluck," says Strong, heading for the plucking post at Los Angeles International to take care of the boarding passengers. "I like to set the tone for the trip. Plus, I'm a stickler on baggage. And I'm really pretty fast at pulling."

Mostly, though, plucking is a chance to indulge in twenty minutes of nonstop joke-telling.

One man wants to know if he can be upgraded to business class. "There is no business class on this flight," says Strong. "If you can find a business-class seat, you can sit in it."

A man tears his ticket coupon out for Strong, but tears it a little ragged, leaving some of the coupon still attached to the ticket. "Oh, that's okay," says Strong, "you can just get off partway."

When the passenger comes through who holds the boarding pass for seat 2B, Strong sings out: "To be or not to be, that is the question! It's a nice saying, but I only get to say it once a flight."

Strong elicits a smile from almost everyone who gets on the plane. She *does* set the tone for what is in fact a fairly unpleasant all-night flight for both passengers and crew, taking a job that has almost no content and turning it into an opportunity. Strong is a delighted, observant student of human behavior.

"When people ask, 'Are H and J together?' I always say, 'Yes, because I is here.'

"It takes them till they get halfway down the Jetway—then

I'll hear them laugh. And the funny thing is, the women catch it before the men do."

About two dozen passengers board in Los Angeles. The whole process is quick enough that flight #74 is back on schedule before it leaves. The last boarding passenger is a woman carrying a cup of frozen yogurt. "Can I take this with me?" she asks.

"Yes, you can take that on, as long as you share," says Strong. The woman heads down the Jetway laughing, calling over her shoulder, "I only have one spoon . . ."

Joni looks at the gate agent, who nods that everyone is aboard. "Ready to hit it? Let's hit it!"

ALL YOU NEED ARE A FEW GOOD VOLUNTEERS

Not every task that needs to be done is best assigned by management. American Airlines has figured out that leaving some tasks to volunteers (that is, the crew) means that those best-suited for a particular job will often end up with it. Many managers often talk about building teamwork but never give the team a chance to work together as a team. An essential ingredient of teamwork is allowing members of the team to create an air of cooperation without the interference of management.

Another lesson to be learned regarding volunteerism is that one should never assume that a particular task will be undesirable to everyone just because most people find it undesirable. While most flight attendants prefer to wait on the airplane and defer coming into contact with the passengers until the last possible moment, Joni Strong volunteers for plucking because she can't wait to meet and entertain new people.

Flight attendants come together as crews for each set of flights—they may work with the same person every week for a month, and then not work again with a person for years.

The chemistry of a crew is important to the tenor of the

flight—for both passengers and flight attendants. "One flight attendant can change it, can bring everyone up," says Strong.

Each impromptu crew is headed by a lead flight attendant—called a premium or number one at American—who volunteers for that role. Being the lead flight attendant involves a fair amount of bureaucratic work, and also means making the public-address announcements and taking care of passengers who utterly exasperate the other flight attendants. Like plucking, it is rarely a job flight attendants vie for. "It's usually the most junior person," says Strong. "Nobody wants it."

IT'S ALL IN THE PACKAGING

American Airlines has identified a task that most flight attendants will avoid at all costs. It is a job that not only requires the individual to do a lot of extra paperwork, but it also carries with it the responsibility of dealing with the problem customers. On the one hand the airline knows that because of these factors it is highly likely that the most junior flight attendant will pull this duty. On the other hand, the airline doesn't want an unhappy passenger thinking he or she is dealing with a neophyte. So, what do they do? They call the position "lead flight attendant." They refer to the person as a "premium" or "number one." The company has not only thought of a creative way to package this junior flight attendant to the public, it has also made the job a little more palatable to the employee.

The advantage to this overnight flight into Dulles is that it is usually quiet. There is only snack service, and most passengers make an effort to sleep.

Strong unstraps from her jump seat about ten seconds before the captain rings the chime telling the flight attendants that the plane is passing through ten thousand feet and that it is okay to go to work.

Strong is almost obsessive about keeping the plane galley neat. She reorganizes it before the passengers board, putting supplies where she wants them, setting up her coffee service.

"I hate it when I come in and everything is a mess," she says. "I can't stand everything messy. I want everything tidy—which is why I redo everything." Among other things, she makes sure all her coffee stirrers are facing in the same direction. "I put all the stirrers in the same direction so it's not pick-up sticks," she says.

"It's an illness," explains Cindy Barwick, a fellow flight attendant, with mock sadness. (Barwick is hardly one to talk—she sets up her galley wearing yellow kitchen gloves to protect her hands.)

On flight #74, Strong moves carefully, because within moments of takeoff, most of the thirty-three tourist-class passengers are sprawled across seats, trying to sleep, their heads and feet sticking out into the aisles.

Strong sells only one headset for the in-flight movie—for four dollars—despite the offer to one passenger to sell him "one ear for two dollars." Food is no more popular than the movie—the four flight attendants in tourist class give out only two sandwiches and two drinks. One man asks for an extra cookie. Strong eyes him skeptically, as if trying to decide whether he merits an extra cookie, then fetches him one. Strong finds one passenger asleep with his reading light on, and carefully reaches in around him to turn it off so he doesn't wake up to an unpleasant glare.

Within forty-five minutes of taking off, every passenger is asleep, and the galleys are almost ready for landing. Strong, who usually naps a little the day before an overnight flight, remains bright-eyed throughout the night. She is a small woman, looking more the age of an energetic aunt than a fifty-seven-year-old grandmother. She keeps her blond hair short, and an old picture identification she carries in her wallet shows that as a young woman, she was beautiful, with a kind of sparkling, show girl's good looks.

"When I was hired, you couldn't wear makeup," she says. "You had to be a natural beauty." She waits a beat. "Some of us were hired by phone."

Joni Strong grew up in Waterville, Maine—her voice has a hint of down-easter brogue—and was raised largely by her paternal grandparents. Her mother, a nurse, and her father, an electrician, divorced when she was young. Her mother moved to California. Her father died at forty-six, Strong's fourth year flying.

Strong started working to earn pocket money at age twelve, baby-sitting and waitressing during the summers in camps. It was about then she decided she wanted to be a flight attendant. The fifties were a time when plane travel still had an air of glamour and excitement about it—passengers wore suits and ties, and there was allure and prestige to being a stewardess.

She saw her first flight attendant on Groucho Marx's television show, "You Bet Your Life." "He had one on, and I thought, 'That's what I want to do.'"

FULFILLING LIFELONG AMBITION

It's really nice when people have the opportunity to fulfill childhood dreams—particularly when it comes to the job they end up doing for years and years. The odds that someone will be great at what she does certainly go up if it's something she wanted to do all her life.

You might want to think about adding one more question to your company's job application: when did you first decide that you were interested in doing this job? That question, when properly followed up in an interview, can give you tremendous insight into whether this person is simply looking for a job or interested in pursuing a career.

In high school, Strong was athletic, outgoing, and popular. She played French horn, was president of the band, and was voted both most athletic and class wit. Although she didn't have much contact with her mother growing up—something she says "I had a hard time with"—she says she and her mother "are like two peas in a pod. People think my mother is a stitch."

But while it was assumed that Strong's brothers, one older, one younger, would go to college, she says, it was equally assumed that she would not. "In high school, I didn't think about going to college," she says. "I figured, and I think they figured too, that I was the girl, and I would get married and settle down."

There is a wide streak of New England independence in

Strong, however. Somehow, she learned of a junior college near Boston, Mount Ida, that offered a stewardess-preparation program.

"My grandparents were all for it—there just was not the money to send the boys to school, and me to school," says Strong. "I knew I could make enough money in the summers to pay for it, though." And that is precisely what she did.

She applied to American Airlines as she was coming out of school—at a time when the airlines were accepting only one of every hundred stewardess applicants. Only one other person from her class at Mount Ida got a job right out of school.

After six weeks of training at American's flight-attendant school at Midway Airport in Chicago, Strong started flying out of Boston.

"My first trip was Boston to Cincinnati, with thirteen stops along the way, on a Convair 240. It was like a local train." There was only one flight attendant on the forty-person plane.

"We served beverages from big jugs, and lunch and breakfast on little trays. But my main job was to make sure no passenger slept through his stop."

SERVICE IS MORE THAN A QUIP AND A SMILE

The companion flight to #74 is #75, which retraces the same route west—Dulles into Los Angeles and then back to Strong's home base, San Diego. When Strong and her fellow flight attendants fly into Dulles at six in the morning, they turn around and fly back out at six that same evening. They spend the daylight hours in a Holiday Inn, sleeping. They must be downstairs, ready to return to the airport, at four in the afternoon.

The van ride back to Dulles—with five female flight attendants and one male—is almost nonstop hilarity, with Strong leading the way. It's not bad preparation; the westbound flight has full meal service, and a full load, and is far more taxing than the eastbound leg.

This flight, too, is heavy with business people. Before the

door is even closed, a woman in the back is using the plane's cellular telephone. "Are you talking to someone I want to talk to?" Strong asks.

"It's just phone mail," the woman says.

Washington passengers are notorious for bringing too much carry-on luggage and then refusing to put it under the seats in front of them because it reduces their legroom. It takes imagination to get the luggage stowed. In anticipation of the usual Washington attachment to too many belongings, Strong and her colleagues relocate some of the drink carts from a rear storage area to the center galley, opening up the rear storage bin for excess baggage.

Being a flight attendant is hard, often thankless work. After thirty-five years, Strong makes only about thirty thousand dollars per year (she could make more—up to forty-five thousand dollars—if she wanted to work more). American gives no merit raises after fourteen years of service, she says, and so she hasn't had one since 1970. If she were to retire now, her pension would be only about a thousand dollars per month. The work is physically demanding, and not just because of the deadening flying schedule. Fully loaded drink carts weigh in excess of two hundred pounds, and pulling them up an aisle in a plane that is climbing through twenty-five thousand feet is not easy—it's like pulling them up a steep hill.

By and large, the work of being a flight attendant is repetitive and pressured: get the drinks served so you can get the meals served so you can collect the meal trays so you can serve coffee so you can make sure the tray tables are up for landing.

Strong deals with the numbing routine by trying to connect with the passengers. Her humor is infectious, and it is also a good technique for dissipating tension—both hers and the passengers'.

Before Strong can do the drink service on the flight back across the continent, a man rings his flight-attendant call button.

"I'm sorry," he says sheepishly when Strong appears. "I couldn't see which was the light, I hit it by mistake."

"This is what happens to people who do that," she says, and playfully slaps his hand three times. Then she leans over, turns off the call light and turns on the reading light. The buttons are right next to each other on the armrest. "Whoever invented this needs to be hanged," she mutters.

Strong doesn't see her role as being simply a human vending machine. Her sense of humor hides a strong mothering instinct, and she is constantly watching for what might make passengers more comfortable. During the drink service, a man's miniature bottle of red wine keeps sliding toward the end of his tray table. Strong makes a little friction pad out of two damp napkins, and sets the bottle on top. It stays put.

Working her way down the aisle with the meal trays— "lasagna, or chicken?"—she notices a man in a sling struggling to open the bag containing his silverware.

"Can I take that out of there for you?" she asks, and promptly presents him with his silver. She also opens his salad-dressing pouch. The man then asks for a carton of milk. "Do I have to open this for you, too?" Strong asks. The man and several surrounding passengers burst out laughing as Strong presents him with an open carton of milk.

For Strong, the goal on most flights is to get the service done in time so she can take out Dudley and entertain a little. Dudley flies along with Strong in his own bag, and is known throughout the American system.

Flight crews, Strong says, "love having him on board. While I do Dudley, they can eat, or whatever. I do all my work first. And they will pick up the last few trays so I can do it. They love it."

Indeed, immediately after Dudley comes out of his bag in the cockpit on this flight, he has to spend a few minutes schmoozing with Strong's fellow flight attendants in first class before he can go back and visit with the passengers.

It was American Airlines staff in Dallas who made Dudley his official American Airlines identification. Another crew of flight attendants once kidnapped him, ransoming him back to Strong for two dozen gourmet chocolate chip cookies.

Dudley—whom Strong named for an American copilot who was paralyzed in a motorcycle accident—is Strong's alter ego. She claims to be a fundamentally shy person—she doesn't like having to do public-address announcements, for instance—and Dudley gives her some license to be a little theatrical. Dudley does and says things Strong wouldn't do or say herself, and in that sense her performance with him is more reminiscent of ventriloquism than puppetry.

Tonight, Dudley is wearing his San Diego Chargers cap, bill in back, catcher style.

He and Strong work their way down the aisle, leaving a ripple of smiles and laughter in their wake. People light up when they see him.

Dudley spots a man working on a computer.

"I know how to use that!" he cries excitedly.

"Can you make coffee?" the man asks.

"Coffee?!" Dudley sneers. "I know how to fly this plane!"

A blond woman blows Dudley a kiss, which causes a sudden convulsion of shyness in him. He buries his head in Strong's armpit.

Strong gives Dudley wonderful, realistic head movements, and her ventriloquism isn't bad.

"We had a guy on a DC-10 once," says Strong, "he was ranting and raving about that lady having an animal on board the plane.

"He was sitting way in the back, and he just went on and on about how someone let this lady on with an animal, and how could you do that?

"The flight attendants in the back just smiled and let him go on and on. I was only one or two rows away when he finally realized it was a puppet."

Passengers talk to each other *about* Dudley as much as they talk *to* Dudley and Strong. "What a riot," says one woman. "She's entertaining the troops."

The man next to her is shaking his head. "For a minute there, she had me going. I thought that was a child, but I thought that child was certainly hairy."

Dudley has been flying with Strong for more than ten years. "I was flying San Diego to O'Hare in 1981, and over the seat back I saw this little face come up," says Strong. "The woman had a puppet. I said, 'Where'd you get that? That's adorable!' She said she made them. And I bought it right there, I paid twenty or twenty-five dollars for the original one.

"I was on the first leg of a three-day trip, and the reaction was so unbelievable on that first trip—I used it on all six legs. The reaction was just fantastic, the smiles he brought out."

The parting words of her lead flight attendant after that trip, Strong says, were, "Make sure you bring it on the next flight."

The woman who makes the puppets, Georgia Lee Waggoner,* has become a friend of Strong's, and Strong routinely passes her name and address on to passengers who ask where they can get their own versions of Dudley.

As effective as Dudley is—particularly for quieting crying children—no one at American has ever suggested issuing a puppet as standard equipment on every flight. Indeed, without having seen Joni Strong at work, most airlines would wince at the idea of a flight attendant doing a ventriloquism routine for an airplane's captive audience.

LET PEOPLE BE THEMSELVES

American Airlines has been smart enough to let Joni be Joni. Indeed, the airline routinely praises her performance, acknowledging—in writing, if not financially—that she goes well beyond what is required of her as a flight attendant, and that the airline is the beneficiary. There is hardly a profession that seems to encourage conformity among its members more than being a flight attendant. And yet Strong does her job so well precisely because she isn't afraid to be a little antic, to surprise her customers. American Airlines realizes that Strong's independence is no threat to the company—quite the contrary, it is good for the company's reputation and its performance.

The magic that Strong is able to work with Dudley is a function of her personality, her sense of humor, and her judgment. But it also shows how valuable working outside the normal margins of one's job can be, and how easy. For Strong, Dudley is just one more way of refusing to give in to the cattle-car atmosphere

*If you would like to purchase a puppet like Dudley from Georgia Lee Waggoner, you can write her at: 1833 Allen Lane, Anderson, Indiana 46012.

of modern air travel. He not only brightens the ride for the passengers, he makes the jobs of Strong's fellow flight-crew members easier, and he makes Strong's job far more gratifying.

Strong has a virtually endless supply of stories of Dudley's antics.

"One guy on a DC-10 forgot to zip his fly after coming out of the rest room," says Strong. "Dudley said, 'Hey! You forgot to zip your fly!' He never took his eyes off the puppet, he just reached down and zipped his fly.

"We had a kid the other night, he was coming over from the Philippines, he was about six, he had a brain tumor. There had been no response from him all day—and when I took out the puppet, he made noises and smiled. Then he laughed and laughed. His mother said, 'You really made my son's day.'

"He changes the complexion of the trip."

Strong takes her job seriously—she has, for instance, not only never missed a single flight in thirty-five years, she's only been late twice (and she arrived before flight time in both cases)— "and that's why I have fun. You can't let it get to you. You have to have fun, and you can bring other people into it."

And Dudley even manages to persuade the skeptical. Ted Koppel was on a flight one night from Los Angeles to San Diego. "He said, 'You look kind of funny walking around with that monkey on your arm,'" says Strong. "And the next thing you know, he was talking to it."

WHAT'S JONI STRONG WORTH?

Joni Strong represents a real revenue opportunity for American Airlines. Like hotels, the airlines are high fixed-cost businesses. In fact, the cost of one more passenger is probably less than 25 percent of most ticket prices.

Joni likes to fly the long-haul routes (more time for fun with her captive audience), so it's probably fair to estimate an average round-trip ticket price of $500. Joni comes into contact with thousands of fliers over the course of a year. Let's say that just 50 of those choose, on future trips, to fly American instead of a competitor as a result of the excellent service and the fun time they received from Joni, and that these customers fly twice per year. What are they worth?

$500 per ticket

× 75 percent (incremental margin)

× 2 trips per year

× 50 customers

= $37,500

$37,500 of pure profit per year as a result of one flight attendant and a stuffed monkey? Gives "Something Special in the Air" a new meaning.

HOW DO YOU FIND JONI STRONG?

Simply audition her.

There is no way Joni could provide an extraordinary experience for a customer at the boarding ramp or on the airplane if she can't provide an extraordinary interview.

CHAPTER 14

MANAGING FOR

MAXIMUM

SERVICE

photo by Henry André

MARIAN GOODMAN

THE GRADUATE SCHOOL OF SERVICE

We set out to find some of the best frontline service workers in America, and to write a book explaining what made them special, what motivated and satisfied them. We also wanted their insights about how bosses could create a working environment in which high standards would be the norm, in which customers would be treated like a blessing instead of an inconvenience, in which creativity, innovation, and, not incidentally, profits would flourish.

We purposefully didn't go looking for *managers* who embodied these qualities, because most of the business books of the last decade have been devoted to managers.

We wanted to hear what the people who actually do the *frontline work* think, we wanted to see the world the way they see it. Indeed, many otherwise exemplary people who were nominated for the book were excluded simply because they weren't frontline workers. They were supervisors.

Now, we present a chapter that features a supervisor—Marian Goodman, assistant store manager of the flagship Bloomingdale's in Manhattan. She is in this book for a simple reason: she treats her employees not as if they are her subordinates, but as if they are her customers.

What first caught our eye about Marian—what intrigued us enough so that we didn't simply set her in the stack of rejected supervisors—was a story in her nomination packet about her assisting a visiting dignitary in shopping at Bloomingdale's, including personally delivering the purchases to the woman's hotel room. Her job description made her sound like a senior manager; her performance made her sound like a superstar salesclerk.

We determined to investigate this unusual combination, and the woman we discovered is the perfect exclamation point to the people in this book who have come before her. Like Marie and Keith and Jorge, she was once a world-class frontline service worker. Now she illustrates how to carry the values of such a worker into the supervisory ranks.

Marian Goodman does by talent and instinct what we have attempted to do through painstaking study. She has taken the ideas presented in the preceding thirteen chapters and applied them not only to customers, but to employees as well. She creates the kind of environment where the people you've met so far in this book could flourish.

Quite simply, Marian has her priorities right. When she is talking to her boss (the store manager) and one of her associates pages her, she stops the meeting with the boss to call the associate; when she is talking to an associate on the selling floor and a customer needs help, she stops talking to the associate to take care of the customer.

Much of the value and prestige of advancement in much of American business seems to be in getting as far away from the customers and the front lines as quickly as possible. Marian embodies exactly the opposite philosophy. She knows that the way a manager learns to keep a business current, nimble, and responsive is to be out where the business is done: on the floor.

Marian Goodman started out selling men's underwear and socks at Bloomingdale's. She has moved up in her store without moving away from her core ethic—taking care of customers. And she has discovered something more managers need to discover: as you rise, the definition of customer needs to be broadened—to include your employees.

Managing the Unmanageable: Service amid the Tumult at Bloomingdale's

The big Bloomingdale's on Fifty-ninth Street in the heart of Manhattan is the New York experience concentrated into a single building—a store as vast as the desires of New York City's richest residents, a place that brings the tumult and variety of the city's streets right inside, where the cognoscenti navigate with slightly haughty familiarity, as if the store were theirs, and where the tourists often stand gaping, jostled by the crowds, unable to remember what floor they're on, let alone what they came in for.

This Bloomingdale's, the flagship store of the chain and in some sense the archetypal American department store, seems as impossible to subdue as New York City itself. People just find their favorite places—the gourmet-foods department, women's casual sportswear, the designer boutiques—and learn to navigate to those, trying not to be distracted by what they pass along the way.

As this store embodies what is so fascinating and so frustrating about New York City and about mercantile America—the energy, the choice, the impossibility of finding a salesclerk when you actually want to buy something—so Marian Goodman embodies the essence of Bloomingdale's, the expansive personality of the place, the charisma, the quickness, the confidence.

Marian Goodman is only thirty-eight years old, but she has already spent sixteen years working for Bloomingdale's. She has complete mastery of the Fifty-ninth Street store, where she is now assistant store manager and presides, among other things, over all of women's fashion, from T-shirts to haute couture. The store is as big as a medium-sized regional shopping mall: eleven selling floors, a million square feet. It does four hundred million dollars in business per year, well over a million dollars in sales every single day.

Goodman has 17 department managers reporting to her—doing an average of five to seven million dollars per year in sales—35 assistant department managers, 250 sales and support people. Goodman's chunk of the store does one hundred million dollars worth of its annual business. As assistant store manager, Goodman also has broader responsibilities—for four of the seven special shopping services Bloomingdale's offers, for much of the renovation that seems to be constantly under way at the store.

Her desk is stacked with rolls of blueprints. One of her current projects is new women's dressing rooms. "Fitting rooms are a pet peeve of mine," she says. "I want them immaculate.

"We are redesigning new fitting rooms—making them larger. You have to think like a customer. What does a customer come in with? A purse, a coat, maybe eight garments, maybe a friend. So you want places to put things, you want places to hang things, maybe a chair. We're putting in phone jacks so there can be a phone in the rooms, we're putting in three sets of bars to hang things, a table so when they take off their jewelry there is a place to put it down.

"Otherwise you're spending millions of dollars renovating it and if you don't think it out, you don't accomplish anything."

Not long ago, Goodman was wandering through the store and it struck her suddenly that with all the tourists and immigrants the store serves, the directory signs should be in more than one language. "P.S.," she says, using one of her signature expressions, "today they are multilingual, six languages."

THINKING LIKE A CUSTOMER

There is a big difference between thinking like a manager and thinking like a customer, and most managers miss it. Thinking like a customer is a never-ending process.

The typical department store's dressing room is tiny and stripped bare—making it convenient and cost-effective for the store and inconvenient for the customer. Goodman applies her own experience as a shopper to thinking about the dressing rooms—and the rest of her store. The result is a store that's more user-friendly.

She also realizes that no matter how many times she goes through the store, there are always things she's missed. So she's constantly on the lookout for things to improve. It took sixteen years for it to suddenly dawn on her that multilingual directory signs were a good idea.

The job, and the store, never seem to get out ahead of Goodman. Unlike most people, who are exhausted by the place, Marian Goodman draws her tremendous energy directly from the selling floor. She has routinely turned down the chance to manage her own Bloomingdale's so she can stay on at the carnival on Fifty-ninth Street.

"The fact that she can retain the type of energy she has for as long as she has says just about everything about Marian," says her current boss, James Gundell, manager of the Fifty-ninth Street store and a man Goodman helped hire. "This store can eat you alive—this is just what it's like, 365 days a year. She loves the commotion, she loves the pace, she loves the fanfare."

Goodman is a tall woman with a long, quick stride. She talks fast, and she has a big, easy laugh and an open face that instantly communicates what kind of mood she's in. She is a New York woman—there is about her just the faintest gloss of glamour, and an air of indisputable competence. She is consistently good-humored—she can be cheerleadery, she can be wry, she can be twinkly. But when she has to be, she can also be tough as nails.

Goodman's job demands a fantastic array of management skills—from taking young, gum-snapping girls straight out of

college and turning them into managers of high-fashion boutiques to being the personal shopper for the European and Asian
royalty who periodically descend on Bloomingdale's with their
entourages to buy a few things.

You only have to watch Goodman for a few minutes to discover that in fact she sees no difference between her greenest
salesclerk and a European princess. On a cold winter morning,
she is meeting with Gundell in his office ninety minutes before
the store is to open.

Three times during the thirty-minute meeting, Goodman's
beeper goes off. Each time—whether she or Gundell is speaking—she gets up immediately, often in midsentence, and she has
a phone in hand before the beeper finishes beeping. Each time
she's paged it's a question from one of her managers or assistant
managers; she can usually tell which one by the extension displayed on the beeper. And each time she greets the person—"Hi,
Cheryl!"—not as if she were in the middle of a meeting but as if
she'd been waiting for just that page.

"Sometimes that drives me crazy," says Gundell. "But I know
why she does it."

"Obviously, if someone is beeping me, it's important," Goodman says. "It doesn't matter what I'm doing. Whatever is on
their mind, it's important for me to solve at that moment. Otherwise they would have just left me a message." It is the difference
between seeing the people who work for her as interruptions and
seeing them as the very reason she has a job.

Goodman is the same way on the selling floor, where she
spends more than half her day.

"She'll be talking to us," says Annie Seale, one of her department managers, "and a customer will come up and say, 'Where is
lingerie?' and she'll say, 'I'll show you,' and walk her to the lingerie department."

Goodman sees herself not as a manager who presides over
one of the biggest stores in the world but as a service worker—
taking care of the people who work for her, and taking care of
the customers. Whatever she's talking to Gundell about can wait
if one of her assistant managers has a question, and whatever
she's talking to her assistant managers about can wait if a customer has a question.

"What does customer service *mean?*" Gundell asks, explaining what Goodman has taught him. "It's not a store's commitment, it's not a company's commitment, it's an individual's commitment."

Goodman is more direct. "My job is just one big 9-1-1 number!" she says with a laugh.

ALL EFFECTIVE MANAGERS ARE FRONTLINE SERVICE WORKERS

If you don't take care of your employees' needs, they can't take care of your customers. Your workers are, in fact, your customers. And by taking care of their needs, you become a model for how you expect them to treat their customers. The way Goodman answers her beeper is exactly the way she wants her sales associates to answer the questions of the store's customers.

At the same time, a manager can never be above taking care of the regular customers. If the manager is too good to take care of the customers, that sends a message that the customers don't matter that much—that if you rise high enough in the company, you become more important than the customers themselves. When Goodman is out on the floor, her attitude and readiness to help send a clear signal that the customers are more important than anything. Her customer interactions are the best lessons possible to teach her managers and associates how to handle problems.

The people that Marian Goodman interacts with in the store are all in a pecking order in her mind. For her, the customer is most important, and she'll stop anything she's doing to help a customer. Her employees are next, and she will interrupt a meeting with her boss to answer their questions. Her boss is last. He comes after everyone else is taken care of. Many managers worry about their boss first. Marian Goodman knows that managing down is much more important than managing up.

THE "FLASH" AND THE SCORE

Marian Goodman says often that it is only the customer that counts.

But before the customer arrives in the morning and after the salespeople have left for the night, there is something else that matters very much: the numbers.

Retail lives and dies by the numbers—today's sales, period-to-date sales, year-to-date sales against last year, against plan, against the Boca Raton store. You can be great with customers, you can be a wonderful trainer, you can know what's on your department's display racks better than what's in your closet at home—but if it isn't reflected in the numbers, if the skill doesn't become sales (and pretty quickly too), you can forget it. Because in the end, retail is about the numbers.

And Marian Goodman's work life reflects this central fact. She comes to the store between six-thirty and seven each morning, working her way through the empty, half-lit aisles to her tenth-floor office, and the first thing she does after she settles in is prepare something she calls "The Flash."

It is a four-page breakdown of the sales at Fifty-ninth Street the previous day, department by department. It includes comparisons to last year's sales on the same day, and how the departments at Fifty-ninth Street are doing against similar departments of Bloomingdale's in the rest of the nation.

Because she doesn't have a computer printer in her office, Goodman prepares the Flash each day by hand, writing each number in the proper box on a grid of her own making, her shorthand categories easily decipherable: coats, swim, intimate, Chanel, Calvin, Kamali.

Actually transcribing the figures every morning gives Goodman an almost scholarly intimacy with them, and they become one of the critical benchmarks against which she judges her people, and against which they judge themselves, day to day. The Flash is photocopied and distributed to the store's senior managers, and although it is something Goodman started doing for her own purposes, its numbers set a standard for the whole store that is difficult to argue with.

"Did we have a great day or a bad day?" says Goodman. "That's what the Flash tells us. It's like your daily report card.

"On a day like the day after Thanksgiving," says Goodman, "we check to see how we're doing hour by hour by hour."

On a more typical day, Marian Goodman takes to the floor well before the store opens, to visit her department managers (DMs, she calls them), her assistant department managers (ADMs), her salespeople, and to see how the merchandise is displayed, talk about what the customers are buying, what the numbers reveal.

Even when the store is not yet open, there is plenty of bustle in Bloomingdale's. Mornings are the time when the place gathers itself to do a million dollars worth of business—the aisles are crowded with boxes and racks from which the employees are stocking shelves. The store shields those inside from any sense of the outside world—the weather, the time of day. It is like a vast ship in which one is always below deck.

Goodman has much the air of a cheerful first mate on early inspection tour as she patrols the second floor of the store, greeting salespeople enthusiastically, her eyes constantly watching for things out of trim.

She whips through the *bloomies* insignia department. "Hi, Laura," she says to a young woman who is stocking *bloomies* T-shirts. "This is a big area for us," Goodman says. "A lot of tourists shop here. Laura, this is too close," she says, repositioning a basket of miniature soccer balls on the floor. "People will trip on it."

She moves from place to place without lingering. Still on the second floor, Goodman points to a new area, the vintage-dress shop. The vintage-style dresses hadn't been selling well—until they were collected into their own area.

"Just relocating and concentrating them doubled their sales," says Goodman. This is part of the mystery of retail—it wasn't that customers didn't want to buy the vintage dresses, they just wanted them displayed a little differently before they'd buy them.

As Goodman works her way around her departments, and as the hourly workers begin to arrive in anticipation of the store's 10 A.M. opening, Jim Gundell comes on the store's public-address system for what sounds like a Bloomingdale's version of the high school principal reading the morning announcements. In Gundell's case, it's the review of yesterday's commodity movements and today's pep talk.

"We had $850,000 for plan yesterday," Gundell says. "We did $843,000. We're close, we're getting better. We're behind plan this week about $300,000." Gundell is not talking loudly, but his voice is everywhere, as if he were standing at your elbow, murmuring.

"We did pick up 2 percent compared to last year, that's good news." It sounds as if he's reading straight off the Flash. "The coat department was up 50 percent, large sizes were up 22 percent, swim-wear was up 2 percent, accessories were up 20 percent." As Gundell goes through each department, there are outbursts of applause from the associates in the departments that have done well. "And congratulations to Jennifer on the big sale of the day . . ." Gundell goes on for well over five minutes.

"The staff loves it," says Goodman, continuing her rounds. "It was Jim's idea. It's like a dose of adrenaline in the morning."

ANNOUNCE THE SCORE EVERY HALF INNING

There is no substitute for letting people know how they're doing. Retailing may provide an extreme example, but employees can't try harder, or try different tactics, if they don't know they're not performing up to expectation. Set the goals, communicate them, and then provide the feedback. Constantly tell your employees how they're doing, and what they need to do in the future. Goodman's morning Flash and Gundell's morning announcements ensure that every Bloomingdale's employee always knows the score.

FROM ARMANI CREPE TO CONTROL-TOP PANTY HOSE

As the store opens, Goodman heads to the fourth floor, where the designer boutiques are. Stephanie Zorzy—a young woman who has just been promoted from DM for Armani, Chanel, Ungaro, and Lacroix to associate buyer—comes up to Goodman.

"We have a package that's just gone," Zorzy says of a customer's purchase that has disappeared. "It was three pieces of navy wool crepe, Armani." She means three separate items—a jacket, a skirt, and pants. The Fifty-ninth Street store is out of stock and Zorzy wants the okay to replace the items.

"You have my American Express number, right?" Goodman asks. Her DMs and ADMs routinely use her American Express card for just such problems.

"Yes," says Zorzy, "but they don't have it at Chestnut Hill."

"Well, if they don't have it, buy it at retail and have it shipped here overnight."

Zorzy wheels and heads off. "The worst thing to say to a customer is 'We lost a package,'" says Goodman.

"Last Christmas, a customer had a Chanel sweater delivered, and it was stolen from her doorstep. The customer was just devastated. We looked around, and only one store had it, the Chanel boutique in Hawaii. We bought it there at full retail and had it sent in."

This is hardly the kind of service for which Bloomingdale's is known. If anything, the Fifty-ninth Street store has a reputation for being a wonderful retail cornucopia, but a place where it takes determination to shop.

"It requires a tremendous amount of energy to be a customer here," says Gundell. "Logistically, there are times there are too many bodies on our floor. When it's cold out, and the people are ten deep at the glove counter, how do you provide a great experience in that?

"That is something we'd like to change, to make it more comfortable for the customer."

Make It Right—Then Figure Out What Happened

Goodman doesn't make excuses when her store loses a package. She makes it right, and she shows her employees how important that is. Being able to see the store like a customer sees it rather than as an employee is absolutely necessary to being able to improve customer service.

Both Goodman and Gundell are well aware that the Fifty-ninth Street store is overpowering, but they haven't simply shrugged and decided that it was that way when they got there and it's not their fault and there's nothing they can do about it. Despite the store's size and the crowds it attracts, they are constantly searching for ways to make it more accessible and more human.

The atmosphere of Bloomingdale's is something Goodman works to change every day, although she has been assistant manager of the store and operating vice president for just two years, and changing the culture of Bloomingdale's is a little like trying to change the course of a supertanker with a canoe paddle.

It's one reason Goodman feels so strongly about spending at least half her day out on the selling floor: She can talk ceaselessly about customer service, but nothing makes the point more vividly than letting people see her deal with customers.

Goodman is now down on the selling floor of the store's Metro level—one of two selling floors below ground level. The Shop for Women, Bloomingdale's large-size department, is on the Metro level. "Their motto is, 'Style should not be a size,'" says Goodman.

Goodman spots a woman wandering through the Shop for Women, obviously looking for something she isn't finding. There is not a salesperson in sight.

"Is there something I can help you locate?" Goodman asks.

"I need stockings," the woman says.

"Any particular kind?" Goodman asks.

"Control-top," the woman says. She seems a little skeptical. Meanwhile, Goodman plunges into the panty-hose display, plucking out packages.

"How can you tell which are control-top?" the customer asks.

"Here, let me show you," Goodman says, ripping open a package to show her the control-top. Goodman's search takes her into a drawer below the display. "What color?" she asks.

"Black," the woman says, "and some kind of bone."

Goodman proceeds to offer up a selection of off-whites—sandalwood, seashell, beige delight—with a discussion of the virtues of each.

"How much are these?" the woman asks.

"The regular ones are five dollars," Goodman says, "the control-top is six-fifty."

Goodman's patience doesn't flag during the ten minutes she spends with the woman. Eventually, a sales associate comes up and Goodman gently hands the woman off to her.

Before heading back upstairs, Goodman pokes her head into the back-of-the-house area of the Shop for Women and tells an ADM doing paperwork there, "You need [sizes] 2X and 3X, black and navy, control-top panty hose. There's nothing in stock. Could you see if we have any?"

On Memorial Day 1989, Goodman was in the men's store when she noticed a pack of suited men with earphones moving through the store. "I went over and said, 'Hi, is something going on?'" The men turned out to be State Department security sweeping the store in advance of the arrival of a princess from an Asian country with an entourage of fifteen. Goodman ended up escorting the Princess throughout the store. "She shopped for probably two hours," says Goodman, who earns no commission. "She wanted everything hand-delivered to her hotel. She was so nervous it would get lost, I carried it up to her room myself."

For Goodman, the numbers are the way she starts and ends her day, but service is how she spends the time in between, and there is no question in her mind about the connection between one-on-one service and strong sales. With competition as diverse as Barney's, the Gap, and the Madison Avenue designer boutiques belonging to the same designers who supply Bloomingdale's, there is no choice but to provide service.

"I always think like a customer," she says. "There is far more product out there than there are customers—or disposable income.

"The customers should feel as good about buying a five-dollar pair of panty hose as they do about buying a five-thousand-dollar gown. She should get the same service—that's my goal."

THERE CAN BE ONLY ONE
STANDARD FOR SERVICE

There is no difference in a panty-hose customer and a designer-gown customer. One day, the panty-hose customer may need a designer gown; tomorrow, the gown customer may be downstairs buying panty hose. Setting a double standard for service—one level for inexpensive stuff, one for expensive—drives away the customers for both. Bloomingdale's has a personal shopping service that's designed for people that have more money than time. But it's available to everyone in the store, not just "big spenders."

You must have a baseline of service you want delivered, regardless of the customer or the purchase. Goodman has in her mind an ideal of the Bloomingdale's shopping experience—she wants shopping at Bloomingdale's to mean something, to stand for a particular level of attention, quality, and service. And she wants customers to have the Bloomingdale's experience regardless of what floor they're on, what department they're in, or how much they're spending. Otherwise, there's no reason for customers to come to Bloomingdale's.

THE GOODMAN GRADUATE SCHOOL
OF BUSINESS

Despite her attentive, almost busybodyish, presence on the floor, one of Marian Goodman's strengths as a manager is that she knows how to hold her tongue. She tries to let her managers bring their problems to her—giving them a chance to figure out that something is a problem and wrestle with it a bit, asking for help only if they need it.

It is just after three in the afternoon, and Goodman is holding a series of regular weekly meetings in her office with her department managers. Goodman's nurturing personality notwithstanding, the meetings are remarkably free of idle chatter. There is no gossip, no talk of what people have done the previous night or the previous weekend. Equally important for inexperienced women managers, there is of course no flirtation or sexual charge in the air. The meetings are all business, and one of the things Goodman's managers are subconsciously learning is what it feels like to be treated with respect and responsibility, what it's like to work in a totally professional atmosphere.

First up are Lisa Conwell, twenty-six, a DM in designer sportswear, and Stephanie Zorzy, twenty-seven, who hasn't yet taken up her new duties as a buyer. Each woman comes in with a list of issues to work through with Goodman, and Goodman sits at her desk with her pen in her mouth, listening.

Zorzy is frustrated with a buyer. Her salespeople know their customers and are ordering to fill their needs, but the buyer hasn't been supplying enough merchandise to fill the orders.

"We need twenty-eight Armani size-fourteens, and she's buying six size-fourteens," Zorzy says. The suits cost three, four, and five thousand dollars each, and for some reason, although Zorzy and her associates have actual customers for each of the twenty-eight suits, the buyer doesn't realize that and is simply nervous that size-fourteen Armanis will not sell.

Goodman—who has been a buyer among the ten jobs she's held in sixteen years at Bloomingdale's—suggests an alternative to Zorzy just telling the buyer the number of suits she needs. "Get the profiles of the customers' desires to the buyer before the buying trip, actually let them know exactly who the customers are." That is, prove to the buyer that the suits she's buying are already sold.

Zorzy nods.

Conwell's list is relatively short, and she moves through it quickly. She explains why she marked down merchandise during the week. "Saks and Bergdorf's had reductions, we issued emergency paperwork to meet the prices."

Goodman asks about a couple of salespeople. Conwell asks for leave to change the lettering on the wall in one of her departments from silver to gold, to match the rest of the area's design.

To Zorzy, Goodman expresses concern about a line of high-fashion clothes that is moving poorly, but is about to go on sale. "The customers don't want to pay full price on the skirts because there is such confusion on skirt lengths this season," Zorzy explains.

Goodman just wants to know if Zorzy's salespeople are pre-selling for the sale—telling regular customers that the merchandise will soon be discounted, and making sure the customers are lined up for it then.

Zorzy assures her that Oscar—one of the store's top salespeople—is doing just that. "Oscar, he dresses these women," she says. "He picks out their outfits, he calls them when they're going on sale, and he says, 'I have a gift for you.'"

Goodman nods. "Open issues?" she asks.

"I need to give a customer a skirt," Zorzy says. "She tripped and fell and tore her Armani skirt, five hundred and fifty dollars. How do I charge that?"

"Charge it to petty cash," says Goodman.

There are smiles all around, and the women excuse themselves, dipping into Goodman's candy jar on the way out.

LET MISTAKES HAPPEN

One of the key elements of being a good manager is leaving people alone, letting them bring their problems to you in their own time. The only way people can learn to manage is to tackle those problems themselves. Goodman sets up a mechanism for people to tell her what's going on—regular meetings—and in those meetings, she lets them set the agenda. As a manager, you can always step in and deal with something. But you need to give people the chance to deal with things themselves, to learn the consequences of both their action and their inaction.

Obviously, no manager wants to sit back and watch serious problems develop that may affect the viability of the company. Those kinds of problems need management supervision instantly. But most situations are not life-threatening. Part of a manager's job is to be able to tell the difference.

Retail is an unusual business in that young people can get very large responsibilities very quickly. Both Conwell and Zorzy run groups of departments—essentially small businesses—that do five million dollars per year in sales. The next step up—the associate buying job that Zorzy is about to move into—involves traveling the world, buying clothes for Bloomingdale's, spending the company's money and deciding what will be on the shelves and the racks in the coming season. Many of the people in such jobs are between twenty-five and thirty years old, and many of them have learned the business, and discovered their own confidence, at Goodman's elbow.

After the meetings, Goodman heads down to one of her departments that is having a fashion show to bring in customers and showcase new merchandise in one of the store's better-sportswear departments.

The area is roped off, a portable fashion runway is set up, champagne is being served, and the people are streaming in. Sales associates have confirmed eighty-five regular customers for the show by telephone, but the number in attendance quickly goes well above that. Goodman moves around, occasionally greeting a customer she knows by name.

Not all her managers do fashion shows, but Susan Celentano, the manager in charge of this department, likes them. She has even arranged to have a seamstress on hand to make alterations immediately on clothes customers purchase.

"The goal," says Celentano before the fashion show starts, "is to sell merchandise. We've sold seven thousand dollars today already. A normal day is three to four thousand."

Celentano, who was recruited out of college, has responsibility for six departments.

"Thank God for Marian's beeper," Celentano says. "Marian is so supportive. I must see her a dozen times a day. I probably beep her more than anybody else. She always takes the extra step, she always goes the extra mile.

"The most important thing—she's a team player. She wants us to be creative, so you're not afraid to propose an idea. She'll say, 'This is great!' Or, 'Super idea, but you're forgetting this.' She's always positive."

By the close of business, the department having the fashion show sells ten thousand dollars worth of merchandise, three times a normal day's sales. "I didn't worry about it at all during the day," says Goodman. "I let Susan handle it."

T H E   B E S T   I D E A S   A R E   R A R E L Y
Y O U R   O W N

Not all people have the same style or approach, and there are many paths to success. Goodman is smart enough to give her managers and associates the leeway to do their own things. Susan Celentano's fashion shows work for her—and Goodman lets her handle them, from start to finish. One of the main reasons they work is because they're Susan's idea. Goodman doesn't interfere, nor does she then impose what seems to be a successful idea on the rest of her managers.

If managers will simply set the objectives—Susan's department needs to increase sales—and then let those responsible come up with the tactics to accomplish the objectives, the results will be a lot better than if the manager attempts to set the objectives and design the tactics as well. Give people the chance to develop their own ideas and you'll probably find they work for them a lot better than your ideas do.

M A I M O N I D E S   M E E T S   B L O O M I N G D A L E ' S

As much as Goodman enjoys seeing the numbers move in the right direction on the Flash, or being returned to the role of sales associate for a morning by an Asian princess, what gives her the most pleasure these days is training the next generation of managers for Bloomingdale's.

"I love training people," she says. "We're in the people business, we're only as good as our people. I try to develop my junior managers so they become department managers or buyers, because they are the future of Bloomingdale's."

She meets with the assistant managers as a group once a week alone—without their managers—"to hear what's going on, to solve problems, to challenge them.

"There's an old saying, 'If you give a person a fish, he can eat one meal. If you teach the person to fish, he can eat for the rest of his life.'" Maimonides would surely be flattered to know his eight-hundred-year-old philosophy has some relevance for Bloomingdale's.

Goodman had only one real job before coming to Bloomingdale's, working part-time for Herman's sporting goods while going to Villanova.

"I loved it," she says. "I sold tennis rackets. I didn't know a
goddamned thing about tennis rackets. There was a guy who
took me under his wing, who taught me everything.

"I liked dealing with customers. I sold tennis balls to my girl-
friends' fathers. I would let the customers know when the tennis
balls were going on sale. I learned how to presell, to a customer
who says, 'I like this, but I don't want to spend this much
money'—to tell him when there was a sale.

"And I learned never to leave the department at night looking
like a mess. I had a boss who was a fanatic about that. He
wanted the hangers in the same direction, and every ski jacket
zipped up to the same point.

"It's not as controllable here, but I know it's possible."

Goodman went to Catholic grade school and high school and
grew up in a relatively typical upper-middle-class New Jersey
home, the middle of three children, the only girl.

She was hired straight out of Villanova by Bloomingdale's.
"When they took me, I remember screaming, 'My God! My God!'
I think I started at $173 a week."

The day after the fashion show, Goodman addresses a small,
nervous lunch group of young men and women who are in almost
the same position she was when she got that $173-per-week job:
they are the spring's recruits, being interviewed by Bloomingdale's for after-graduation jobs.

"My first assignment was men's socks and underwear," she
tells the college students. "This was when men's underwear was
white jockeys, and the socks were blue and brown. With some
white socks in the back.

"It was a rude awakening. I had spent four years in school,
and there I was in men's socks and underwear."

Goodman—who is only beeped once during her twenty-
minute speech—goes on to lay out the steps of her career—men's
clothing, associate buyer in men's designer, sweater buyer, trips
across Europe and the Far East.

The group is a little intimidated. Goodman asks for questions. "Was anything you bought a flop?" one woman asks.

"Oh, yeah!" Goodman says, laughing. "I always felt like I was buying my markdowns.

"I bought fifteen hundred units of a sweater that was selling twelve hundred units a week. He kept shipping, and we kept buying. I didn't have the insight to say, 'This is gonna stop.' I was like twenty-three years old.

"It stopped as fast as it started. I owned ten thousand sweaters, and we couldn't move those sweaters. But everything has a price. We marked those down to $4.98 to get rid of them. I still remember that last blue sweater being sold."

SETTING THE STANDARDS AND LETTING PEOPLE RISE TO THEM— OR TRIP OVER THEM

Before nine in the morning in her office the next day, Marian Goodman takes a call from a store executive. He had witnessed an incident the previous night. A customer in a wheelchair approached an associate to return something that didn't come from the department the woman was in.

The rule at Bloomingdale's is that associates take all returns, regardless of the department. "The sales associate looked at her and said, 'Take it to the second floor,' " says Goodman.

Goodman calls Susan Celentano, who has responsibility for the department where the associate works, explains the incident, and asks Celentano to find out who the offender is. Celentano calls back with the name—a person who has had some trouble before, and for whom this may well be the last straw.

"Bring her to the office at one," says Goodman, "and then we'll go to personnel"—her way of saying the woman will be fired.

Goodman talks to the woman, with Celentano present, before she is sent to personnel to be formally fired. The associate doesn't even attempt to defend herself, Goodman reports.

"I said, 'Did this happen?' She gave us an obnoxious look and said, 'Yeah, it happened.' She couldn't have cared less. I asked her, 'Would you like to have been treated like this?' She said, 'No.'

"I said, 'Well, you've really left me no choice . . . I want you to realize how seriously we take this.' She was so obnoxious, I was ready to throw her out the window."

It is not enough, obviously, to set standards for service and attitude, they must also be enforced. A sales associate snubbing a customer is an extreme example; Goodman draws much finer distinctions.

"We had an associate in coats," she says, "who was a top producer. But the associate only gave customer service when it was convenient." He could just as easily be rude or peremptory as helpful. "He got good letters, but for every one of those he got, he got two bad customer-service letters," says Goodman.

"He sold a lot of coats, but he didn't do it with good customer service. He did a lot of things that weren't good for Bloomingdale's." He left before being fired.

GREAT CUSTOMER SERVICE ALWAYS HAS A PRICE

There's a big difference between selling a customer something and providing customer service. An associate who sells a lot but "burns" customers in the process does far more long-term damage than short-term good. It's important to realize that good customer service often has short-term costs. These can include firing someone who sells a lot of sweaters or replacing a stolen item—but these costs are trivial compared to the value of the purchases a happy customer will make in a lifetime.

You can never afford to make the daily numbers at the expense of next month's or next year's numbers. Too many managers are managing for the next earnings statement instead of managing for the future.

Moreover, service standards are of no value if they are not enforced. There must be penalties—discipline, firing—for anyone failing to treat customers the way you want them treated. This policy has to apply to the best salespeople as well as those who are only average.

The example Goodman sets is not just how to treat customers, but how to manage employees.

Annie Seale, one of her department managers, came to Bloomingdale's straight out of college. "She would see me from the opposite end of the store," Seale remembers, "and then she'd be right next to me, and she'd say, 'Annie, you're chewing gum. Why are you chewing gum?' "

Seale in fact drove Goodman crazy before she finally stopped chewing gum on the selling floor. "I said to her, 'How are you going to be a leader if you're chewing gum?' " Goodman says. "I was tough on this kid. She couldn't even figure out which train to take. She probably went home half the time in tears. But she stuck it out. She's super. It is such a pleasure to see someone like that grow up before your eyes."

Seale is unscarred by the gum experience. "I've always been very impressed by Marian. I've grown a lot. She's taught me that every situation has to be handled differently. I've seen her deal with customers, I will watch her handle a situation, and that's how I learn.

"She, to me, is Miss Bloomingdale's. She puts her heart and soul into Bloomingdale's. She comes in at six-thirty or seven every morning. She's been here since she was a trainee. She's a great role model.

"She speaks her mind. She encourages that from us.

"You want to make her proud," Seale says, "because one day you want to be like her."

WHAT'S MARIAN GOODMAN WORTH?

Marian Goodman is simply priceless for Bloomingdale's. She sets standards that make it possible for the store to sell $400 million in merchandise a year. More important, perhaps, she trains generation after generation of sales assistants and future managers imbued with those standards, young people who carry what they've learned from Marian to other Bloomingdale's stores.

At this stage of her career, Marian's influence is surely

reflected in tens of millions of dollars of sales a year for the company.

HOW DO YOU FIND MARIAN GOODMAN?

1. The best place to find Marian Goodman is right under your nose. Marian, for instance, has never gone looking for work since she got her first postcollege job at Bloomingdale's.

    Inside your organization, you can find Marian by looking for frontline workers who not only know how to take care of customers, but who have leadership skills and a global sense of your business. And who are ambitious. But there has to be balance—Marian has never let her ambition confuse her priorities. She knows that at every point, the customer is more important than she is.

2. We have cautioned in several places throughout the book that great frontline workers don't necessarily make great supervisors of great frontline workers, that the skills of one are not necessarily transferrable to the other.

    But it is also true that the best supervisors of frontline workers have usually been frontline workers themselves. They understand the pressures, problems, and pleasures of the frontline jobs, and they understand what a boss can best do for those people. In the ideal case, like Marian Goodman, such supervisors understand that the best strategy is to treat the frontline workers the way you would want the frontline workers to treat your customers.

    So how do you apply this somewhat contradictory advice—that not all great frontline workers make good supervisors, but that the *best* supervisors often come from the front line?

Judgment. You have to look for people with a larger vision of your business than just their small jobs (as Jorge Alvarez does, for instance), you have to look for people who set a good example, who have leadership skills, and who understand not just the difference between being a supervisor and a frontline worker, but the similarities as well.

THE CARE AND FEEDING OF THE REAL HEROES OF BUSINESS

If you've read this book from beginning to end, something extraordinary has happened: you now likely know more about the people in this book than you know about virtually anyone you work with—your colleagues, your subordinates, your boss.

We have done this on purpose. We wanted you to know as much as possible about these people, almost as much as we know about them, because in learning about this group of individuals, we discovered some vital lessons and patterns.

The stories of the people are as important a part of this book as the lessons, because the stories taught us a very simple lesson ourselves: the better you know the people you're thinking about hiring, the more likely you are to hire outstanding workers.

Would you have hired Phil Adelman—laid off, unemployed, with no hotel experience—if he had applied to you for a door-man's position? Would you have hired Paula Doricchi after she flunked the preemployment liquor-knowledge test at your restaurant? Would you have hired the polite, deferential David Greene to be a direct salesperson? Would you have hired Jorge Alvarez, with his modest English, to be the final quality-control check for airplanes your company catered?

Once you *know* Phil and Paula, David and Jorge, of course, you know how good their work is going to be. Almost anyone would hire them after meeting them in this book.

But the people who hired them were often anything but certain. They were taking a risk. They were relying on some intuitive sense, a bit of instinct, having spotted a spark in these people not present in the typical applicant.

If that's how you're doing your hiring—just relying on instinct (and we admit that, too often, that's how we have done our hiring)—you're on the right track, but you're still missing out. You're missing the opportunity to consistently hire the very best people you can. And that's the gap that can give almost any business the chance for competitive advantage—not simply hiring on instinct, but actively seeking the qualities Paula's and Phil's managers stumbled onto.

For unless you know almost as much about the people you are considering hiring as you do about the people you've just read about here, you are shooting craps with your hiring decisions.

Finding out about job candidates doesn't require you to spend several days with each potential candidate, following them around, writing down every move and thought, as we did. We didn't know what we were looking for in advance, so we had to do this the hard way.

It does require asking the right questions—and listening to the answers. In an appendix that follows, we provide a list of some of those questions—open-ended questions that require a little thought, that may give your candidates a chance to reveal themselves.

Because although Phil Adelman the doorman and Keith Spring the car mechanic seem like completely different kinds of people, as different as David Greene the salesman and Joni Strong the flight attendant seem, their similarities are more striking still.

It is those similarities that are the real key to consistently finding people of this quality, this loyalty, this commitment.

It is those similarities that provide the opportunity for you as a manager.

Having read about these people, it is easy to spot some consistent qualities. While this is a decidedly unscientific sample of people, the remarkable range of qualities they share can't be coincidental. Many, for instance, are early risers, most are high-energy, most have type-A personalities. And these are only the most obvious similarities.

The specialness of these fourteen people—and all the people they represent—lies in their overlapping traits. And if you can find job candidates with a similar set of qualities, you vastly improve your chances of finding not just good employees, but real heroes.

What World-Class Service Workers Are Made Of

In one way or another, everyone in this book had a remarkable childhood. If you ask the right questions of any of them—What was your first job? When did you first start working? What impression of work did your parents give you?—you will hear a story that reveals respect, even passion, for work, born very early:

Phil Adelman, remembering his father patiently rising from the Sunday dinner table to go deliver heating oil to a customer running low.

Paula Doricchi, as a teenager, working in a clothing store, so concerned about beating last year's sales that she bought clothes with her own money.

David Greene, as a boy, selling drinks at a college football stadium, figuring out that what his customers really wanted was ice, not soda, and making sure they got it.

Joe Sabelli, working in the fields before he was a teenager to support his family, then joining the Navy before he was old enough.

Joni Strong, who started working at twelve, determined even at that age to become a flight attendant.

Marian Goodman, working in retail while in college, selling sporting goods to the fathers of her friends, and zipping up all the ski jackets to the same point.

It's not just that each of the people we found can talk about such early experiences. Everyone can. It is the *way* these people remember those moments and the passion with which they talk about them—these were important experiences, and the people in this book remember them in tremendous detail, decades later. That should tell you something about what kind of values these people bring with them—and it will say something similar about people you interview.

All the people in this book have hung on to a work ethic developed early. They are powerfully motivated in circumstances where even the two of us (both incurable workaholics) can only look on in awe: Phil Adelman, a devoted, disciplined, imaginative doorman, working at a second career that his friends were skeptical of, and earning a very modest wage; Alan Wilk, working all night on Christmas Eve to fix someone's drain, without a thought of leaving before the problem is solved; Paula Doricchi, working six nights per week, fifty weeks per year, for a decade, as a waitress earning roughly twenty thousand dollars per year to support her family and begin sending her husband to chiropractic school.

Despite the hours they put in, and the sometimes modest financial rewards, all of the people in this book are wonderfully good-natured and love their work. They are all, in one way or another, charming. They are easy to like.

To be sure, their charm is individual. Keith Spring is different from Alan Wilk, Marie Williams is different from Jorge Alvarez. But they all come to work enthusiastic, even cheerful. In almost every case, their colleagues and supervisors said they couldn't recall ever seeing any one of these people in a bad mood at work.

This, too, is revealing. It's not that these people lead charmed lives. All these people are real, they have problems, conflicts, low moments just like everyone else. But they manage to leave those problems at home when they come to work. They have developed the ability to compartmentalize their moods—they understand that it is important not to let what's going on in their personal lives spill into their work lives. This means they are not moody employees, who take out their bad moods on their customers and colleagues.

Of course, most people can manage to be pleasant, even charming, in an interview. But this points out an important issue to take up with a job candidate's references. Almost to a person, the people in this book are so consistently good-humored that their colleagues and supervisors found it striking. Many supervisors seemed to envy the ability of these people to come to work in a good mood without fail. It is something prior employers would surely have noticed as well.

Every one of these people sees his or her world, and job, from the customers' point of view. They are trying to take care of the customer, and they almost never bend the work world to suit their own needs at the expense of the customer. Jorge boards the extra meals rather than inconvenience the flight attendants. Wally will drop whatever stocking or ordering task he's in the middle of to go into the cold room and get a fresh avocado for a customer if the ones on display aren't good enough. Danny Williams works all night to restore phone service—then goes to work as usual when the sun comes up. Joe Sabelli will make change, even though that's not his job.

You can find out how potential employees feel about customers in all kinds of ways—but just asking them to talk about their contact with customers in previous jobs will be tremendously revealing.

These people trust their customers. When someone tells Keith Spring there's a noise in her car, he believes her, and goes about finding the noise. When someone tells Joe Sabelli that he only got change for a ten-dollar bill when he had handed over a twenty, Joe believes him. That trust infuses each encounter these people have with customers.

It is a level of trust that creates an atmosphere that makes customers feel welcome and respected. And it is an unusual atmosphere. Salespeople, waiters, service people all too often give the impression that they are suspicious of customers, that they think everyone who walks in the door is trying to rip *them* off. But all you have to do is listen to Paula Doricchi or Rich Ciotti or Marian Goodman talk about customers for a little while to hear the seriousness with which they take them. It is not always possible to measure the sincerity of such sentiments perfectly in advance of seeing people interact with customers, but you can get a pretty good idea.

We've noticed, in fact, that a key element in the way these service performers related to customers is that they almost all take a very long-term view of their relationships—they aren't worried about the immediate payoff. Phil Adelman isn't expecting a tip from everyone, but he is determined to treat everyone as if he'd been tipped in advance. Rich Ciotti doesn't try to sell people furniture they don't really want or need (and given his skill, he could) because he doesn't want a sale from his customers, he wants a relationship with them. He doesn't care if they buy furniture from him this Sunday afternoon—as long as they ultimately buy all their furniture for the next five years from him. Alan Wilk isn't racing to finish one call so he can get to the next one and make another dollar. He takes his time, not only doing what's necessary to solve someone's drain problem, but also cleaning up after himself, and doing what's necessary to reassure a customer that the unpleasant experience is really over and unlikely to recur. His long-term financial situation is much more secure that way—he's built himself a devoted customer following who specifically request him.

For almost all these world-class performers, financial rewards are a by-product of good performance, not the goal of good performance. They have confidence that investing in secure relationships ultimately pays off. Their own experiences prove they are right.

This kind of patience may be the hardest thing to nurture in employees. These fourteen people understand this idea instinctively—but they had help realizing it. Phil watched how his father treated his heating oil customers; Rich learned it when he was first delivering groceries, and he had it reinforced on his first furniture-selling job, at a store that cultivated relationships with customers, not transactions with them. Almost all these people have had mentors or role models—and they can talk eloquently about what values those people passed on.

This should tell us two things. It's worth asking applicants who their role models are. And it's vital to use your best employees as mentors, as trainers, as role models. They can transmit to your new employees the ethic you so value in them.

Among the more remarkable common traits in this group is that in a world where no one seems to have the time to do anything right the first time, these folks always have time to do it right.

Jacob Smith understands that a rejected loan without an explanation is a spurned customer, someone who is not only lost to the bank, but may do word-of-mouth damage; a rejected loan with a careful explanation may end up being a salvaged customer, someone the bank can help get a loan. Jorge Alvarez understands that the best marketing for Caterair is a group of satisfied flight attendants, and no matter how pushed for time he is, his patience for the flight attendants never flags. He always has time to replace a missing potholder (someone else might snip, "Couldn't they just use a towel or napkin?") or to offer an extra six-pack of diet Coke. Marie Williams doesn't throw up her hands in frustration when a patient gives her the wrong insurance information—she just gets on the phone and finds out what she needs to know herself, often without the customer even realizing it. Each of these people wants to find ways to do the job, not excuses to avoid doing it.

This willingness to get the job right inspires another common characteristic among world-class service workers. Almost universally, they have a talent for seeing what's missing and racing to supply it: Phil Adelman's cards imprinted with directions, Paula Doricchi's insistence on keeping iced-tea glasses full, David Greene realizing that a company on a "green" campaign might want recycled paper products, Joe Sabelli fixing the slot machines, Wally Bojorquez's cut-melon program, Marian Goodman realizing that Bloomingdale's needs multilingual store directories.

Indeed, almost all of these workers—and certainly almost all the workers you'd want to hire—have put themselves and their companies on a miniature continuous-improvement program. Without any seminars or prompting, they have internalized the Japanese notion of kaizen. They are tinkerers, never satisfied with their own performances, or with the processes by which they get things done, and they are constantly looking for better systems, for better ways to do things.

Alan Wilk, with his truck, his gadgets, his constantly improved equipment, is the most obvious example of this. But you have Keith Spring, reorganizing the auto dealer's service department that has existed for decades, and heading off into the lot to look at new cars and see if he can find anything wrong with them. You have Danny Williams wiring future areas of development for telephone service before anyone has broken ground. You have Joe Sabelli, at age eighty-five still looking for ways to redefine his job to take on more responsibility and to serve more seamlessly his casino's customers.

These people in large measure embody an interesting contradiction. While they are never satisfied with their own performances, or their own ability to deliver service, many of them are quite content to be frontline workers, with little ambition to "rise" into areas where they perceive the "hassle-factor" will also rise. Not everyone fits this pattern—David Greene, Danny Williams, Jorge Alvarez, Marian Goodman all want supervisory roles. And this is not an endorsement of hiring people specifically because they do not have managerial aspirations—that can be a disaster. But it is striking how many of these people have resisted efforts to get them into higher management jobs. Even Marian Goodman has turned aside several offers to head her own store. World-class service workers like customers—they do the work they do because they like it, not necessarily because it is a prerequisite for the next level.

Finally, one of the most critical and striking similarities among these people is that in some ways almost all of them don't, at first blush, seem all that well-suited to their jobs (Phil Adelman, Marie Williams, David Greene, Joe Sabelli, Jorge Alvarez, Jacob Smith). That's a reminder not to judge too quickly.

And it is vital to recognize some of the things this group does not share: some are old, some young; some have extensive formal education, some dropped out of high school; some are immigrants or first-generation Americans, some come from families that have been here for generations; some have only had one kind of job, some have had a half dozen different jobs.

Which brings us full circle—you have to approach the hiring process with an open mind, you have to gather as much relevant information about candidates as you can, you have to ask the right questions, you have to listen to the answers, and you have to know that what you're looking for is not always prior experience.

You need to listen for the clues of excellence, the clues to an energetic personality, an innovative approach, a competitive nature, an insistence on excellence and quality.

WHAT CAN BE TAUGHT VERSUS WHAT MUST BE HIRED

Service businesses in particular have fallen into an unfortunate habit of thinking that since almost anyone can be a waiter, or a security guard, or a retail sales clerk, or a telephone repair technician, it doesn't matter who you hire to do those jobs.

One reason for this confusion is that the technical details that need to be mastered to do these jobs can be taught to almost anyone who wants to learn.

But the group of service performers we've assembled shows how short-sighted this view is. Because with only a couple of exceptions, what makes these people so special is not their mastery of the particular skills their jobs require (opening the door, stringing phone wire, handing out soft drinks and peanuts). Indeed, in many cases what makes these people so special are things that *cannot* be taught, qualities that are intrinsic to the people, qualities they would bring with them to any employer.

This only reinforces our argument that the key moment in the quality of your service delivery is the moment when you hire people, because the real service performers to a large degree bring their greatness with them, at least in raw form.

For that reason, it's important to clearly understand which qualities can be trained, and which have to be hired.

As we've noted several times, direct previous experience (except perhaps in sales), is almost irrelevant. These job skills can be taught.

Energy, though, cannot be taught, it has to be hired. The same is true for charm, for detail orientation, for work ethic, for neatness. Some of these things can be enhanced with on-the-job training. And employees can be shown the virtue of being neat, or have incentives built in to enhance their energy or work ethic. But by and large, such qualities are instilled early on, and you don't want to have to struggle with a low-energy person in a job like Jorge Alvarez's, which requires constant scrambling.

Two things that can and should be taught are problem solving and customer orientation. Someone who comes in with Marie Williams's attitude, but without her sense of how to deal with the insurance bureaucracy, or confused customers, or balky doctors' offices—such a person can be shown how to solve the problems encountered every day. One of the best ways to train such people is simply to plant them at the elbow of someone with the experience and improvisational skill of Marie Williams.

Good jazz improvisation, good comedy improvisation, good political debate, good chess playing are all a combination of innate skill and experience watching masters at work—and working with the masters.

Customer orientation can be taught to the degree that you are able to give your employees a clear set of goals that allows them to focus on what your customers expect. Alan Wilk knows that the goal is simple: unclog the drains, leaving the customer, her mood, and her home restored to at least the condition prior to the drain backing up. Joni Strong knows her goal better perhaps even than American Airlines knows it: to keep her customers relaxed and happy even when things aren't going the way they'd like.

Harrah's could easily refocus the jobs of all the rest of its security guards along the lines Joe Sabelli has outlined, by adding this item to the list of their duties: do what the customers need you to do for them, act as if you were their host. Some of the current security guards might not have the innate skills to handle that role—but those that had the skills could easily be taught to think of their jobs in broader terms.

The key in balancing the qualities that can be taught against those that cannot is knowing the balance of those qualities in the job you're filling. It is vitally important to distinguish what you can give your employees from what they need to come in with.

Surprisingly, when we talked to the managers of the people in this book, they were uniformly modest about their role in nurturing the greatness of their employees. Indeed, the managers deserve a lot of credit for recognizing how extraordinary these people are, for working with them even though less challenging employees are easier to deal with, and for being willing to step forward and claim that one of their employees is among the best in the nation.

Not a single manager claimed credit for anything more than simple technical training. Most said the really important thing they had done to foster world-class performance was get out of the way and provide feedback (both praise and constructive criticism) and recognition. These employees take a lot of stroking.

What the people in this book show more than anything else is how valuable it is to put more time, energy, and care into the hiring process, even in what many perceive to be relatively low-paying, frontline service jobs. It is very costly to let luck decide whether you hire world-class service workers. You end up wasting time, money, and customer goodwill hiring people with the wrong attitude and little interest in their work. And perhaps more important, you run the risk that someone like Rich Ciotti or Keith Spring or Paula Doricchi will slip past, unhired.

THE CARE AND FEEDING OF THE REAL HEROES OF AMERICAN BUSINESS

We've said it throughout this book: people like this can be hard to manage. Even someone as pleasant and fun as Paula Doricchi can be a pain in the neck.

Why?

For precisely the reason that one of Paula's managers pointed out (and that Rich Ciotti's manager pointed out, and Jorge Alvarez's manager, and Phil Adelman's manager, and even Marian Goodman's manager): these people have high standards, sometimes their standards are even higher than their bosses' or their company's standards.

So for a supervisor who is content with things being just fine, for a boss who is comfortable with mediocrity so long as there is no disruption, an employee like this can be a real nuisance.

But in fact world-class service workers are relatively easy to manage, once you learn the trick. They've got the hard things down cold: motivation, standards, customer-focus, attitude.

What people of this caliber—and even people of more typical caliber—need is a job that suits their strengths, and then they need to be left alone. They need support—they need first-class internal service—but they don't need interference.

They need less management and more encouragement. They need to understand what the goals are, what the tools for achieving those goals are, and then they need managers who are smart enough to get out of the way.

As much as good workers need latitude—the right to break the rules to serve the customer, the chance to use their judgment to meet the goals that have been set—they also need feedback. Some of these fourteen people are modest, some of them are acutely aware of just how outstanding they are. But every one of them craves praise. Rich Ciotti proudly wears the ring and the watch that he has been awarded for his sales achievements—not because he couldn't afford to buy them himself, but because he loves the recognition. Jacob Smith is perfectly content to sit at his desk, going about his work, but he unquestionably enjoyed the recognition that went with the Jacob Smith Challenge.

All these people also need to feel like they are a part of their organizations, that someone listens when they speak. Much of the satisfaction Phil Adelman gets from his job comes not from working the front door, but from working the suggestion box. He knows that his suggestions are taken seriously, not just because he gets a response to every one of them, but because Marriott management periodically does just what he says. (Notice something else, too: Phil doesn't expect that just because one of his ideas is good, every one of his ideas is.) Paula Doricchi told Ruby Tuesday that charging for breadsticks was silly, and soon enough the company realized she was right.

The challenge in managing people like this is to figure out

what their high-achieving personalities need, and to give it to them. They all need to be allowed to express themselves. As many characteristics as these fourteen people share, they all need to be managed differently. Keith Spring needs to find constant intellectual challenge in repairing cars. Jacob Smith and Marie Williams need to be able to spend the time necessary to take care of their customers, to explain complicated rules and situations, to listen to complicated, sometimes wrenching, stories. Paula Doricchi needs not just good food and a comfortable restaurant, she needs the schedule that will accommodate her family. Phil Adelman and Alan Wilk need to know that someone cares about their suggestions.

World-class service employees pay all kinds of benefits. Their performance shows up on the bottom line, as we showed vividly at the end of each chapter. Indeed, the most outstanding frontline service workers are so valuable to the profitability of your company, they are generally worth paying more if that's necessary to keep them from leaving, something that is rarely done in the service industry. World-class service workers also provide benefits that are a little harder to quantify, but not at all hard to see. They raise the standard of your entire operation. It is not just as a mentor that someone like Wally Bojorquez or Jorge Alvarez or Jacob Smith is valuable. Their insistence on quality, their refusal to settle for "good-enough," their courtesy and attention to customers, all make it that much harder for other employees to do only marginal work. People like this are the key to ever-increasing profitability. They help you retain satisfied customers, and they help you reduce the cost of service, because the last thing employees like this need is a lot of middle managers "helping" them.

These fourteen people have changed the way we look at the world of work, the way we look at our own work, and the way we think about the people we hire. They still make us shake our heads in wonder. They are a challenge and an inspiration. They set a standard most of the rest of the world can only aspire to.

Finding Service Performers: Twenty Questions to Help Get You There

It is our contention that you can improve your chances for spotting real service performers when they first apply for work—but not just with the standard, two-sided application form. Those forms ask a series of questions the answers to which provide *data*, but not much *information*.

There are two critical elements to finding world-class workers. One is to interview them in person. The only way to gauge energy, attitude, presentation skills, and charm is to meet the people. (The only exception to this rule is when hiring for jobs that primarily involve talking on the telephone—those people should initially be interviewed by telephone).

The second critical element is to ask the right questions. You want to ask open-ended questions that allow people to reveal how they think about their work, their customers, their employers, themselves. If they can't give engaging answers, answers that positively excite you with their detail and their passion, chances are they won't be able to do much for your customers.

There is one more critical element in this process. You need to have the patience to listen to the answers to questions like this, you need to have the skill to ask good follow-up questions. Because it is in the answers that you will hear echoes of Phil Adelman and Marie Williams and Jorge Alvarez and Joni Strong.

1. Tell me about your first job. (Or, for salespeople, tell me about the first thing you ever sold to anyone.)

2. What did you learn about work, and about customers, from that first experience?

3. Who has had the greatest influence on your adult personality? Why?

4. Why are you applying for a job doing [whatever the job is]?

5. How did you get interested in [whatever your business is]?

6. Have you ever had any experience as a customer of a business like ours? Describe that experience. What struck you as important to doing this job well when you were a customer? What do you think businesses like this do well? What do they do poorly?

7. Have you ever had a bad experience as a customer of a business like ours? Describe that experience.

8. Tell me in some detail about the last job you had (or the job you currently have).

9. What were the customers like in the last job you had?

10. Did any of your customers become regular clients, or even friends?

11. What was your goal as an employee in the last job you had?

12. If you could have improved anything about the way your previous employer went about his work, what would you have changed?

13. Who was the best boss you've ever had, and what made that person a good supervisor? Who was the worst boss you've ever had, and what made that person a bad supervisor?

14. In a case where someone is applying for a job very similar to one they've had previously, don't hesitate to walk them through your office or plant, giving a brief tour and asking them what is different about your operation.

15. When you have a job you really like, what is it you like about that job? What do you get from work you really enjoy?

16. What do you think you will get from working here? What do you think you will bring to working here?

17. What do you like to do when you're not working?

18. What would you like to be doing five years from now?

19. Is there anything about yourself I haven't asked you that you think it's important for me to know as I consider whether to hire you?

20. Ask me some questions you must have about our business.

What Are They Worth? Calculating the Value of Your Frontline Workers

At the end of each chapter in the book, we gave a brief accounting of what we thought the service worker profiled in that chapter was worth.

The purpose of that exercise was really twofold. First, we wanted to shock you a little bit—into recognition of just how valuable good frontline workers can be to your business.

We also wanted to show you that the value of almost any service worker can be calculated. The first step in understanding the value of a worker is understanding the value of a customer. So we want to show you how you can do a rough calculation of the lifetime value of a customer for your particular business.

First, establish what the profit margin of an incremental customer is for your business. If you fix widgets, and you have a before-tax profit margin of 8 percent, and your fixed costs (those that don't change by adding an additional customer) are 20 percent, your incremental-customer profit margin will be the combination of the two, or 28 percent.

Next, consider the average size of a customer's order. Our widget fixer's average bill to his customers is $235. Now think about how often your customer places that average order. The widget people are called out 2.25 times per year. This gives an *annual* value of an incremental customer of: $235 × 2.25 × 28 percent = $148.05. Finally, think about how long the life of a typical customer is. To get this you can take your number of customers and divide it by the number of customers who stop doing business with you annually.* That figure will give you the current life of a customer.

If you had higly motivated and well–trained service workers providing superior service and great value, what would that figure be? Use these figures for comparison, and multiply each by the annual value we calculated above. Our widget fixers have an actual customer life of 5 years (customer defection rate of 20 percent each year), and they believe that figure could be 10 years if they improved their service levels and value delivery. What does that mean?

$148.05 × 5 years = $740.25 (value of a customer)

$148.05 × 10 years = $1,480.50 (value of a customer)

Therefore, the value of an employee is the value of a customer multiplied by the additional years that a great employee could keep a customer and/or the incremental customers that a great employee could retain.

* This works well for retail businesses with customers who have basically similar order sizes. If you have a wholesale business where some customers are dramatically more valuable than others, you may want to consider running these numbers using revenue dollars defecting each year, as opposed to the number of customers defecting each year.

And this discussion completely ignores the enormous value of word-of-mouth advertising that comes from satisfied customers. Consider how much more impact the opinion of a trusted friend or relative about the quality of a service has on your own purchasing behavior, compared to an advertisement, or any marketing strategy. It is very difficult to quantify, but the effect is significant. Remember Alan Wilk at Roto-Rooter.

∎

We've been talking about revenues and profit margins, and we've seen some dramatic numbers. Let's talk briefly now about costs.

What's the cost to your organization of employee turnover? It's higher than you think. In fact, recent research indicates that it's higher than most people think. Again, let's develop a model that you can apply to your own company to help understand how high these costs really are.

Research performed by J. Douglas Phillips* indicates that the costs traditionally associated with turnover, advertising, hiring, training and so on are only the tip of the iceberg. The significant costs associated with turnover are rarely even considered.

Phillips conducted two studies on turnover costs. In the first, costs averaged 150 percent of the annual wages for the position being filled. In the second, costs were 75 percent of the annual wages for the position. The two studies were eight years apart. In his article, Phillips estimates that costs may run as low as 50 percent of wages, particularly for less skilled, hourly workers. He also estimates that costs may run as high as 200 percent of annual wages at the other extreme.

What did Phillips consider that so many personnel officers have ignored? Let's go down his list: inefficiency of incoming employees (in contrast to average employees), inefficiency of coworkers closely associated with incoming employees, relocation costs, inefficiency of positions being filled temporarily while vacant, inefficiency of departing employees and their close colleagues, and costs associated with processing (human resources and non–human resources).†

* See "The Price Tag on Turnover" in *Personnel Journal*, December 1990.
† Ibid.

While the total cost figures vary widely depending on which study you consider and what positions you look at, they make a very loud statement: turnover is significantly more expensive than anyone realized, and money spent to reduce it is likely money well spent.

What does this mean for your company? The equation would be: annual wages for position × 50 percent (to be highly conservative) = cost of turnover, per employee leaving and being replaced.

Given the cost, there are significant economies in reducing turnover.

And this model completely ignores one very important factor: the cost of poor service delivered to the customer. The above considers the costs from the standpoint of an employee's reduced efficiency. There are also significant losses due to the alienation of customers as a result of new or inexperienced employees serving them, employees who are generally not as good at serving customers as those with years of experience.

All of these measurements—of the value of an employee, of the lifetime value of a customer, and of the cost of replacing even average employees—are useful for managers at every level of an organization. Help your managers, colleagues, and subordinates to understand what a customer is worth to your company, and to understand the cost of turning over employees. Then consider some of the suggestions in this book for maximizing customer retention and reducing employee attrition, suggestions inspired by world-class service providers. All of a sudden, treating people, both employees and customers, with dignity and respect, as you would like to be treated yourself, starts to pay—a lot. Try it. It's doing well by doing good. And the best part is, it works.

INDEX